In/visible Sight

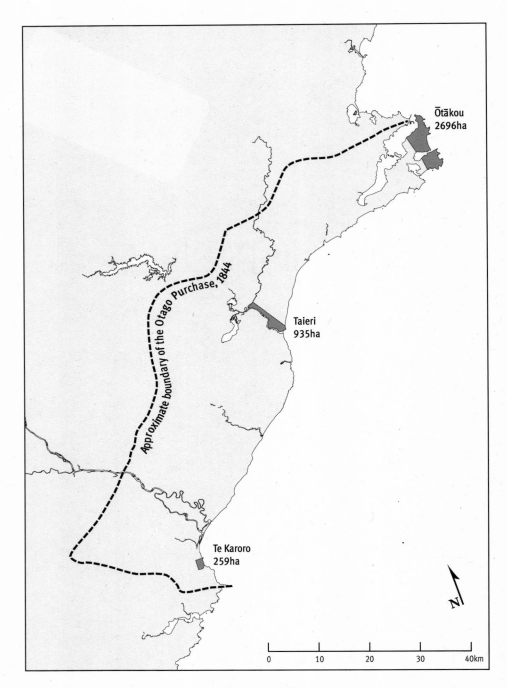

The Otago Purchase 1844, showing the native reserves at Ōtākou, Taieri and Te Karoro.

The Mixed-Descent Families of Southern New Zealand

In/visible Sight

Angela Wanhalla

AU PRESS
Athabasca University

© 2010 Angela Wanhalla

Published by AU Press, Athabasca University
1200, 10011 – 109 Street
Edmonton, AB T5J 3S8

First published in 2009 by Bridget Williams Books Ltd.
PO Box 12474, Wellington 6144, New Zealand.
ISBN 978-1-877242-43-4

Library and Archives Canada Cataloguing in Publication

Wanhalla, Angela, 1976-
    In/visible sight : the mixed-descent families of Southern New Zealand / Angela Wanhalla.

Bridget Williams Books
Includes bibliographical references and index.
Also available in electronic format (978-1-897425-87-9).
ISBN 978-1-897425-86-2

    1. Kai Tahu (New Zealand people)--New Zealand--South Island--Relations with Europeans.
2. Europeans--New Zealand--South Island--Relations with Kai Tahu (New Zealand people). 3. Interracial
marriage--New Zealand--South Island. I. Title. II. Title: Invisible sight.

DU423.F48W35 2010   305.800993'7   C2009-907342-0

The publication of this book was made possible by grants from the BWB Publishing Trust, Creative New Zealand
and the G & N Trust. Support was also provided by the author's Royal Society of New Zealand Fast Start Marsden
Grant and PBRF (Performance Based Research Fund) Enhancement Grant from the Humanities Division,
University of Otago.

The publishers are grateful for this support.

ARTS COUNCIL OF NEW ZEALAND TOI AOTEAROA

Permission to reproduce photographs was granted by the families, libraries and museums listed in the captions.
The author and publishers warmly thank these groups. Any further information about these images would be
gratefully received.

Maps on pp.ii, x-xi, 12, 23 and 70 were created by Geographx; those on pp.ii and 70 are based on
Harry C. Evison, *The Ngai Tahu Deeds: A Window on New Zealand History*, Canterbury University Press, 2006, pp.
15 and 45. Those on pp.x-xi, 12 and 23 are based on the work of Tim Nolan, from information supplied
by Angela Wanhalla.

Versions of several chapters in this book have been published previously: Chapter 2 as "'One White Man I
Like Very Much": Intermarriage and the Cultural Encounter in Southern New Zealand, 1829-1850', *Journal
of Women's History*, Vol.20, No.2, 2008; Chapter 4 as "'*My Piece of Land at Taieri*": Boundary Formation and
Contestation at the Taieri Native Reserve, 1844-1868', *New Zealand Journal of History*, Vol.40, No.1, 2007,
pp.44-60; and Chapter 7 as 'In/visible Sight: Maori-European Families in New Zealand Cities, 1890-1940',
Visual Anthropology, Vol.21, No.1, 2008, pp.39-57.

Edited by Alison Carew
Design and typesetting by Mission Hall Creative
Printed and bound in Canada by Marquis Book Printing.

Contents

List of Maps and Tables

Maps

Tables

In memory of S. G. W. (1943–2005)

Acknowledgements

Many acts of kindness have made this book possible. Bridget Williams is the best publisher one could hope to encounter as a first-time author. Her energy and encouragement have brought this book to life. Katie Pickles and Ann Parsonson, who supervised the doctoral thesis on which this book is based, gave me timely advice, guidance, encouragement and support, and continue to do so. I thank them for their ongoing generosity. Numerous colleagues, whom I am lucky to call my friends, have given much-needed support to this project. Jim Miller read my doctoral thesis long before I even contemplated revising it as a book, and offered advice on beginning the process of transformation. Keith Carlson, Bill Waiser, Lissa Wadewitz, Mark Seymour, John Stenhouse and Tony Ballantyne have all made suggestions at crucial moments on several chapters, while Barbara Brookes read the draft as a whole. Judy Bennett and Claire Freeman have provided me with mentorship and advice since my arrival at the University of Otago, and I thank them for their generosity.

I owe a particular debt of gratitude to many former and current postgraduate students of the Department of History at the University of Otago, who have all taken an interest in my work, particularly Rachel Standfield, Michael Stevens, Marjan Lousberg, George Davis and Sue Heydon. Discussions with my own postgraduate students, especially Kate Stevens, Marc Ellison, Kenton Storey, Tara Gimpel and Sarah Carr, have helped me to formulate my ideas about interracial intimacy and postcolonial history. I thank Adele Perry, Sarah Carter, Pat Grimshaw, Judith Binney, Charlotte

Macdonald, Atholl Anderson, Te Maire Tau, Bill Dacker and Garth Cant for taking a keen interest in my project and providing me with much-needed advice. Terry Ryan of the Ngāi Tahu Whakapapa Unit helped me trace the whakapapa of the Taieri families. I wish to thank the staff of the various archival institutions I have visited in the course of researching this book, all of whom have provided crucial support over the past few years.

I am grateful for the financial support of several institutions, which enabled me complete this book. A Royal Society of New Zealand Fast-Start Marsden Grant allowed me to finish my research and to move towards publication. A University of Otago Humanities Division Performance Based Research Fund Enhancement Grant and a Humanities Division Research Grant also proved crucial. A Canadian Research Council post-doctoral fellowship, held in the Department of History at the University of Saskatchewan, allowed me to start rethinking my doctoral thesis as a manuscript for publication.

I have come to know the history of Taieri and southern New Zealand in a very personal way. I am grateful to the numerous people who have passed on family information and allowed me to rummage through their photograph albums, and welcomed me into their homes and into their lives. My friends Rani Kerin, Kriston and Megan Rennie, Christine Whybrew, Chris Brickell, Paerau Warbrick, Judith Collard, Michael Allen, Robert Peden, Matt Morris, Sarah Dowling, Joanie Crandall, Heather Watson, Leedom Gibbs and Sarah Coleman have listened patiently to my ideas, and calmed me down at crucial moments. Three very important people, Lachy Paterson, Christopher Burke and Hayley Brown, have been cheerful, gracious and utterly kind during the writing (and rewriting) of this book. My life is greatly enriched for knowing them. Most importantly, I could not have completed this project without the support of my family, especially my father, Stanley Gordon Wanhalla, who came to know the history of the Taieri families much better than I do. This book is for him.

Angela Wanhalla
November 2009

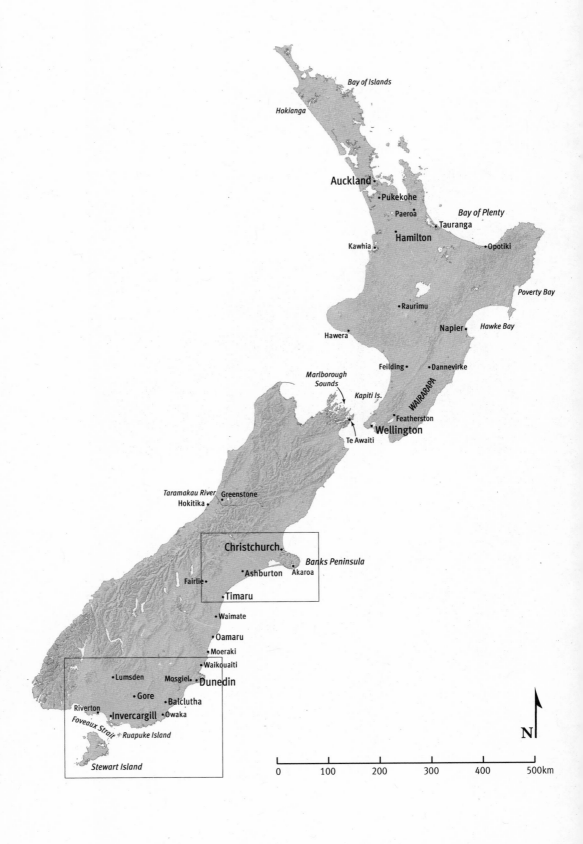

Bay of Islands

Hokianga

Auckland
• Pukekohe
Paeroa •
Bay of Plenty
• Tauranga
Kawhia • Hamilton
• Opotiki
Poverty Bay
• Raurimu
Napier • Hawke Bay
Hawera •
Feilding • • Dannevirke
WAIRARAPA
Marlborough
Sounds
Kapiti Is.
• Featherston
Wellington
Te Awaiti

Taramakau River
Hokitika • Greenstone

Christchurch •
Banks Peninsula
• Ashburton Akaroa
Fairlie •
• Timaru
• Waimate
• Oamaru
• Moeraki
• Waikouaiti
• Lumsden Mosgiel • • Dunedin
• Gore
Riverton • • Balclutha
• Invercargill • Owaka
Foveaux Strait
• Ruapuke Island
Stewart Island

N

0   100   200   300   400   500km

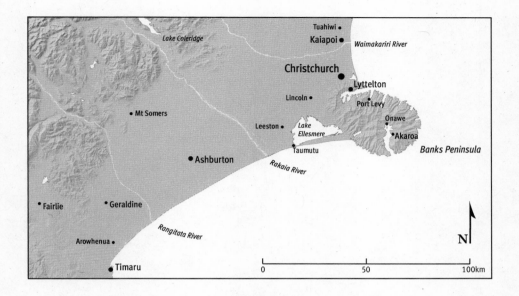

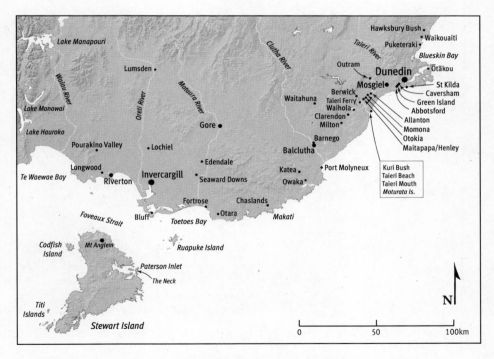

Maps showing key locations in the text: New Zealand (opposite), Canterbury (top), Otago and Southland (below). The families from Maitapapa settled in towns and cities throughout New Zealand, but particularly in the southern regions. Outward migration in search of employment began in the late nineteenth century, and by the 1920s few people remained in the settlement.

Elizabeth Garth, Thomas Garth and Teone Wiwi Paraone (undated). Elizabeth was the daughter of Robert and Jane Brown. In 1878, at the age of 14, she gave birth to her only child, Teone, who was raised by his aunt, Eliza Koruarua, at Taumutu. In 1901 Elizabeth and her husband, Thomas Garth, adopted a son, whom they named Thomas David Lauder Garth. [Photograph courtesy of David Brown]

Chapter 1. Intimate Histories

Historical research can be transformative, and often very personal. My father's life has framed and influenced the research and writing of this book. Born in 1943 to a Māori mother and Pākehā father at Lincoln, a small rural community on the southern edge of Christchurch, he grew up in 1950s rural Canterbury. That childhood experience and his later youthful escapades in Christchurch were shaped by his ethnicity. Ambiguous in appearance, and with an unusual surname, Dad was rarely identified as Māori. Commonly mistaken for Dutch Gypsy, German or Jewish, he recast his identity at will in response to people's puzzled reactions. My mother was one of many to be confused: on first meeting him in 1968 she enquired if he was Indian, and he replied, 'Cherokee'. In these brief moments of transformation my father engaged in a practice adopted by many mixed-descent people in New Zealand since the mid nineteenth century.

Stories of transformation are at the heart of this book. My father's identity, like that of the families described within these pages, underwent numerous changes. Many other Ngāi Tahu experienced a similar kind of ambiguity. Their lives were overshadowed by a history of interracial marriage in the South Island that is largely unexplored and little known. *In/visible Sight* traces the experiences of mixed-descent families in southern New Zealand from the 1830s until 1940. It explores the ways in which interracial families engaged with the government, and sought to create and define their own identity, which for some meant the denial of Māori ancestry. My father belonged to a generation that lived in cultural poverty, with tenuous ties to their Ngāi

Tahu ancestry and identity. Not all people of mixed descent from the lower South Island had similar experiences, but the overwhelming narrative that emerges in this book is one of absence as well as shame, followed by attempts to recover the past and to reassert Ngāi Tahu identity.

My father was raised in a family where stories circulated, myths abounded, ancestry was shadowy, and family photographs largely absent. Misinformation was rife. Dad knew only that his maternal grandfather was named John and his grandmother was Mabel, but was uncertain whether they were both Ngāi Tahu. The last few years of my father's life were spent immersed in research for this book, which began its life as my doctoral thesis; the subject was the history of the mixed-descent community at Maitapapa, in the Taieri region, where my great-grandparents, John Brown and Mabel Smith, were born. As the thesis took shape, as a community emerged from the records, and individuals were anchored to a social world, my father found the confidence to claim a Ngāi Tahu identity. The experiences of those families who lived at Maitapapa are the central focus of *In/visible Sight*, within the broader cross-cultural history of the southern regions. More specifically, the book investigates the processes whereby community and individual identity were transformed by a sustained pattern of inter-racial marriage. In combination with state policies of amalgamation and assimilation, interracial marriage shaped the social and economic possibilities of the families concerned.

Marriage and intermarriage

Marriage is a central institution in Māori society, and in the eighteenth and early nineteenth centuries it followed distinct protocols based on the status of the individuals concerned. Arranged marriages were not unusual. Such alliances usually involved a negotiation, in which the genealogies of both parties were examined to ensure that their rank and status were appropriate.[1] Most pre-contact marriages took place within the tribe, as marriage outside the group had important consequences for land ownership.[2] In some cases, particularly in times of war, high-ranking women entered into arranged inter-tribal marriages in order to forge political alliances or underpin peace settlements. Aristocratic marriages included a ceremony of

Left: My mother, Coralie Wanhalla (née Noonan), in Christchurch, May 1973. When my parents married in 1970, interracial partnerships were becoming increasingly common in urban New Zealand. Until the mid twentieth century, it was relatively unusual for Pākehā women to marry Māori or mixed-descent men. Right: My father, Stan Wanhalla, with his youngest sister, Ruth-Ann, in a photo booth on New Brighton pier, Christchurch, in the late 1960s. [Author's collection]

blessing, followed by a feast with speeches and gift-giving.[3] But regardless of rank, the community's approval or agreement was required before any marriage could take place, because a well-conducted marriage negotiation brought prestige and wealth to the group as a whole.[4] Marriage was thus an important social event, involving obligations to the community.[5] Yet there was room within Māori society for marriage based on love and attraction. Indeed, 'flexibility in the system permitted love matches where mutual attraction led to the flouting of the usual conventions'.[6] Public recognition was still key to a couple being accepted as married, across all social classes. Commoners chose to enact this facility by being discovered together so that formal community approval was bypassed.[7]

The practices and protocols surrounding marriage reflected the way Māori society was organised, and the 'inherent flexibility' that underpinned its economic success and social cohesion.[8] That success, achieved through the complex mechanisms of resource management, exchange and trade, revolved around chiefly authority. In the contact era, the ability to forge alliances with newcomers and to integrate European technology and knowledge represented a continuation of the chiefly role. There was, in fact, a great deal for Māori society and its leaders to gain from a controlled engagement with newcomers, but the process had to be managed carefully if the social and cultural fabric of Māori society were to be retained.

For the purpose of this book, 'intermarriage' refers to a process sanctioned by the tribe and the family, carried out in accordance with certain cultural and social protocols, and designed to integrate newcomers into the tribal group. In the case of inter-tribal or inter-hapū alliances, these newcomers would of course be Māori. In the contact era the process was expanded to encompass non-Māori, and such alliances are referred to as 'interracial marriage'.

During the early contact period (1790–1840), Ngāi Tahu took a leading role in forging significant economic and social relationships with the newcomers, mainly sealers and whalers. Lacking the interracial conflict prevalent in the North Island in the 1860s and 1870s, the South Island is generally regarded as having been peacefully settled by Europeans. Sustained and extensive interracial marriage is often invoked as evidence of harmonious race relations in the southern regions, and is what distinguishes Ngāi Tahu from the trajectory of culture contact experienced by northern tribes.[9]

Ngāi Tahu chiefs encouraged interracial marriage for a range of purposes. One was the continuation of a tradition whereby marriage was used to make alliances and cement peace deals during a previous era of inter-hapū and inter-tribal wars. For example, the migration of Ngāi Tahu into the South Island from the eighteenth century was partly achieved through, and consolidated by, marriage with Ngāti Mamoe, the existing inhabitants.[10] It was through marriages with high-ranking women that political alliances were forged, peace deals were brokered, and access to resources was gained. Māori women took an active role in negotiating marriage alliances within tribal society, and continued to participate in the process in the new resource-based economies of sealing, trading and whaling.

Interracial marriage thus offered Ngāi Tahu an opportunity to regulate economic and social encounters with newcomers. Marriage to a Ngāi

Tahu woman guaranteed, through kinship ties and the responsibilities they entailed, that the single, mobile whaler would be drawn into the community. It was a strategy employed by Māori communities wherever newcomers established themselves in New Zealand. In Hauraki, for example, interracial relationships were part of the culture contact landscape from the 1830s. Sometimes referred to as the 'my Pākehā' phenomenon, these alliances were of strategic importance to Māori communities, giving them a measure of social and economic control over newcomers.[11] The strategic value was mutual, with newcomers benefiting from the kinship bonds thus acquired. Richard (Dicky) Barrett, for example, living at Te Awaiti shore whaling station in the Marlborough Sounds, was 'related by his wife to all the influential chiefs living at Port Nicholson [Wellington]'.[12]

Māori women themselves actively used interracial marriage to create social, economic and political alliances. Indeed, the arrival of newcomers opened up the marriage options of Māori women, especially as these men were highly valued and sought after as additions to a community. Tokitoki, niece of southern Ngāi Tahu chief Honekai, famously protected the young sealer James Caddell in 1810 when his ship was captured, and eventually married him.[13] In the North Island, Moengaroa of Te Hikutu chose the Hokianga trader Frederick Maning as her partner.[14] In this new era, a number of Māori women became significant economic and political agents, especially as business-owners. Ruawahine's marriage to the Tauranga trader John Lees Faulkner in 1842 represented an affective tie, but it also established them as trading partners. Such women were able 'to manage tribal business interests and ensure optimal economic opportunities for their communities'.[15]

Yet despite evidence of women's agency, interracial relationships in early New Zealand have often been interpreted as a form of trade and exchange, over which Māori women exerted little control. While Michael King characterised the relationship between Māori communities and newcomers as one of exchange and interaction with mutual benefits, he paid little attention to the role of Māori women in fostering such alliances.[16] Some have argued that the first decades of cross-cultural contact saw a flourishing 'sex industry' involving Māori women.[17] Ngāi Tahu used terms such as 'o te parara' ('out of the barrel') to describe children born of relationships between whalers

'Stewarts Isle', *c.* 1860s (photographer unknown). During the nineteenth century many Ngāi Tahu families of mixed descent lived on Stewart Island, particularly at The Neck and Paterson Inlet. European-style houses such as this were becoming typical of communities on the island. On his regular visits, missionary Johannes Wohlers reported on the state of the houses, particularly their domestic arrangements. Clothing, standards of behaviour, and cleanliness were all used as evidence of the shift towards Christian family life and respectability; other signs were appropriate gender roles, engagement in Christian marriage, and baptism. [E-296-q-158-3, Alexander Turnbull Library, National Library of New Zealand/Te Puna Mātauranga o Aotearoa]

and Māori women, thus hinting at a trade in women's bodies. But that trade was not extensive, being restricted mainly to the ports visited by bay whalers in the Bay of Islands. Bay whaling, which is characterised by short-term encounters along the shoreline, was not common in southern New Zealand, making 'sex trade' an inappropriate description for relationships that grew out of shore whaling. Where that trade did exist in New Zealand, it was short-lived, whereas interracial relationships formed in the sealing and shore whaling era survived long after those economies had disappeared.

Like the alliances formed between indigenous women in North America and European fur traders around the Great Lakes and in Western Canada,

Māori women's relationships with newcomers were much more complex than was first believed, encompassing violence, barter and trade. Indigenous women in a range of contexts and localities were crucial to the survival of frontier industries.[18] Interracial marriage played an important social-economic role in the North American fur trade, for instance, giving traders access to resources while uniting indigenous communities and traders in joint endeavours.[19] But the predominant interracial relationships that emerged from the fur trade were characterised by 'tender ties': long-term marriages built on mutual love and attraction.[20] New Zealand's early interracial encounters were sometimes violent in nature, and trade in women's bodies did occur; but as in North America, the relationships that emerged out of cross-cultural contact in southern New Zealand were more likely to be tender than violent.

Just how many of those relationships were romantic alliances in which Māori women were active agents is impossible to know. Despite the central role that indigenous women have played in opening up resource frontiers to newcomers, it is notoriously difficult to interpret their lives and experiences because of the relatively few sources available. Shore whalers were often illiterate, and rarely left personal records that have made it into the archives; and where they have, Māori women appear very rarely, or only 'in statements about sexual hospitality, companionship and domestic service'.[21] This 'archival silence' limits the extent to which historians can gain direct evidence of interracial relationships and their internal dynamics in the early contact period.[22]

Despite these constraints, the evolving pattern of intimate interracial encounters can be traced in southern New Zealand from the 1790s. Those that developed in Otago, Southland and Stewart Island were often short-term liaisons based on seasonal industries along the southern coastline, particularly sealing. By the late 1820s, a new kind of encounter began, centred on the shore whaling industry. What emerged was a range of interracial relationships, encompassing informal unions that lasted only as long as the whaling or sealing season; short- or long-term marriages undertaken for economic purposes and according to Māori protocol; and legal Christian marriages formalised by the local mission station or church.

'Taieri River between Titri and Taieri Mouth', painted in 1880 by Samuel Edwy Green. The width of the river indicates its importance to the development of local resource economies, and as a communication route. Also notable is the steep terrain, which restricted Ngāi Tahu and British settlement to the interior plains and along the coast. [A-250-002, Alexander Turnbull Library, National Library of New Zealand, Te Puna Mātauranga o Aotearoa]

With the arrival of the New Zealand Company, Ngāi Tahu embarked on a new phase of encounter, one that led to the systematic British settlement of the South Island. The New Zealand Company purchased large tracts of the South Island in the 1840s, and by 1864 representatives of the British Crown had completed the purchase of Ngāi Tahu territory; in both cases, blocks of land were set aside as native reserves. It is this process of 'sale' and subsequent settlement that has largely occupied historians of Ngāi Tahu, together with the economic and social impact of colonialism in the post-contact era. What has been demonstrated is the economic and cultural loss resulting from colonial practices. By the end of the nineteenth century, widespread land loss and inadequate reserves had brought poverty and marginalisation. In 1876 tribal leaders established a fighting fund called Te Kereme (The Claim) to press for an official investigation into the land purchases, and contributions were received from all Ngāi Tahu families. Throughout the 1880s and 1890s, government-appointed commissions of inquiry were conducted into the 'land question' in the South Island, but little was achieved.[23] While the life-ways of Ngāi Tahu communities over the nineteenth and twentieth centuries were characterised by land aliena-tion and poverty, there are other aspects of colonialism that have yet to be explored as fully.

People and place

The history of interracial marriage in Otago, Southland and Stewart Island provides the context for a more detailed examination of the lives and expe-riences of the mixed-descent individuals who lived in the small Ngāi Tahu settlement of Maitapapa in Otago between 1830 and 1940. More commonly known as Henley, Maitapapa is located on the southern Taieri Plain. More specifically, it lies on the northern bank of the Taieri River at the entrance to the lower Taieri Gorge, where the Waipori and Taieri rivers converge and feed into the sea. The Taieri is the third largest river in Otago, and is fed by eight tributaries. From its headwaters in the Lammermoor range in Central Otago, it travels through mountains and the upper Taieri Gorge, crosses the Taieri Plain into the lower Taieri, where it joins the Waipori River near Maitapapa, then flows through a second gorge and runs into the sea at Taieri Mouth. This river system includes Lake Waihola and Lake Waipori, which today form part of a wetland of 2,000 hectares. Originally the wetland included three further lakes – Potaka, Tatawai and Marama Te Taha (Lake Ascog) – which were drained in the early twentieth century. These waterways shaped settlement patterns at Maitapapa, and influenced early economic development in the region.

New Zealand Company surveyor Frederick Tuckett and his companion, David Munro, provide a glimpse of what the wetland looked like in 1844. Looking down on the lower Taieri, Munro described a plain

> ... stretching away to the southward for at least twenty miles [and] bounded on all sides by naked hills of rounded outline. This plain, we learnt from the natives, was called the Tairii [sic]. Its general colour was a brownish yellow, broken only by the black hue of one or two patches of wood, and by the glitter of the water, which seemed in some places to form lagoons, in others to wind about with many sinuosities.[24]

Munro also noted the deep depression of the valley. On reaching the summit of a ridge on the northern bank of the Taieri River, he declared that he had 'never seen any place which more strongly warrants the supposition of its once having been a lake'.[25] Tuckett and Munro had much difficulty in travelling through this environment. They had to 'wade through fern and coarse grass over our heads, to say nothing of swamps – while, if we took to the side of the hills, they were so steep, and the footing so bad, that progression was almost fatiguing, and fumbles frequent'.[26]

It was this environment that Ngāi Tahu frequently passed through, and eventually inhabited. They settled the lower Taieri from the eighteenth century, their permanent settlements being Tu Paritaniwha (near Momona), Omoua Pā, Maitapapa (on the flat land below Omoua), and Takaaihitau (Taieri Ferry). A fishing village, Te Au Kukume, was located at the mouth of the Taieri River, on its northern bank. Other seasonal settlements were located at Palmer's Gully, Excelsior Bay and Craigie's Island. Ngāi Tahu from Otago Peninsula travelled through the Taieri on a seasonal basis, stopping off at camping sites along the banks of the river and at Taieri Mouth. This seasonal pattern continued, despite Maitapapa being occupied by 'northern people' from Kaiapoi, fleeing from Te Rauparaha in the 1830s.[27]

Ngāi Tahu from the southern reaches of New Zealand also began to arrive at Maitapapa in the late 1830s, attracted by the trading opportunities that emerged with the arrival of whalers.[28] Some came to Maitapapa as the partners of whalers, bringing children and extended family with them. By the time the whaling station was finally abandoned in 1844, a group of people with kinship connections to Canterbury and Otago had settled at Maitapapa on a permanent basis. Living with them were a handful of ex-whalers and their Ngāi Tahu wives, and their large families. It was this grouping of people, with a complex set of kinship connections, that the New Zealand Company representatives found living at Maitapapa in 1844 when the Otago Deed of Purchase was signed. Under that purchase, the northern bank of the Taieri River was set aside as a native reserve, comprising 2,310 acres. When the reserve came under the operations of the Native Land Court in 1868, Ngāi Tahu with connections to Kaiapoi and to the Foveaux Strait region had been living at Maitapapa for around thirty years;

in addition, the children of the whalers had grown into adulthood. All were determined to protect their interests in the reserve before the Land Court, as disagreements, claims and counter-claims came to light (see Chapter 4).

Interracial marriage developed in a sustained manner at Maitapapa from the 1830s: by the early 1890s, around 90 per cent of its 170 inhabitants were of mixed descent. This high rate of interracial marriage differentiates the community from numerous other Ngāi Tahu settlements in Otago and elsewhere, among them Riverton, Bluff and The Neck (Stewart Island), many of which certainly had large mixed-descent populations. But it was the sustained pattern of interracial marriage that defined the Maitapapa community, to the point that extensive outward migration in the early twentieth century led to its disappearance as a physical entity by the 1930s. The role played by interracial marriage in bringing a group of people together, the social bonds that forged these families into a community, their experience of living as mixed descent during an era of great pressure to assimilate, and the reasons for the community being disestablished are all part of the history traced in *In/visible Sight*. For the Pāma/Palmer, Paraone/Brown, Overton, Wellman, Garth, Drummond, Crane, Smith, Crossan, Stevenson, Robertson, Robinson, Gibb, Milward, Matene/Martin, Williams, Low, Bryant, Sinclair, Tanner, Campbell and Sherburd families – some of the many people of Ngāi Tahu descent who lived at Maitapapa throughout the period under investigation – interracial marriage and being of mixed ancestry are fundamental to any understanding of their colonial experience.

In/visible sight

In other colonial settings, the role of interracial relationships in forging new societies has been explored in great detail; so too has the power accorded to indigenous women through interracial relationships, and what they lost in this process.[29] In New Zealand, much of the historical scholarship relating to Māori is framed by Māori–government–settler interaction, and the individual encounters that constitute interracial contact are often neglected. Far more is known about the Crown and Māori, about patterns of resistance to colonial authority, and about processes of land dispossession, than the experiences of individuals, families and communities.

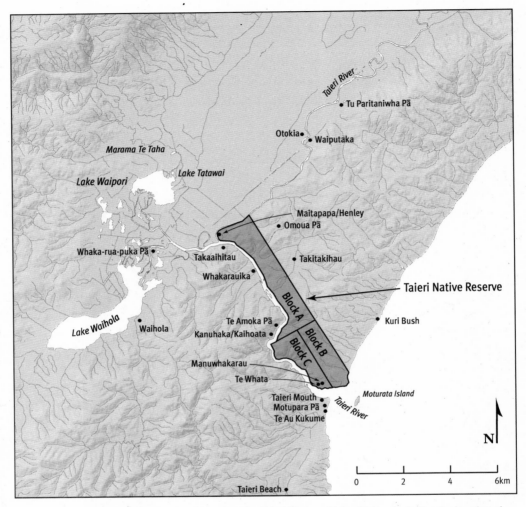

Map showing significant settlements near the Taieri River and inland lakes, including the location of the Taieri Native Reserve, set aside under the Otago Purchase of 1844. The 2,310-acre reserve was divided into three blocks in 1868, in an attempt to resolve conflicting claims to the land.

This book sets out to explore the less visible side of colonialism by tracing the history of interracial marriage in a part of the country where such relationships are most intensive. Patterns of interracial marriage from the 1830s to 1940 are revealed, as are the contexts that produced them. The internal dynamics of these relationships and the experiences of interracial families are also examined.

In Otago, Southland and Stewart Island, the newcomers of the late eighteenth century quickly formed relationships of exchange and mutuality with the people living there. Like the hapū of Hauraki,[30] Ngāi Tahu in southern New Zealand engaged with the newcomers on their own terms, forming relationships through trade as well as through affective and intimate ties. It was the establishment of shore whaling stations, with their semi-permanent population, that had the most significant impact on Ngāi Tahu society, ushering in an extended period of widespread interracial marriage. The male-gendered and seasonal nature of shore whaling meant that interracial intimacy played an essential role in shaping the industry's fortunes. The first station was established in 1829 at Preservation Inlet, and by the late 1830s twelve stations were in operation along the southern coast of New Zealand. The stations varied in size, and were a significant fixture of the Ngāi Tahu landscape for a period of twenty years. Small stations had crews of six to twelve men, while the larger stations, such as Ōtākou and Waikouaiti on Otago Peninsula, employed crews of up to forty or more.[31]

Shore whaling stations were at the hub of cross-cultural exchange. The long whaling season necessitated the establishment of semi-permanent settlements, often located near Ngāi Tahu villages. In order to gain access to the land, newcomers engaged in customary marriage with Ngāi Tahu women, usually with the strong encouragement of Ngāi Tahu leaders. Such an alliance was often with a woman of high status, in order to gain the protection of the chief and access to the necessary resources. Interracial relationships were mutually beneficial: the whaling industry fostered new trading relationships for Ngāi Tahu, bringing wealth to communities as well as to chiefly families, and marriage drew whalers into a network of economic, political and social obligations. While these exchanges took place within the context of new trade conditions, what emerged from the shore whaling era were permanent, rather than temporary, interracial relationships.

In recent years, historians have re-examined conjugal relations, sexuality and family life in light of colonial practices and experiences. Within this context, they have sought out indigenous women's stories of cross-cultural encounter, and have found that interracial marriage gave women significant social and economic roles in resource economies such as the North American fur trade. Chapter 2 examines 'Maori women's agency in cultural encounters',[32] by demonstrating their important contribution to the shore whaling industry in the early nineteenth century. It draws upon individual women's stories to demonstrate the complex range of relationships that thrived in resource economies of the 1830s and 1840s. In so doing, it opens up the internal dynamics of interracial relationships to reveal a more complex history than has been previously understood. Pātahi's story is used to illustrate how such relationships worked, especially the extent to which they were romantic arrangements. How relationships were formed, and women's experience within them, have remained elusive aspects of the interracial experience. Yet Pātahi's story makes it clear that Ngāi Tahu women sought out relationships with male newcomers, often on their own terms, thus belying the typical interpretation of these encounters as a form of trade in women's bodies.

By 1840, 140 male newcomers had founded mixed-descent families in southern New Zealand, and had fathered 596 children.[33] By 1864, 68 per cent of the Ngāi Tahu population of Foveaux Strait were of mixed descent, suggesting that an interracial community, and even a separate ethnic and cultural identity, was emerging.[34] Given these statistics, it makes sense to explore the complexity of the interracial experience in the locations where Māori and Pākehā (Europeans) intermarried.[35] This is particularly so for Otago and Southland, where extensive and sustained interracial contact between newcomers and Ngāi Tahu makes it 'an important case study in intermarriage and the production of "half caste" children'.[36] Chapter 3, therefore, explores the social world the newcomers entered, as well as the world that was created from sustained interracial contact.[37] It demonstrates the importance of marriage in creating kinship ties between interracial families, and examines why a distinct identity based on physical and cultural intermixing did not eventuate in southern New Zealand, despite the increasing demographic dominance of interracial families.

Interracial marriage and mixed-descent families are the obvious outcomes of cross-cultural contact. But what impact did the arrival of male newcomers have on Ngāi Tahu communities in terms of land retention, especially once systematic colonisation began? The relationship between colonisation, land loss and interracial marriage is explored in Chapter 4, which investigates how Ngāi Tahu coped with the growing mixed-descent population in the context of land alienation and resource depletion. By the 1840s Ngāi Tahu were dealing with the impact of new land settlement practices, particularly the marking out of native reserves. While Ngāi Tahu welcomed interracial marriage and appeared to integrate people of mixed descent into their communities, the conflict over boundaries and rights to the Taieri Native Reserve demonstrates that economic integration and acceptance had their limits. Interracial relationships, and the children born from them, generated conflict within communities left with inadequate reserves and limited resources, reframing the ways in which communities interacted. Indigenous perspectives on interracial marriage are not easy to elicit, especially when official records are often silent on such matters, but there is evidence to suggest that Ngāi Tahu communities struggled to accommodate mixed-descent people economically at a time when land was scarce.

Beyond the confines of the native reserve, interracial relationships were of concern to government officials, even though interracial marriage was never outlawed in New Zealand. But the lack of legal prohibition does not mean that officials were relaxed about such relationships. Private life in nineteenth century New Zealand was structured by colonial policy. Marriage, for example, was both a private and a public event. As a public event it was subject to legislation, which defined boundaries of citizenship by determining who could or could not marry.[38] Marriage, as a public institution, was also 'the place where the state most directly shaped gendered authority'.[39] Officials worried a great deal about the implications of illegitimacy for the inheritance rights of mixed-descent children, and as a result sought to encourage legitimate relationships. Official attitudes to interracial relationships were also mediated by prevailing views about masculinity and respectability. As Chapter 5 demonstrates, New Zealand officials certainly regulated, monitored and policed interracial relationships as soon as colonial government was established, and sought to generate loyalty to the Crown through the provision of land grants to white men who entered into Christian marriage.

The Wellman brothers' band was a great favourite of the Taieri communities, and played at many local events and weddings. The man on the right, holding a violin, is John Wellman, with William Richard Wellman on the left. The two women are not identified, although the pianist may be John and William's sister Elizabeth, who often accompanied them. [Photograph courtesy of Shirley Tindall]

Meanwhile the census enumerators worked to generate information on the size and extent of the mixed-descent population, which officials then used to proclaim the success of colonial assimilation policy. As the Ngāi Tahu population absorbed increasing numbers of people of mixed descent, tribal identity and authenticity began to be questioned, leading to a view of Ngāi Tahu as the 'white tribe'.[40] By the 1890s, census reports were positioning Ngāi Tahu as the most 'European' of the Māori tribes, based on genetics, their 'way of living', use of English, and Western-style dress and appearance. In the New Zealand census, racial terminology (notably 'three-quarter-caste' and 'quarter-caste') was used to quantify the changing ethnic make-up of the indigenous population, at a time when social scientists were interested in the implications of the crossing of the 'races'. But as Chapter 6 demonstrates, southern Ngāi Tahu did not accept these racial categories, and in fact used the census to assert Ngāi Tahu standards of identity and inclusion. By the late nineteenth century, people of mixed descent were active participants in tribal politics, and their everyday lives undermined any official attempt to categorise them racially. Nonetheless, the language of race and racial classification seeped into everyday life, and had a material impact on the economic and social futures of mixed-descent families, marking them as 'white' in official eyes.

Officials used the census not only to highlight the extent of assimilation through interracial marriage, but also to trace the resulting 'disappearance' of people of mixed descent. Chapter 7 focuses on the urbanisation of mixed-descent families as they migrated to southern towns and cities in the early twentieth century, and examines the multiple ways in which they were supposedly 'invisible' in urban settings. While living as mixed descent was a highly visible experience during the nineteenth century, this increasingly gave way to invisibility during an era of state assimilation policy, which sought to erode Māori identity and culture through integration into main-stream society. For many such people, invisibility was a strategy for survival as well as for the attainment of economic and social success. Oral histories, in conjunction with a rich visual record, demonstrate however that people of mixed descent were actually 'hiding in plain view' in urban spaces.[41]

New resources and a new approach are required to open up the history of Ngāi Tahu and interracial relationships to an intimate lens. Because indi-vidual experiences are at the heart of this book, it draws on two important sources: oral histories and the family photograph album. The wealth of visual resources available demonstrates the visibility of mixed-descent people in nineteenth century New Zealand, not just in southern New Zealand but across the country. Oral histories highlight the meaning of visual records to families, while also providing an explanation for how visibility was eroded from the beginning of the twentieth century. These two sources help to reveal a history of silences, disappearances and loss, as well as one of resilience and strength. They provide a very different picture from the one conjured up in official records – particularly the national census and the racial categories it employed to define the mixed-descent population. Combining the visual record with family history creates an intimate archive, one that opens up colonial history to complex and competing perspectives, and provides a powerful way to interrogate the impact of cross-cultural encounter and colonial practices on indigenous peoples.[42] This is the way that historians must approach the history of southern Ngāi Tahu, because the families and communities involved have important and relevant stories to tell.

Chapter 2. Pātahi's Story

Long time ago when I was young girl, big ship came to Otakou [Otago], it have lot of men to catch the whale, they stay at Otakou, then go away catch more whale ... one white man I like very much, he very kind to me and by and by he say you be my wife. I say by and by when I get big and older. Next time you come. The ship she go away and I very sorry, the Maori Chief at Otakou he big strong man, he make big fight when Te Rauparaha the big chief come with lot of canoes and men from what you call North Island and kill lot of Maoris, the Maoris of Otakou kill a lot too, and then they call the chief, Bloody Jack [Tūhawaiki], after the ship gone, Bloody Jack he say I want you for my wife. I say no, I like the Pakeha Palmer, and when the ship come back I going to be his wife, the Chief he very angry, and many times he get very angry. All the other Maoris say I must marry Bloody Jack, so one night I left Otakou and go to Moeraki, stay four moons [months], then I go to Waikouaiti and every day I make a look out for the ship, by and by it come, then I go to Otakou and I be Mr Palmer's wife. I stay on the ship – then we build a whare [house] and live there and a Maori go instead of Mr Palmer. I very happy then, for long time we live at Otakou and I have one girl, then another.[1]

This is Pātahi's story. The events took place at a time when her tribe was forging significant economic and social relationships with newcomers through the sealing, whaling, flax and timber trades. Of these, shore whaling was the most important, drawing large numbers of European men to southern New Zealand from 1829 until 1850. Pātahi's relationship with trader and

This studio portrait of Jane Brown, daughter of Edwin Palmer and Pātahi, with her granddaughter Mabel Smith, was probably taken in 1889 as part of the celebrations associated with the marriage of Jane's son George to Helen McNaught. A much-treasured family photograph, it is the only known extant image of Mabel, the daughter of Beatrice Brown and James Smith. Mabel is the great-granddaughter of both William and Edwin Palmer: her mother descends from Edwin through Jane, and her father is the son of Mere Kui, one of William Palmer's daughters. Mabel married Teone Wiwi Paraone in 1900. [Photograph courtesy of David Brown]

whaler Edwin Palmer typifies the first phase of interracial marriage in the region, in which the participants were white men and 'full-blood' Ngāi Tahu women. Shore whalers were the group that had the most intensive interaction with Māori, and they left an indelible mark on Ngāi Tahu whakapapa (genealogy), trade relations and settlement patterns. Their target was the right whale, hunted for its oil and bone during a season that lasted from May to October.[2] The newcomers founded whaling stations on the coast, near Māori settlements, creating infrastructure in the form of houses, gardens, boats and landing places. The long-established whaling stations in southern New Zealand – Moeraki, Waikouaiti, Ōtākou, Bluff, Aparima – depended not only on shelter, an abundance of whales, landing places, and a source of fresh water, but also on the labour of Māori men and women.[3] Ngāi Tahu settlements in the interior were soon abandoned in favour of the coastal stations and the trading opportunities they provided, thus ushering in an intensive period of culture contact and economic exchange.[4]

As in other frontier societies, newcomers and indigenous people inhabited the same terrain and depended on each other for food and clothing, and for much-needed labour during the whaling season.[5] Stations attracted settlement around its hinterland, and visitors noted that their relations within the industry were marked by mutuality and exchange. Edward Shortland, the Sub-Protector of Aborigines, visited the southern regions in 1844, and reported that Ngāi Tahu were attracted to the stations 'coming from other parts of the country for the sake of tobacco, clothing, & c., which they could here obtain in exchange for their labour, or for pigs and potatos'.[6]

Pātahi and Palmer are associated with the Taieri region, having been drawn there by its shore whaling opportunities and agricultural potential. George and Edward Weller were the first to establish a whaling station on Moturata Island, at the mouth of the Taieri River, in 1838. It was fitted out and manned later that year, preparing for full operation in the New Year under its first manager, David Cureton.[7] Newcomers and local Ngāi Tahu undertook the day-to-day working of the station, among them names such as Murray, Bradbury, Whylie, Apes, Williams, Fern, Brown, Patterson, Russell, Antony, Robinson, Cory, Bowman, Happy, Teoto, Rua Keony, Harris, Morris and Richards. Given the smallness of Moturata and the limited supply of

View of Moturata Island, across the Taieri River mouth. From the 1890s, the Taieri Mouth and its surrounding districts became a popular recreation area. In 1927 the river was described as 'a boatman's paradise', and the 'splendid level beach' as 'one of the safest bathing spots in the Dominion'.[8] This dry-plate negative was reproduced in 1906 as a postcard.
[C.0105991, Museum of New Zealand Te Papa Tongarewa]

whales, alternative forms of resource exploitation were clearly essential to the station's longer-term survival. The economic importance of the abundant timber on the mainland was soon realised. In a letter to his brother George, Edward Weller described

> … a sample of pine timber, which is growing at Taiari [sic] and from 50 to 60 feet long, much superior to Otago pine. Banks the carpenter approves of the wood for boat building and that natives say they will assist in getting timber tho they cannot be depended on.[9]

Despite his cynicism, the development of the timber industry depended very much on the labour of local Ngāi Tahu. By December 1840, with local whaling in 'a most reckless and unprotected state', a thriving secondary economy had developed near the inland lakes, with 'the Natives' employed in the cutting and counting of logs.[10]

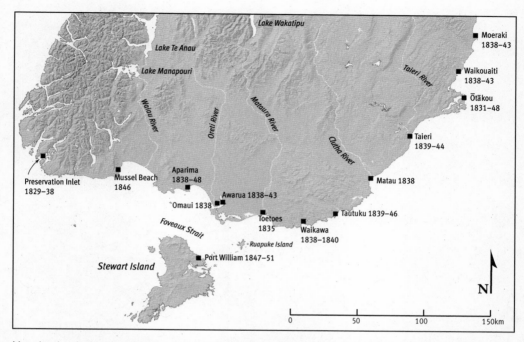

Map showing the location of shore whaling stations in southern New Zealand, and their years of operation.

As the newcomers came into contact with Ngāi Tahu women, many entered into intimate relationships with them. There are no statistics on the extent of interracial relationships during the whaling era, but anecdotal evidence suggests it was extensive. In 1844, New Zealand Company surveyor Frederick Tuckett estimated that from Banks Peninsula to Riverton 'two-thirds of the native women, who are not aged, are living with Europeans'.[11] When Tuckett visited Moturata in 1844, he found Tommy Chaseland and his Ngāi Tahu wife Puna keeping 'a very comfortable fireside, not the less so from the bleak barrenness which surrounds their dwellings; nowhere, perhaps, do twenty Englishmen reside on a spot so comfortless as this naked inaccessible isle'.[12] When the station was abandoned in 1841 and again in 1844, many of these men, such as James Wybrow, John Kelly and William Russell, briefly settled inland with their Ngāi Tahu kin, only to disperse in pursuit of economic opportunities as they arose.

Interracial alliances brought mutual benefits. For the newcomers, 'marrying in' had an integrative function, providing access to the land on

Marriage patterns in southern New Zealand were shaped partly by demography. During the 1830s and 1840s, European women were a rarity in Otago and Southland, but once large numbers of single white women arrived in the region the marriage patterns of whalers shifted. Captain James Wybrow, seen here with his mixed-descent son David, was one of a number of former whalers who sought the companionship of a European woman after the death of his Ngāi Tahu wife.
[E2904/10, Hocken Collections/Uare Taoka o Hākena]

which to establish a whaling station, and ensuring its ongoing protection. The level of protection conferred depended on the woman's status, which meant that whalers not only had to 'marry in', but had to marry well. Unsurprisingly, many of the Ngāi Tahu women who entered into such relationships in the first phase of contact were the daughters of chiefs or other well-connected women. Edward Weller, owner of the Ōtākou and Taieri whaling stations, married Paparu, daughter of the powerful warrior chief Taiaroa, to demonstrate his attachment to the Ngāi Tahu community.[13] In 1836 John Hughes, with his crew of William Haberfield, Peter Chevatt, John Thompson, Richard Burn and John Knox, established a whaling station at Onekakara, near present-day Moeraki.[14] Both Hughes and Haberfield married Ngāi Tahu women, and after the death of their wives remarried into the local Ngāi Tahu community. Haberfield's first wife was Merianna Teitei, niece of the Ngāi Tahu chief Te Maiharanui, and thus of high rank. The marriages of such women of status brought about the permanent settlement of male newcomers in the southern regions.

The recording of Pātahi's story

The scarcity of sources makes it extremely difficult to interpret the lives of indigenous women in the early contact period, and particularly their experience of interracial relationships.[15] But Pātahi is different. Her story is accessible because William Martin recorded her narrative, and left a diary and his unpublished reminiscences. Little is known about Martin's background before he arrived in New Zealand. His memoirs do not record his early life, but dwell instead on the excitement of the gold-rush years. We know much more about his later years: he eventually settled in Oamaru, and during the 1880s worked as a bailiff for the District and Magistrate's Court before taking up employment as an usher at the Supreme Court in Dunedin. After his retirement in 1898 he became a Justice of the Peace.

Martin's knowledge of Māori people, language and culture was minimal until the gold-rushes brought him into contact with their world. It was 'the first time most of us had had an intercourse with the Maoris, and we were determined to hold aloof from them and keep them at arms length'. But having encountered their generosity and hospitality, he concluded that

View of the Southern Alps from the mouth of the Taramakau River, c. 1867 (artist unknown). It was on the banks of this river that William Martin began prospecting for gold in the early 1860s; and it was near here that he met Pātahi. [A-048-025, Alexander Turnbull Library, National Library of New Zealand/Te Puna Mātauranga o Aotearoa]

Māori were 'very different from what we expected. Instead of being hostile and thieving, we found them kind and careful of us and our goods'.[16] Martin learnt some of their language and was able to converse in it, although a Māori lay preacher was available to act as mediator and translator. Communication difficulties were also allayed by the fact that southern Māori were already familiar with the English language, having come into regular and sustained contact with newcomers from the 1790s. Māori interest in literacy and the written text emerged in the 1830s, culminating in the appearance of Māori language newspapers in the North Island from 1842. Māori soon became a highly literate people; indeed, two-thirds of Māori adults could read and write their own language by the 1850s.[17]

When Martin met Pātahi in 1863, southern Māori had been in contact with missionaries for nearly twenty years. Nonetheless, Martin 'had often wondered how it was that Pata[h]i was the one who spoke our language so well'.[18] One night, having remarked on her 'superior knowledge of our speech', he asked her if she had ever lived with or near Pākehā, and in due course 'drew from her the following explanation given as near as I can in her own words'.[19] How far Martin retained 'her own words' is difficult to assess, but her narrative does follow the style of nineteenth century Māori literacy, in which written and oral traditions converged.[20] Letters published in Māori language newspapers from 1842 to 1863, for example, are 'more oral than written in style', with embellishment, metaphor, symbolism and other common features of spoken Māori.[21] While Martin attempted to replicate Pātahi's broken English, there is little such embellishment in the text, nor any of the songs or incantations usually associated with Māori oral tradition. Some oral elements are present, however, notably a personal connection with the audience, and little distinction between past and present in the recounting of events.[22] Pātahi's narrative is a speech, but it does not follow Māori protocols of whaikōrero (formal speech-making).[23]

But despite Pātahi's involvement, this is ultimately a Western text, controlled by a male newcomer. Martin did not simply 'record' her story objectively; he intervened, interpreting and shaping it to tell the story of an indigenous woman subjected to the cruelty of a white man. In his concluding comments, he described Palmer as her 'betrayer', who 'flung away the purest richest gift to man – a woman's pure love – whether the giver be black or white'.[24] However, his emotional embellishment does not alter the truth of Pātahi's story. Family records and historical evidence confirm the existence of Pātahi's relationship with Palmer and its eventual demise, as she described them to Martin. While the origins and authorship of this text are complex, Pātahi's story does provide a rare insight into the private world of an indigenous woman in the early contact period.

Pātahi's decision to marry Palmer took place in an era of great conflict and major social and economic shifts for Ngāi Tahu. In the late 1820s and early 1830s, Ngāti Toa from Kapiti Island, led by Te Rauparaha, made a series of raids on the tribes of the northern and central South Island, including Ngāi Tahu. Te Rauparaha succeeded in destroying the Ngāi Tahu stronghold of Kaiapoi in 1831, closely followed by the rout of Ōnawe pā, in Akaroa Harbour. These attacks caused widespread devastation among Ngāi Tahu in Canterbury, and extensive depopulation as a result of death or migration.

Edwin Palmer (1802–86). Three Palmer men played a significant role in the history of whaling and agriculture at Taieri. All three married Ngāi Tahu women and fathered large families. Edwin married Pātahi, his brother William married three Ngāi Tahu women, and his nephew Ned married Sarah Brown, the 'half-caste' daughter of Te Wharerimu and the sealer Robert Brown.
[E1795/36, Hocken Collections/Uare Taoka o Hākena]

Pātahi's reference to the Ngāti Toa raids places her meeting with Palmer in the late 1820s, and this is confirmed by the birth of their first child, Betsy, in 1829, followed by a second daughter, Jane, in 1830.

What is most interesting in Pātahi's narrative is her rejection of Tūhawaiki, the most important of the southern Ngāi Tahu chiefs, in favour of Palmer. Her people were clearly anxious for an alliance with Tūhawaiki, and Pātahi's freedom to reject him demonstrates her status. Pātahi has been remarkably difficult to find in published Ngāi Tahu whakapapa, suggesting that her rejection of Tūhawaiki had long-term consequences. However, her whakapapa can be pieced together from a number of sources. She was a descendant of Tūrakautahi, the builder of Kaiapoi pā, from whom many contemporary Ngāi Tahu leaders also descend, and his first wife, Hinekakai. Tūrakautahi's son, Uruhia, married Hineari, a descendant of Tūrakautahi's second wife, Te Wharepapa. Their great-grandson, Kaioneone, was the uncle of Pātahi. Her parents' names were not recorded.

Pātahi's story illustrates the central role of female agency in the intimate history of New Zealand's colonial past. As such, it provides an intriguing insight into a relationship based on mutual love and attraction, yet one that does not fully fit the usual pattern of interracial relationships as they are currently investigated in New Zealand and elsewhere. Pātahi's experience shows that interracial marriage was not always explicitly about strategic alliances and access to resources. Pātahi's people were not, in fact, interested in 'marrying in' a Pākehā whaler and trader: the value they attached to a marriage with Tūhawaiki, the foremost chief of Ngāi Tahu, was clearly far greater. Nor did interracial marriage always have a protective function; indeed, for Palmer it was potentially dangerous. Pātahi's decision to marry him, rather than Tūhawaiki, would certainly not have guaranteed him the protection usually conferred by such a union. Her relationship with Palmer, and others like it, illustrate the degree of flexibility in Māori marriage customs. While high-ranking women did enter into arranged marriages of benefit to the tribe, they also had the power to seek alliances on their own terms. Yet Pātahi's experience shows that interracial marriage, for all its benefits, was not to be undertaken at the expense of traditional protocols, rankings and kinship obligations.

Palmer's background was similar to that of many traders and whalers who frequented the southern districts of New Zealand. Many whalers in the region were escaped convicts from the Australian colonies, or the children of convicts who had gained their ticket of leave. Edwin was born in Sydney in 1802, the first child of Richard Palmer and Elizabeth Tetley. Both were English convicts who had been transported to New South Wales in 1800 and 1801 respectively.[25] Little is known about Edwin's childhood, but his adult life was peripatetic. Having settled with Pātahi at Ōtākou in the late 1820s, by 1832 he was whaling at Preservation Inlet, and had spent some time at the Tautuku whaling station where his brother, William McLeur Palmer, was manager. In the 1840s Edwin managed the farm of whaling magnate Johnny Jones, near Waikouaiti in Otago.[26] This mobility is not atypical. Once a whaling station had been abandoned, the whalers often moved on to other work. Palmer travelled up and down the southern coast, following job opportunities in trade and whaling as they arose. How Edwin and Pātahi met, whether they remained together during this mobility, or the nature of their relationship during this period is not the subject of Pātahi's narrative.

Pātahi's relationship with Palmer, and the frontier conditions that fostered it, underwent a rapid shift with the arrival of Scottish colonists in the region from 1848, and the founding of the city of Dunedin as part of the Otago Settlement. Pātahi described to Martin how her life changed:

> By and by two, three, ships come, bring lot of white people, they go up the river make a lot of houses, by and by Mr Palmer go often away in boat to see them, lot of other ships come, then Mr Palmer go to Taieri, build house, take lot of cattle with him, I want to go too, but he say no, sometimes he no come for a long time and when he come he very cross; and by and by he say he no married to me like white people then he say he married to white woman and he come for the children, he take them away from me. I very angry and make a long cry, the Maori say 'Me no good better you had married Bloody Jack.' About a year after Toby a Maori he take me for his wife, but many times I cry.[27]

Palmer's own version of events is contradictory. Never having formalised his union with Pātahi in a Christian marriage ceremony, his commitment may have been the weaker. In January 1851 the Reverend Thomas Burns,

Presbyterian minister to the Otago Association, found Palmer residing with his 'half-caste' daughter Jane at Maitapapa; he also noted that Palmer's Māori wife had 'run away'.[28] Some years earlier, when Palmer was living at Waikouaiti, Edward Shortland recorded his Ngāi Tahu wife as 'dead'.[29] But Pātahi was very much alive. She was baptised Irihāpeti/Elizabeth in November 1851 at the Holy Trinity Anglican church in Lyttelton, and was married there on 13 January 1852 to Toby.[30] By 1863, Pātahi was living at Greenstone on the banks of the Taramakau River, on the West Coast, and it was there that she encountered William Martin. She went on to marry for a third time, to Haimona Tuangau from Hawke's Bay, who was the Māori Catechist at Port Levy on Banks Peninsula.[31] Pātahi died in 1887. Meanwhile, in December 1851, Palmer had married Scots-born Beatrice Fowler, twenty years his junior, and settled into a more respectable life as a large landholder in the prosperous farming district of Otokia, only a few kilometres away from Maitapapa.[32] Together he and Beatrice raised a family of five sons and one daughter.[33]

Abandonment was not an uncommon outcome of interracial marriage during the whaling period. Among 'Pākehā Māori' – male newcomers who married into and lived in Māori communities in the contact era – abandonment increased after 1840 as their economic and political influence grew.[34] It was also a feature of interracial marriage in connection with the Canadian fur trade and, as Sylvia Van Kirk has noted, was usually driven by the male partner's desire for respectability as settler society began to emerge from frontier conditions.[35] Yet marriage records indicate that many relationships formed in the early nineteenth century between whalers and Ngāi Tahu women were long-lasting. While a number of men lost their wives during childbirth or through introduced disease, many of them, like Hughes and Haberfield of Moeraki, chose to remarry women of Ngāi Tahu descent. Edwin Palmer's brother, the whaler William Palmer, whose first two wives were Ngāi Tahu, married for a third time to Ann Holmes, of mixed Ngāi Tahu/European descent.[36]

The status of Pātahi's relationship with Palmer is complex. As a woman of rank, Pātahi had an important social and political role to play through her marriage. Yet she rejected the expectations of her community, and the marriage customs were never observed in her alliance with Palmer. Thus the relationship was never sanctioned, because she entered into it on her own terms. In the eyes of her community, Pātahi was not married. In her own eyes, however, she *was* in a marriage, a belief reflected in her subsequent feelings of abandonment. Significantly, she never returned to her people at Ōtākou after Palmer abandoned her, but moved to Banks Peninsula. This suggests that her failure to bring honour and prestige to her community by contracting a marriage with a leading Ngāi Tahu chief had long-term consequences.

Adding to her experience of abandonment was the pain of losing contact with her daughters after Palmer refused her access. With her second husband, Pātahi had travelled to the Taieri to see them:

> We stop in the bush all night, next morning I go near the grass field and see Mr Palmer's house, but the bush hide me, by and by I see one little girl, she come near … I make a call as I see her come, she no see me, then I come nearer and called her, she come and we both make a cry … by and by the white woman sees us and tell Mr Palmer, then he come down and say, what you do here. I say I come to see my little girls. He look very angry and say 'You no stop here.' I say 'No.' He say, 'Well, you come get some breakfast then you go away.' I went to the house … He give me lot of food and some tobacco then he took us to the road and say 'Goodbye. No you come again.' That is the last time I see my little girls … They not little now, they all women now. I am long way from them. I am getting old. I think I never see them again.[37]

The subsequent marriages of Betsy and Jane reflect the fluidity of race and class in early Dunedin. Both achieved high-status marriages within whaling society and Ngāi Tahu respectively. In 1846 Betsy married Richard Sizemore, the brother-in-law of whaling magnate Johnny Jones, and had four children with him before her death in 1858.[38] Jane married Robert Brown/Pāpu Paraone, the mixed-descent grandson of Tapui, a chief of the Foveaux Strait region. While these marriages in the mid 1840s suggest a frontier society in which race and class intertwined, and where the colonial elite emerged out of the whaling economy, by the 1850s this had been superseded by a new colonial order, in which respectability and morality

William Palmer (1815–1903), Edwin's brother, started his career as a whaler in Foveaux Strait, eventually becoming manager of the Tautuku whaling station. He married three times: first to Titi, then to her sister, Te Haukawe. After Te Haukawe's death he moved his family of five daughters to Taieri, where their kin resided, and there he met his third wife, Ann Holmes, daughter of James Holmes and Tamiraki. The Crane, Campbell, Smith, Bryant and Tanner families are all descended from him. [F402/12, Hocken Collections/Uare Taoka o Hākena]

were equated with white womanhood. Just as marriage was a key institution in Māori society, and was used by Ngāi Tahu as an assimilation tool in the contact era, marriage was central to the creation of a civil society on the colonial frontier.[39]

Although Pātahi's subsequent marriages suggest that she recovered from her abandonment by Palmer, this did not mean that her own people regarded her as a suitable marriage partner. These new relationships did not draw her back into Ngāi Tahu society, but were with men from northern tribes. As noted in Chapter 1, inter-tribal or inter-hapū marriages were not common in Māori society, and were undertaken only for political purposes. They also had significant economic implications, because high-ranking women took their resource rights with them. Bruce Biggs has found that out-group marriages in traditional Māori society were a 'possible source of quarrelling, especially in view of the great value, sentimental as well as practical, with which land was invested'.[40]

The conflicts over land that arose from such alliances continued into the contact era, as marriage to newcomers was integrated into customary marriage practices. This is evident in Pātahi's abandonment and its implications for her children. Historian and ethnographer Herries Beattie was told one version of Pātahi's story in February 1915:

> It was claimed that Ned [Edwin] Palmer married a Maori wife and got land through her and later married a European wife, one Beatrice Fowler, a regular harridan by all accounts. In his will I am told he left the land to his European children, ignoring the halfcaste children through whose mother he acquired it. If this be true it was a most unfair and unjust proceeding.[41]

The story of Pātahi's abandonment was also well known among the river communities surrounding Maitapapa. Accounts collected by Margaret Shaw during the late 1940s focused on the economic consequences for the family.[42] William Adam, who farmed at Waihola from the late nineteenth century and employed many local Ngāi Tahu, told Shaw that Edwin Palmer 'had dismissed his Maori wife and his two daughters' to marry 'Beatrix Fowler a hardy Scottish woman from East Lothian'.[43] Thelma Smith, a descendant of Pātahi, told Shaw that before dissolving the relationship, 'Edwin and his

Dunedin grew rapidly during the gold-rush years of the 1860s. In this watercolour by W. S. Hatton, dated 1861, a Māori family looks down on the city and its busy harbour. Systematic colonisation of Otago from 1848, as well as the rush of newcomers in the 1860s, offered economic opportunities for Ngāi Tahu, but also marked a shift towards Pākehā political, social and cultural dominance. [B-078-007, Alexander Turnbull Library, National Library of New Zealand/Te Puna Mātauranga o Aotearoa]

second consort prudently [had Pātahi] sign over her considerable southern property first – the foundation of their wealth'.[44]

Palmer did not, however, escape the scrutiny of his neighbours, many of whom were former whalers living with their Ngāi Tahu wives and mixed-descent children at Maitapapa. Nor did interracial marriage prevent mixed-descent children being accepted into Ngāi Tahu society. Pātahi's daughters did not lose their Ngāi Tahu rights, nor the social and economic responsibilities that their whakapapa entailed. Despite the belief of locals, there is no evidence that Palmer actually gained land through his marriage to Pātahi. Generally speaking, interracial marriage gave whalers the patronage and protection of a chief and occupation rights, not land ownership rights. Palmer's marriage to Pātahi certainly brought him no protection, and it is unlikely that he gained any land from it.

Edwin died in March 1886 at his home 'Tahora', in Upper Walker Street, Dunedin, leaving his estate to Beatrice and his sons. The existence of his surviving daughter from his first marriage was not acknowledged.[45] The children from his second marriage maintained the farm after his death, and remained in the Taieri district, near the settlement where their half-sister Jane and her children lived. The two families rarely came into contact: the children and grandchildren attended different schools and socialised in very different circles. Thelma Smith warned Margaret Shaw that 'it would not be polite to mention the Maori past' among descendants of the 'second Palmer family'.[46]

. . .

Pātahi's interracial relationship is not easy to define. It was neither a brief encounter, nor a relationship of exchange; and the fact that it was not sanctioned by her community makes it difficult to see it as a customary marriage. From Pātahi's perspective it was a relationship of mutual love and attraction, albeit one that was never formalised. A range of interracial relationships took place in southern New Zealand in the early nineteenth century, and such alliances were not always a form of trade in women, based on gaining access to resources. Sometimes women repudiated custom and chose to marry for personal reasons. Pātahi's experience suggests that tribal responses to interracial relationships were not always positive, and that the outcome could, in fact, be cultural and personal dislocation. For Pātahi, the decision to marry a whaler resulted in abandonment, loss and displacement.

Pātahi was a woman of strong character, who defied her community and the expectation invested in her as a woman of rank in order to enter into a relationship that her community refused to recognise. Despite her subsequent abandonment, she continued to live according to traditional seasonal patterns, and maintained her connection with her culture, though not with her kin. Her story of interracial encounter is significant because it demonstrates the power that a woman of status could wield when it came to marriage; but in this case her decision had serious consequences. It is also an emotional story, as we hear in 'her own words' the impact of her abandonment, leading to immense suffering in the loss of her kin and children. Pātahi's narrative makes explicit the complex nature of interracial intimacy – something rarely encountered in the study of culture contact.

Chapter 3. Interracial Families and Communities

The interracial relationships that developed between male newcomers and Ngāi Tahu women in southern New Zealand were welcomed by officials and Māori alike. Such relationships were mutually beneficial: Ngāi Tahu welcomed whalers because the industry brought new economic opportunities, while marriage with Ngāi Tahu women drew whalers into a network of reciprocal obligations. For newcomers, rank was no barrier: all levels of the station hierarchy, from managers to coopers, carpenters, sailors and clerks, engaged in interracial relationships, including customary marriages; indeed, station owners placed no restrictions on such unions. Ngāi Tahu leaders, on the other hand, intervened in and mediated this marriage market, identifying men of rank and status with whom they wished to make alliances. As Atholl Anderson has noted, daughters of chiefs occupied the top tier of women who 'married in' members of the whaling elite such as the Wellers, owners of numerous stations along the southern coast.[1] This marriage hierarchy would shape the fortunes of many of the first generation of mixed-descent families.

While many affective ties were contracted within the context of a relatively short-lived industry, the shore whaling era produced long-term interracial relationships, and a mixed-descent population with strong familial bonds and cultural ties to Ngāi Tahu. Like the Canadian fur trade, another industry in which interracial relationships were crucial to success, shore whaling was 'not simply an economic activity, but a social and

Clockwise from rear left: Stephen Watson, Theophilius Daniel, John Howell and Lewis Acker. These men were leading figures in the Aparima (Riverton) community, which Howell had established as a whaling station in 1838. Both Howell and Acker married Māori women, while Daniel and his wife, Elizabeth Stevens, fostered a number of mixed-descent children. [83/0728, Hocken Collections/Uare Taoka o Hākena]

cultural complex' based on physical hybridity, and cultural, economic and technological intermixing.[2] What emerged in Western Canada, and in other frontier regions such as the Great Lakes, was a set of relationships based not on 'casual, promiscuous encounters but the development of marital unions which gave rise to distinct family units'.[3] But whereas in North America there has been a strong interest in the mixed-descent communities that emerged out of the fur trade, in New Zealand the history of early interracial communities is less well known. Atholl Anderson has called for detailed regional and community studies in order to understand the impact of interracial marriage,[4] and his challenge has been taken up by historians of settler colonialism.

By tracing the history of interracial families in detail, particularly the networks they formed, we can reconstruct the social world in which they lived. The experiences of such families, during an era in which many Māori suffered great loss, needs to be understood in terms of class and its intersection with race and colonial policy. During the 1860s and 1870s, for example, the mixed-descent families in the Bay of Plenty lived within the context of war, a brutal policy of land confiscation, and an aggressive assimilation policy, and those who professed their loyalty to the Crown achieved some social and economic prominence. In her sensitive study of the interracial families of southern New Zealand, Kate Stevens demonstrates that the social and economic success of such families often depended on access to land, which was itself a product of a good marriage alliance. An elite class of interracial families emerged in the region by the 1860s, but they were small in number. Most families lived on the economic margins, and within Ngāi Tahu communities, sharing with their relatives a colonial experience of land dispossession.[5] Most importantly, through marriage, the first generation of mixed-descent children formed a kinship network that connected Ngāi Tahu and newcomers into a social world of family and community obligations.[6]

The emergence of a mixed-descent population

In the late 1840s, with shore whaling in decline and agriculture becoming established in the southern regions, newcomers had already altered the demographics of the Ngāi Tahu population.[7] On his 1844 journey through the South Island, Edward Shortland, the Sub-Protector of Aborigines, noted that the 'number of half-caste children is, as yet, very trifling; probably little more than three hundred'.[8] This was hardly a 'trifling' number, within a population that hovered around two thousand. What is most interesting about Shortland's journey is the evidence he found of extensive economic and social interaction between Māori and Europeans in the vicinity of shore whaling stations – something that early settlers in northern New Zealand had noted in the 1830s. Joel Polack, a Jewish trader at the Hokianga, claimed that in 1838 there were 'innumerable' Europeans dwelling in the South Island – mostly 'old men living there for the last forty years on the coast'.[9]

The interracial communities that developed around the whaling stations were indeed thriving. In 1844, twenty European men, thirteen Māori women and twelve 'half-caste' children were living at Aparima (now Riverton), where John Howell had established a whaling station in 1838. There was a similar-sized community at the Tautuku whaling station. In 1844 surveyor Frederick Tuckett noted that the men at Tautuku had 'erected some good houses', and that William Palmer, one of the community leaders, had a wife of 'very prepossessing appearance and manners, the mother of two or three fine children'.[10] The Ōtākou station was home to eighteen newcomers, ten Māori women, and nine 'half-caste' children. There were also sizeable interracial communities at Waikouaiti and Moeraki in Otago, both the sites of large whaling stations.[11] In total, Shortland identified 170 male newcomers living among Ngāi Tahu in 1844.[12]

In May 1845 Johannes Wohlers, the Lutheran missionary at Ruapuke Island, noted the considerable number of European men living on the region's shores, and that 'more and more remain here'; all of them 'amalgamate with the natives' and co-habit 'in marriage according to the New Zealand way'.[13] By December that year the southern coast was 'crowded with fisheries and many whaling ships are cruising around here'.[14] At that time The Neck, the major settlement on Stewart Island, was 'inhabited by Europeans who are married to New Zealand women', and who had fathered, Wohlers claimed, at least a hundred 'half-caste' children.[15] Just two months later, he counted 150 such children living 'in the surroundings of Foveaux Strait'.[16]

Ōtākou whaling station, on Otago Peninsula (undated). Whaling stations were bustling villages, centres of trade with a vibrant social life. Established by the Weller brothers in 1831, Ōtākou was one of the oldest and most successful whaling stations in the southern region, attracting a large labour force comprising both newcomers and Ngāi Tahu. [E2181/-, Hocken Collections/Uare Taoka o Hākena]

Numerous mixed-descent families lived on Stewart Island in the 1840s and 1850s. Indeed, in 1844, 72 per cent of the mixed-descent population of southern New Zealand were living in the Foveaux Strait region, and 28 per cent in Otago.[17] While seasonal mobility was a feature of the shore whaling industry and the lives of its workers, Stewart Island came the closest to developing a distinct mixed-descent community, primarily because former whalers and their families settled permanently on the island, where they farmed, or worked in the shipping industry. Many were still living there in 1864, when surveyor and Land Commissioner Theophilius Heale visited the area. He described the ex-whalers as

> … aged men, but they are generally surrounded by half-caste families, who constitute a little community which has grown up entirely without aid or care from the Government, and which is remarkable for the general good conduct of its members.[18]

Among the mixed-descent families living on the island at that time were names such as Moss, Davis, Cooper, Chaseland, Antoni, Goombs, Joseph, Thomas, Brown, Goodwilly, Watson, Leech, Owen, Newton, Wybrow, Cross, Lowry, Anglem, Gilroy, Parker, Joss, Bragg, Honor, Whitelock, Lees and Bates. Native Commissioner Alexander Mackay recorded 94 'half-castes' living at or near The Neck in 1867, 'most of whom are grown up, and have families'.[19] By the 1880s the mixed-descent population around Foveaux Strait had grown substantially, and was largely located at the mainland settlements of Riverton and Bluff, and on Stewart Island. In 1881, of the 295 people living on the island, 111 (37%) were 'half-caste', making it one of the largest mixed-descent populations in southern New Zealand.[20]

Enumerating 'half-castes'

It is difficult to account for this mixed-descent population statistically, owing to inconsistencies in the national census. Enumeration of the Māori population began on a national basis in 1874, but the Māori census was held separately from that of the non-Māori population and was not comprehensive, with officials initially preferring estimates rather than precise figures.[21] To confuse matters, under the Census Act passed in 1877, the mixed-descent population was to be classified as 'half-castes living as European' in the general census, and 'half-castes living as Maori' in the Māori census. Separating 'half-castes' along these lines drew on a tradition established by officials in the 1840s and 1850s, who classified mixed-descent children according to whether they were recognised by their European father, or 'brought up in Maori fashion by the Maori mother'.[22] When former Attorney General William Swainson claimed that five hundred individuals of mixed descent were residing in Auckland in 1857, he was referring to those acknowledged by their fathers and living in settler society.[23] Nor was the decision to categorise a person as 'half-caste' evenly applied by census officials, because people of mixed descent were not enumerated on the basis of 'race' alone. Local enumerators also drew on visual appearance, dress, and place of residence.

While the census was not precise, the results give a general indication of the size and location of the mixed-descent population. 'Half-castes' were recorded in the first national census in 1871, and totalled 1,465; by 1874, the number had increased to 1,860, and by 1881 to 2,004.[24] Even though the first Māori census was held in 1874, the category 'half-castes living as Maori' was not included until 1886, allowing a much fuller picture of the total mixed-descent population across the two categories. The combined figure was 4,212 in 1886, 4,828 in 1891, and 5,762 in 1896.[25]

Census figures also demonstrate that interracial marriage was largely experienced in Māori communities, with many tribal groups absorbing the mixed-descent population. From 1886 to 1896, the total mixed-descent population was only 0.7 to 0.8 per cent of the non-Māori population, but accounted for a much larger proportion of the Māori population; in 1886, for example, it was 5.3 per cent.[26] The proportion also varied between tribes, reflecting the extent of interracial contact in each region historically. People of mixed descent were a much larger proportion of the Māori population in the Bay of Islands, Bay of Plenty and lower South Island, where whaling and trading stations were clustered in far greater numbers than elsewhere in New Zealand during the early nineteenth century. When the 'half-caste' figures are analysed by tribal group, it is clear that interracial marriage was far more common in some regions than in others. According to the 1891 census, 32 per cent of the Ngāi Tahu population was of mixed descent, followed by Ngāti Maniapoto (11.1%), Ngāti Porou (6.8%), Ngāti Kahungunu (5.2%), Ngā Puhi (4.9%), Arawa (4.8%), and Waikato (3.9%). By 1896, the mixed-descent population was living increasingly among Māori, with only 39 per cent recorded as 'living as Europeans', compared with 45 per cent in 1891. All tribal groups experienced an increase in their mixed-descent population that year: the Ngāti Porou figure rose to 10.3 per cent, Ngā Puhi to 7.4 per cent, and Arawa to 5.1 per cent. In the South Island as a whole, the proportion was 48 per cent.

Shaping identity

While census figures are problematic, they do reveal some important trends. Statistics confirm that Ngāi Tahu increasingly comprised people of mixed descent, and that a sustained pattern of interracial marriage was central to their colonial experience. What differentiates Ngāi Tahu from northern groups such as Ngā Puhi and Ngāti Porou is that the newcomers Ngāi Tahu encountered from the early nineteenth century remained within their tribal territory on a permanent basis, producing a largely mixed-descent population by the latter part of the century. Not only was culture contact in the South Island very different from what was experienced elsewhere in New Zealand, but the extent of interracial relationships in the south also

Lewis Acker, *c.* 1880. One of several American whalers who settled in New Zealand during the 1830s, Acker worked with John Howell at Riverton, and then as a boat-builder and carpenter on Stewart Island. He eventually settled at Otatara, where he farmed. Both his marriages were solemnised in the Christian church, and all his children were baptised. [1/2-190150-F, Alexander Turnbull Library, National Library of New Zealand/Te Puna Mātauranga o Aotearoa]

played a significant role in shaping Ngāi Tahu identity during the nineteenth century and beyond.[27] To outsiders, Ngāi Tahu became 'the white tribe'.

Given the concentration of mixed-descent people in the far south of New Zealand from the 1840s, there was the potential for a distinct mixed-descent community with its own separate identity to develop. This is what happened in Canada with the Mētis, a group formed out of interracial relationships in the fur trade, who developed a distinctive cultural identity separate from those of the aboriginal people and settlers. But in southern New Zealand this did not eventuate, for several reasons. Whalers in the South Island during the 1830s and 1840s were a highly mobile group, lacking a centre of settlement such as Red River or Batoche in Western Canada. As a result, the mixed-descent population they fathered was dispersed across Otago, Southland and Stewart Island. While there were small pockets where mixed-descent populations were concentrated, these people were living alongside, and often absorbed by, the Māori population, taking on tribal affiliations and identity.

A separate ethnic identity, based on distinct cultural and religious values and social practices, gained little purchase when the origins of the newcomers were so diverse. The first wave of 140 newcomers to southern New Zealand were mainly European, but their countries of origin included Australia, the United States, Ireland and Scotland. William and Edwin Palmer were born to English parents in Australia, as was Nathaniel Bates. George Newton was Scottish, and John Kelly was Irish.[28] Others included the American whaler Lewis Acker, Thomas Chaseland, of mixed Aboriginal-European descent, William Apes, a Native American, and Joseph Antoni, who was Portuguese.

By the end of the nineteenth century, Stewart Island had a truly international demographic. Many of the male settlers hailed from the Shetland or Orkney Islands, such as Tom Leask, who was persuaded to settle there in 1866 by James Harrold, a fellow Orcadian.[29] Some, like Frederick Lonneker, were German, and many others were Scandinavian. In 1896 the non-Māori population was 228, and over half of them (140) were men.[30] These male newcomers came from Australia, England, Wales, Scotland, Ireland, France, Germany, Portugal, Russia, Sweden and Norway. There was a similar pattern

Bravo Island on Paterson Inlet, Stewart Island, painted in 1879 by Christopher Aubrey. By the 1870s Paterson Inlet had developed into a thriving interracial community, featuring European-style houses and extensive agricultural development. The house of Portuguese whaler Manuel Goomes (or Gomez) can be seen centre left, with people standing in the doorway. [C-126-010, Alexander Turnbull Library, National Library of New Zealand/Te Puna Mātauranga o Aotearoa]

of diversity at other prominent interracial communities on the mainland, such as Riverton and Bluff. Religious affiliations were also likely to have been varied, something that Wohlers, the sole missionary in the region, had to grapple with as he attempted to draw newcomers and Ngāi Tahu into the bonds of Christian marriage.

The meaning of marriage

Marriage continued to function as an assimilatory tool for Ngāi Tahu well after the whaling industry died out in the late 1840s, as evidenced by the use of marriage to tie together an established network of interracial families across the generations. This was despite the attempts of missionaries to encourage new marriage practices. For missionaries in southern New Zealand and elsewhere, baptism and marriage were central to the conversion of both Māori and newcomers to Christianity, and to the creation

The population of male newcomers who settled permanently in southern New Zealand was characterised by ethnic, religious and cultural diversity. Not all of them originated from Britain. Americans, Europeans, Native Americans, African Americans, and South-east Asians arrived as a result of their employment in the maritime trades, particularly bay whaling or shore whaling. This undated photograph is of Manuel Goomes (or Gomez), who settled on Stewart Island. He was Portuguese, as was fellow whaler Joseph Antoni. Goomes married Johanna Antoni, the daughter of Joseph and Esther Pura, and half-sister of Margaret, in 1858.
[S08-542c, MS1417/001, Maida Barlow Papers, Hocken Collections/Uare Taoka o Hākena]

mr. Wohler's church + schoolhouse, Ruapuke Isla...(march 1896.)

By 1896, when this sketch was made, the Ruapuke mission station was no longer the thriving centre of activity it had been in the 1850s and 1860s. Johannes Wohlers had died in 1885, and by the end of the century many Ngāi Tahu and mixed-descent families had moved to the mainland, settling at Invercargill, Bluff and Riverton. [E5216/17, Hocken Collections/Uare Taoka o Hākena]

of civil society. Wesleyan missionaries James Watkin, Charles Creed and William Kirk were stationed at Waikouaiti, on the Otago Peninsula. But it was the Lutheran Johannes Wohlers who had the most extensive contact with southern Māori. Wohlers had arrived in the South Island in 1843, with three trainees of the North German Missionary Society. With the encouragement of Ngāi Tahu's paramount chief, Tūhawaiki, Wohlers established a mission station on Ruapuke Island, in Foveaux Strait, in May 1844. Ruapuke was the headquarters of southern Ngāi Tahu; but as Wohlers explained, it had certain advantages for a mission site 'because it is a sort of gathering place, where everybody, native or European who crosses through these waters comes ashore'.[31] He lived on Ruapuke for forty years, ministering to both the island's population and dispersed settlements on the mainland.

Like whalers, missionaries lived in close proximity to Ngāi Tahu, and the relationships they developed were often ambiguous. Recognising this, perhaps, Wohlers announced: 'I am not the man to civilize them, on the

Left: Reverend Johannes Wohlers (1811–1885), in *c.* 1870s. [1/2-022563-F, Alexander Turnbull Library, National Library of New Zealand/Te Puna Mātauranga o Aotearoa]

Right: James Watkin (1805–1886), the first missionary to Otago. Having been found guilty of misconduct in Tonga in 1837, he was sent to Otago, where he established the Methodist mission at Waikouaiti in 1840. Four years later he was transferred to Wellington, where he stayed until 1855. [S08-140b, Hocken Collections/Uare Taoka o Hākena]

contrary the natives uncivilize me.'[32] With proximity came temptation, and several New Zealand missionaries, married and single, engaged in sexual relationships with Māori women.[33] Wohlers was not unaware of the risks inherent in the missionary encounter. In May 1845 he noted: 'it is not quite without danger for such an old bachelor as me to come into such close contact with the young New Zealand women who are not invariably amiable'.[34] Of one of his neighbours, a Mrs Sterling, he wrote: '[She is] the crown of the women at Foveaux Strait and one cannot at all notice that she is a halfcaste. She is so pretty, so friendly, so quick and so clever that one might envy Sterling for her.'[35] Wohlers' solution to both isolation and temptation was to marry Eliza Palmer of Wellington in September 1849.

Having introduced the Christian marriage ceremony into southern New Zealand, missionaries were particularly critical of whalers who engaged in illicit relationships. James Watkin viewed interracial marriage as a trade relationship, describing it as 'the practice of selling', thus denying any female agency in such encounters, or the possibility of their being romantic or meaningful connections.[36] Watkin viewed this 'practice of selling' as central to the demographic decline of southern Ngāi Tahu during the 1840s, when in fact inter-tribal conflict, introduced disease and epidemics were more culpable. Wohlers, on the other hand, supported and encouraged interracial marriage, seeing it as a temporary solution to that decline: 'Europeans with their mixed offspring are going to continue the line of the thin population of this region'.[37] These views were typical of colonial musings on indigenous peoples, in which depopulation and eventual disappearance tended to dominate.[38]

Recognising that interracial marriage could not be eradicated or prevented, many missionaries turned their energies to encouraging 'regular unions'. Ngāi Tahu women were commended for enthusiastically engaging in this practice. Wohlers claimed success when he discovered that 'girls who are lucky enough to get a European fiancé insist on being officially married'.[39] Alfred Domett, Civil Secretary in Governor George Grey's administration, linked Wohlers' work in bringing Christian marriage to southern Ngāi Tahu with his 'efforts to civilize and improve the Natives in that District'.[40] In recognition of this work, Ruapuke became a Registry Office in 1849 under the provisions of the Marriage Ordinance 1847, thus ensuring that the rule of law and the authority of the Christian Church were extended to all southern Ngāi Tahu.

However, bringing legal marriage to Māori was as much about controlling newcomers as it was about converting Māori to Christianity. The German naturalist Ernst Dieffenbach noted that, in northern New Zealand, 'the missionaries seem to have been actuated by a desire to check the influence of bad characters who may thus connect themselves with a tribe'.[41] Exasperated by the behaviour of former whalers, Wohlers claimed that they 'don't lift a finger to civilise their wives. The most they do is buy them a European women's dress, whether it fits or is becoming or not'.[42] Just seven months later, in December 1845, Wohlers recorded some success, claiming that the men, 'especially those who already have several children', were seeking to have their families baptised 'and to get married to their wives in the Christian way'.[43]

Marriages undertaken by newcomers in the southern regions were, for the most part, monogamous. Any deviation from this path often attracted censure from the local missionary, who fostered and publicly celebrated a brand of masculinity among newcomers that encompassed Christian marriage, the absence of violence, and the provision of economic security for the family. Although many of the existing unions were of long standing, and accepted by Ngāi Tahu because they followed local custom, the broad acceptance of Christian marriage by newcomers 'was probably influenced in part by the desire to retain social standing within the emerging colonial society'.[44] While some newcomers saw no need to formalise their union, most took advantage of the opportunity and travelled great distances to do so. Among them was James Spencer, who with Mere Kauri travelled from Bluff to the mission at Waikouaiti to marry in January 1841.[45]

There is also evidence that polygamy existed. In 1844, for example, Bishop Selwyn found Joseph Honour living with two Māori women on Codfish Island, near Stewart Island. Nathaniel Bates, of Riverton, also cohabited with two women, one his legal wife, and the other the wife of another man.[46] Bates had moved Ann Pauley (nee Williams) into his home, which he still shared with his wife, Harriet (nee Watson). Both women were the mixed-descent daughters of whalers. Nathaniel and Ann were together for twenty-three years.[47] Such relationships were, however, the exception. In fact, permanent and monogamous unions, 'acknowledged and supported by the wider community and solemnised where possible', were the norm in southern New Zealand.[48]

A 'new stock shall arise'

During his forty years of living among Ngāi Tahu, Johannes Wohlers produced an extensive written archive, including records of births, deaths and marriages. His writings tell us much about the mixed-descent population in the southern region, and the social world these people inhabited. His register of baptism, for example, records a common practice among whaling families: the adoption of mixed-descent children who had been abandoned by their father. Most importantly, his papers record the transition of whaling stations into colonial settlements, and signal the role of class and race in the forging of settler society. Wohlers celebrated the rise of a mixed-descent population, fervently believing that this 'new stock' would not only slow population decline among Ngāi Tahu, but also play a prominent role in establishing respectable settler society. Caroline Brown's story illustrates this process.

In February 1846 Wohlers undertook a journey to Ngāi Tahu settlements along the coast of Foveaux Strait. At Riverton he encountered Caroline Brown, the daughter of Te Wharerimu and the sealer Robert Brown, and now the wife of John Howell. At the time of their marriage, with whaling nearing an end in the region, Howell was in the midst of developing Aparima (now Riverton) as an agricultural settlement.[49] Wohlers described Caroline as 'a pretty young woman', and commented:

> She lost her father when she was a child and, hence she has grown up amongst the natives without any European education. She does not know any English but that which she has learnt during the few months of her marriage from her husband. Howell wants to civilize her and to make her outstanding among the other women. Hence he does not allow her to sit around among the natives, nor to attend the Maori church services which are led by a native teacher.[50]

Aged thirteen when she married Howell, Caroline (or Koronaki, to use her Māori name) was one of many mixed-descent women in southern New Zealand who, from the mid nineteenth century, 'married out'. Wohlers described Caroline's situation as

> … somewhat lonely; for she does not know how to behave among the European women, of whom there are three in this place and hence she does not feel comfortable in their company. She is not allowed to keep close contact with the natives. Neither yet is she conscious of her status. Hence I tried to fill her with pride and put it to her that she was superior to the other women of this settlement. She was the wife of a gentleman and hence must not associate with the women who stood far below her.[51]

Caroline Howell (right) and Peti Parata were the daughters of Te Wharerimu and the sealer Robert Brown. Robert was part of the 'codfish mob' who settled on Codfish Island, and are regarded as one of the earliest interracial communities in southern New Zealand. Another daughter, Sarah, married the whaler Ned Palmer; a brother, Robert, married Jane Palmer, the daughter of Edwin Palmer and Pātahi; and their eldest brother, Thomas, married Mary Thomas, also the daughter of a shore whaler. [c/n E6361/18, Hocken Collections/Uare Taoka o Hākena]

In the early stages of her marriage, Caroline preferred the company of Māori and the customs and culture in which she was raised. However, the arrival of newcomers and the development of a mixed-descent population did not foster a separate identity. Mixed-descent children were seen to retain 'many of their mother's peculiarities, especially in the colour and quality of hair and eyes. They are generally attached to her race, and of course better acquainted with her language than with English'.[52] As Caroline's early life demonstrates, interracial marriage took place on Māori terms, at least in the 1840s; newcomers lived in Māori communities, and the children were raised by Māori.

Caroline's married life was very different, however. Surviving photographs suggest that she lived in comfort as the wife of a European gentleman. Howell's wealth was derived from whaling in the 1840s, and cattle and sheep farming in the 1850s. His first marriage to Kohikohi, daughter of the chief Patu, gave him access to large tracts of land on which to launch his business ventures. His mercantile success is reflected in the three large properties he owned, which were the centre of social life in Riverton. His status was consolidated by his membership of the Southland Provincial Council, while his brother-in-law, Theophilius Daniel, who was married to Howell's half-sister Elizabeth Stevens, was a member of the Southland and Otago provincial councils. Daniel also served as mayor of Riverton for two terms, in 1879 and 1881. These political ties, combined with material wealth, marked Howell and his kin as the pre-eminent family of Riverton. Their status was reinforced through education: Howell may have supported its provision in the district, but he sent all his children to Dunedin to complete their schooling.

The wearing of Western dress, and other trappings of material prosperity, suggest that Koronaki had assumed a new and stable identity as Caroline Howell. Yet her ancestry and her appearance were something the European world could not erase. Over the course of her life, Caroline's allegiances traversed the spectrum of Māori, European and mixed-descent communities in the southern region. She was part of a network of mixed-descent families with strong kinship ties and cultural links to Ngāi Tahu. At first glance, the photograph of Caroline (page 53) implies assimilation to European social and cultural values. Yet this is a family photograph in which kinship is asserted. Caroline stands next to her sister, Peti Hurene, who married Tame Parata, the son of Koroteke and Thomas Pratt. Parata was immersed in both tribal politics and the colonial political system, representing the Southern Māori electorate.[53] In this photograph, Caroline and Peti connect the mixed-descent families of Riverton, in the far south, and Puketeraki, north of Dunedin, thus demonstrating the resilience of cultural and kinship ties across the southern region.

In pockets of colonial New Zealand, the first generation of mixed-descent children did form a new class of colonial elite: they were often well educated and economically successful, farming their own land, or employed in the colonial civil service as clerks and interpreters. In Poverty Bay and eastern Bay of Plenty, for example, a 'sub-culture' of interconnected mixed-descent families existed by the 1860s.[54] Economic and social prominence was achieved through land ownership, based on the status of Māori mothers, and consolidated by the marriage of mixed-descent daughters to members of the colonial elite attached to government circles, such as surveyors, resident magistrates, soldiers and politicians. Mixed-descent sons achieved social success through the patronage of government officials, who found them employment in the civil service as interpreters.[55] These families moved in very similar circles, and were linked together by friendship and marriage alliances.

Many mixed-descent families in the southern regions lacked the educational and employment opportunities of their counterparts in the north, and were rarely prominent in public life.[56] What the two groups did have in common, however, was a deep concern for their children's welfare, education and economic security. Fathers sought official recognition of their interracial relationships in order to secure the land rights of their children. But it was the men who made the best marriage alliances, gained wealth from the whaling trade, made a smooth transition to pastoralism, and diversified their business interests who could afford to educate their children and secure their economic future.

Nonetheless, respectability was a fragile and often fleeting asset for some in frontier and colonial societies. Andrew Sinclair, on visiting Riverton in February 1860, found that the natives 'have so mixed themselves up with the Europeans that the rising generation is almost entirely half-caste. They are at the same time more European in their dress, speech and occupation than any Maoris I have seen before.' John Howell, he noted, was acknowledged as the principal man among them, 'who is called the father of the place'. However, rivalries of class and status had emerged as British migrants arrived in Riverton and the surrounding districts:

> [Howell] and several others of the same kind are wealthy and still hold some influence, and of course they look with some jealousy on the newcomers, who appear to them as interlopers. They have accumulated considerable wealth though they expend a good deal on the dress of the women and outrageous festivity.[57]

Many Riverton men may have had their union formalised in a Christian church, but this did not protect them from the taint of immorality. Whalers were associated with a certain type of masculinity, characterised by drunkenness and vice, which wealth and property could not erase. William Barnard Rhodes is a good example. Having made his fortune from bay whaling off the east coast of the South Island, he eventually settled in Wellington, where he rose to political prominence as a member of the House of Representatives and of the Wellington Provincial Council; he was also a large landholder, and owned several businesses in Wellington. Rhodes moved in elite circles, but this did not make him a suitable marriage prospect. When Rhodes married Sarah Ann Moorhouse, sister of the former Superintendent of Canterbury Province, in 1869, her family opposed the union because his daughter, Mary Ann, was born to a Māori woman whom Rhodes had never married.[58]

The Howells were among the few mixed-descent families in the South Island who rose in status to circulate among the political and social elite. Another such couple were English-born Samuel Hewlings, a surveyor and later Mayor of Timaru, and his wife Ngā Hei, also known as Elizabeth, with whom he had five daughters and one son. Fathers who could afford it often chose to have their children educated overseas, usually in Sydney or London. Hewlings took his two eldest daughters to England for their education in 1861, and his remaining daughters were educated in Sydney.[59]

William Barnard Rhodes (1807–1878) settled in Wellington in the 1840s, and was a central figure in the city's mercantile development. In this 1858 ambrotype, Rhodes is seated next to his then wife, Sarah King (1834–1862), the daughter of a Wellington solicitor. Standing in front of them is his only biological child, Mary Ann. [PAColl-5601, Alexander Turnbull Library, National Library of New Zealand/ Te Puna Mātauranga o Aotearoa]

English-born Samuel Hewlings (1820–1896) was a surveyor in Canterbury, and served a term as Mayor of Timaru from 1868. He and his wife Ngā Hei raised six children, and mixed in Canterbury's elite social circles. His friend Dr A. C. Barker, the noted photographer of early Christchurch, took several photographs of Hewlings and his children. The glass plate negative of this photograph was made on 7 January 1870 at Barker's residence. [Prudence Barker Collection, Canterbury Museum]

The various forms of marriage functioned to connect individuals into a social network and to forge economic alliances across all levels of Ngāi Tahu society. Many of the interracial relationships associated with the whaling industry took place in the second generation, giving rise to a complex web of kinship connections. The Spencer and Edwards families, for example, were linked through the marriage of James and Charlotte in 1864, while other Spencer marriages linked them to the Coupar and Goomes families. Like fur-trading families in Western Canada, whaling families often inter-married, a pattern noted by a Mr Scott of Dunedin. In 1860 Scott claimed that 'half-castes' tended to 'intermarry with each other, having sometimes large families of children, contrary to what some have asserted, and these children are as fair as most European children'.[60] It was not uncommon for whalers' daughters to marry whalers. Margaret Antoni, for example, the daughter of whaler Antonie Raymond and Pura married Thomas Chaseland, a well-known southern whaler of mixed Aboriginal-European descent, at

Ruapuke in 1850. Former whaler James Wybrow married twice: first to Temuika, with whom he had three sons; and then, in 1853, to Elizabeth, the daughter of former whaler George Newton and Wharetutu.[61] A quarter of that first wave of 140 newcomers who fathered mixed-descent children later entered into a second or third marriage, often with a mixed-descent or European woman.[62] Among them was Wybrow, and also Lewis Acker, whose second marriage was to Australian-born Jane Stuart. William Palmer's third wife, Ann Holmes, was of mixed descent, while William's brother Edwin abandoned his Ngāi Tahu wife, Pātahi, to marry the Scots-born Beatrice Fowler, as described in Chapter 2.

Archival records provide numerous examples of the kinship networks created by the marriages of first generation mixed-descent children. Catherine Acker (1842–85) married Italian boat-builder John Rissetto in 1860. Her second marriage was to the son of a whaler, George Printz (1827–98). Printz married a second time to Matilda Gordon, the daughter of John Howell and Caroline Brown.[63] Nathaniel Bates, a Sydney-born whaler and trader, entered into a customary marriage with Hinepu, and they had three children together before Hinepu's untimely death. In 1848 Bates married Harriet Watson, the daughter of Robert Watson and Parure. Mary Ann Bates, the eldest child of Nathaniel Bates and Hinepu, married John Lee in 1858. Lee's second marriage was to Jane Dallas, the daughter of William Dallas and Motoitoi.[64] This web of kinship extended throughout the southern region, particularly in the 1840s and 1850s, as the mixed-descent children of early whalers entered adulthood and married.

Obviously, marriage tied together families and their resources. But in a context of sustained and extensive interracial relationships, marriage also tied an individual to a tribe. Atholl Anderson has noted that the first generation of mixed-descent daughters tended to 'marry out'. The Ruapuke marriage records compiled by Wohlers suggest that this pattern holds true for the Foveaux Strait region. But outward marriage did not necessarily mean cultural assimilation in the 1840s and 1850s; class and status are crucial to understanding the extent of cultural assimilation in this period. Many of the mixed-descent women who 'married out' did so to men of similar status to their father's – boat-builders, sawyers, sailors, carpenters, labourers and ex-whalers – which kept them connected to the social and cultural world in which they were raised. Wohlers recorded very few mixed-descent women marrying 'gentlemen'.

Interracial families at Maitapapa

The pattern of interracial marriage at Maitapapa in the mid nineteenth century was similar to that in the Foveaux Strait region, and is beset with the same inconsistency of enumeration. Edward Shortland, for example, recorded nineteen people living in the Taieri in 1844, but made no mention of 'half-castes'. Five years later, Reverend Thomas Burns found twenty-seven Ngāi Tahu in residence, as well as thirty-four settlers; the latter were mainly ex-whalers and their children, including the Palmer, Low, McKenzie, Perkins and Williams families. That same year, local settler John Forbes noted that eight white men married to Ngāi Tahu women were living at Maitapapa. By 1852 there were twenty-three Ngāi Tahu living at the settlement, but government enumerator Henry T. Clarke made no reference to a mixed-descent population there. On his 1852 visit Walter Mantell, the Commissioner of Crown Lands for Otago, found a small population of Ngāi Tahu, who had migrated from Southland and Canterbury. Mantell's list is notable for its omissions. His census was taken not long after Thomas Burns made one of his regular visitations to Maitapapa in December 1852. Mantell failed to note the presence of several interracial couples and mixed-descent families at Maitapapa, whom Burns did record. They included Robert and Jane Brown, and their children, Eliza, Thomas and Robert; Sarah Brown and her husband, the former whaler Ned Palmer, as well as their children, Harriet, George and Edwin, and their adopted son William Russell; and William Palmer's children, Eliza and Anna. William's eldest daughter, Elizabeth Crane, and her husband, and Elizabeth's sister, Mere Kui, also lived there as did John McKenzie. Charles, Louisa, John and David Hunter were born at Taieri and lived at Maitapapa until 1860.[65]

Waterways dominate the physical environment at Taieri, and it was along the river that early British settlement was concentrated and zones of contact were established. During systematic colonisation the river system enabled new economies to emerge, based on the agricultural settlement of

Mixed-descent women like Sarah Ann Howell had far more marriage options than their brothers. From the 1850s to the 1880s, the first generation of mixed-descent women in southern New Zealand generally married the mixed-descent sons of whalers; or, like Sarah, they married European settlers. Class was often a key factor. Sarah, the well-educated daughter of John Howell, the founder of Riverton, married Scots-born William Cameron, a lighthouse keeper on Centre Island, who later farmed on the mainland. Mixed-descent men tended to marry Ngāi Tahu or mixed-descent women; marriage to a white woman was unusual, especially with a surplus of single white men in the region as a result of the gold rushes. [83/0726, Hocken Collections/Uare Taoka o Hākena]

the Taieri plains. Most of the millable timber could be found in the south and west of the plains; the river was a natural communication route; and the soil was heavier and more fertile at the southern end of the plains.[66]

When the first census of Otago was held at the end of 1855, there were 459 colonists residing on the Taieri Plain, following a pattern of scattered settlement southwards along its margins.[67] From the 1850s Otokia (west of Maitapapa) and Taieri Ferry (on the south bank of the Taieri River) were the largest settlements in the area. After gold was discovered in Otago in 1861 the river settlements grew, as did trade and river traffic, and accommodation houses were established along the riverbank, notably at the Ferry. Maitapapa, situated at the centre of this activity, became a stopping point for prospectors and travellers seeking their fortunes on the goldfields.

As the waterways brought newcomers into contact with Ngāi Tahu women, a new phase of interracial marriage in the southern regions began, bringing settler and Ngāi Tahu families into a shared social and economic world. William Palmer, for example, was engaged in shipbuilding at Taieri Mouth, with Peter Campbell (senior). It was through this economic relationship that his 'half-caste' daughter Hannah and Peter Campbell (junior) met and subsequently married in 1866.[68] James Crane began his working life as a pit-sawyer before taking up farming in the 1860s. William Overton took part in the fledgling fishing economy at lower Taieri, but after his marriage to William Palmer's daughter Harriet he worked land at Maitapapa village. William Bryant, John Wellman and John Dickson may have been attracted to the Taieri for economic reasons, but it was marriage into the local Ngāi Tahu community that encouraged their permanent settlement.

Census enumeration from the 1870s indicates a growing population of increasingly mixed descent. In 1878, sixty-seven of the seventy-four people living at Maitapapa were recorded as 'half-castes'.[69] By 1886 the balance had altered, with sixty-six of the 113 inhabitants being of mixed descent;[70] the census enumerator reported that the population was steadily increasing as a result of 'contentment, industry and habits of temperance'.[71]

For women of mixed descent, marriage also came to mean migration. While marriage tied migrant men to a community in the 1850s and 1860s, patrilocal settlement patterns became prevalent among the women of Maitapapa from the 1870s. Ian Pool has identified strong matrilocal marriage patterns among male newcomers in the North Island, but after a brief period the families moved to the margins of Māori settlements before settling in outlying townships. Pool claims that South Island mixed-descent families were mainly patrilocal by the late nineteenth century, living in mixed or European communities.[72] In the context of interracial marriage, patrilocality is often associated with mobility, dispersal and assimilation.[73] Most women from Maitapapa 'married out' in the period 1850 to 1900 (see Table 1). Eliza Palmer, the daughter of Sarah Brown and Ned Palmer, worked as a domestic for the Gibb family of Taieri Beach. After the death of the family matriarch, Eliza married the only son, Walter Gibb, in 1876.[74] Eliza's sister Martha married into the Dicksons, a prominent farming family from Kuri Bush. Hannah Campbell's daughter Agnes married Scotsman James Liddell, twenty-five years her senior, in 1888 and raised six children at Akatore, Green Island, where James farmed. These marriages established ties to the settler community, and integrated mixed-descent women into outlying river settlements and respectable farming families.

Table 1: Ngāi Tahu and Mixed-descent Women of Maitapapa, Marriages: 1850–1900

NAME OF BRIDE	NAME OF GROOM	OCCUPATION OF GROOM	BIRTHPLACE OF GROOM	YEAR OF MARRIAGE	PLACE OF MARRIAGE
Elizabeth Palmer	James Crane	Pit Sawyer	Wales	1852	Henley
Ann Holmes	William Palmer	Shipbuilder	Sydney	1853	Henley
Harriet Palmer	William Overton	Fisherman	England	1865	Henley
Hannah Palmer	Peter Campbell	Bushman	Scotland	1866	Henley
Mary Palmer	William Bryant	Labourer	England	1868	Otokia
Eliza Brown	William Neil	Labourer	unknown	1868	Henley
Ann Williams	John Wellman	Farmer	England	1875	Milton
Harriet Palmer	Stephen Bishop	Blacksmith	unknown	1875	Henley
Eliza Palmer	Walter Gibb	Farmer	Scotland	1876	Milton
Sarah Palmer	John Parata*	Farmer	Otakou	1878	Waikouaiti
Amelia Crane	Charles Flutey*	Farmer	Akaroa	1878	Tuahiwi
Elizabeth Crane	Takiana Manihera†	Farmer	Wellington	1881	Lyttelton
Mary Smith	Frederick Cook	Shepherd	Australia	1883	Henley
Martha Palmer	John Dickson	Farmer	Kuri Bush	1883	Dunedin
Mere Bryant	James Tanner	Labourer	Ireland	1885	East Taieri
Jane Brown	James Smith*	Labourer	Taieri Ferry	1886	Waihola
Charlotte Sherburd	Joe Crane*	Farmer	Waihola	1886	Henley
Agnes Campbell	James Liddell	Farmer	Scotland	1888	Milton
Beatrice Palmer	Cornelius Johnson	Fisherman	Holland	1889	Christchurch
Sarah Overton	Robert Stevenson	Stockman	Wanaka	1890	Dunedin
Emma Palmer	George Adams	Labourer	Dunedin	1892	Dunedin
Caroline Overton	John Robinson	Farmer	West Taieri	1893	Berwick
Mary Overton	John Stevenson	Clerk	Geelong	1893	Henley
Jane Campbell	Isaac Yorston	Labourer	Waihola	1893	Milton
Annie Sherburd	Abraham Starkey*	Farmer	Dunedin	1894	Kaiapoi
Sarah Crane	David Given	Stonemason	Dunedin	1895	Waihola
Jane Bryant	Joe Crane*	Farmer	Waihola	1895	Dunedin
Eliza Neil	Teone Paka*	Farmer	Taumutu	1895	Taumutu
Caroline Bryant	George Milward	Japanner	England	1895	Wellington
Sarah Sherburd	William Robertson	Farmer	Dunedin	1897	Henley
Elizabeth Brown	Thomas Garth	Labourer	Henley	1898	Dunedin
Mabel Smith	John Brown*	Labourer	Henley	1900	Mosgiel

* Ngāi Tahu descent
† Māori (iwi unknown)
Source: Registered Marriage Certificates, Department of Internal Affairs.

Table 2: Ngāi Tahu and Mixed-descent Men of Maitapapa, Marriages: 1879–1900

NAME OF GROOM	NAME OF BRIDE	OCCUPATION OF BRIDE	BIRTHPLACE OF BRIDE	YEAR OF MARRIAGE	PLACE OF MARRIAGE
William Brown	Margaret Davis*		Fortrose	1879	Toetoe
George Palmer	Mary List		England	1882	Allanton
James Palmer	Agnes Reid		West Taieri	1884	Dunedin
William Palmer	Jessie Clifford		Otokia	1884	Outram
Thomas Palmer	Hannah Perkins		Kuri Bush	1886	Kuri Bush
Thomas Crane	Ellen Payne		England	1888	Otokia
George Brown	Helen McNaught		Scotland	1889	Henley
William Crane	Charlotte Paipeta*		Tuahiwi	1889	Tuahiwi
James Smith	Emma Robson		England	1891	Taieri Ferry
William Bryant	Fanny Horne		England	1893	Taieri Ferry
Henry Martin	Ripeka Karetai*		Otago Heads	1893	Dunedin
Joe Crane	Jane Bryant*		Otokia	1895	Dunedin
J. C. Crane	Elizabeth Smith		Australia	1897	Sydney
John Wellman	Ann Campbell		Otago	1898	West Taieri
Stephen Bishop	Alice Conlin	Tailoress	Wellington	1899	Wellington
Alfred Palmer	Eliza Vince		Sedgemere	1899	Leeston
William Sherburd	Sarah Mackie		Wales	1900	Mosgiel
John Brown	Mabel Smith*		Henley	1900	Mosgiel

* Ngāi Tahu descent

Source: Registered Marriage Certificates, Department of Internal Affairs.

Marriage patterns for mixed-descent men in southern New Zealand during the same period were very different. Sons of whalers were more likely to marry mixed-descent or Māori women. European women were a rarity in southern New Zealand in the 1840s and 1850s. Wohlers, for example, recorded no cases of white women marrying Māori or mixed-descent men in his registers. But as Table 2 suggests, mixed-descent men began to 'marry out' from the 1870s and 1880s. Some newcomer women certainly found mixed-descent men attractive. In a letter to her sister in 1874, Alice Lees, an English emigrant recently arrived in Oamaru, commented that there 'are no Maoris about here, and the few who pass through the town are like southern Europeans, very handsome, they might easily be mistaken for Italians'.[75] Nonetheless, Māori and mixed-descent men were not generally regarded as serious marriage prospects for newcomer women. In 1878 South Island Native Officer Alexander Mackay wrote that the saving of the Māori race lay with white men and interracial unions, 'as sexual unions between the females and Europeans are usually prolific, but unions with males of their own race are rarely so'.[76] Colonial officials gave little thought to the possibility of unions between white women and indigenous men. In his 1881 census report, Mackay claimed that Māori men's 'habits and modes of life preclude the possibility of intermarrying with Europeans'.[77] However, this was certainly not the case in southern New Zealand, particularly at Taieri, where the possibilities for interracial marriage increased for mixed-descent men as the British settlement of Otago expanded from the 1870s.

The fact that there were fewer interracial marriages among mixed-descent men than among their sisters was due to a lack of available partners and the need to be mobile for economic reasons, as well as to racial prejudice. Marriage choices were, to some extent, limited by a lack of Ngāi Tahu women living in close proximity. Broader demographic factors were also at play in the marriage market. One was the surplus of men in Otago, despite the gold-rush having ended decades earlier: in 1881 there were 161 men to every 100 women in the province.[78] For many men, 'marrying out' or bachelorhood remained as options. But despite the demographic factors, most mixed-descent men who lived beyond their twenties did get married, and bachelorhood was unusual at Maitapapa.

The prevalence of interracial marriage at Taieri does not mean that such relationships were always accepted or tolerated. When James Palmer, a mixed-descent man from Maitapapa, married Agnes Reid in 1888, her wealthy farming family refused to attend the ceremony at Knox Church, one of the leading Presbyterian churches in Dunedin.[79] Their absence demonstrates that attitudes 'toward interracial marriage depend on the gender of the white person involved'.[80] Across numerous frontiers, relationships between white men and indigenous women were tolerated because they 'represented extensions and reinforcements of colonialism, conquest, and domination'.[81] For white women, the rules were clearly different.

Nevertheless, a few European women formed unions with mixed-descent men from Maitapapa including Helen McNaught, who married

George Brown at Henley in 1889. Born in Scotland, Helen had arrived in Dunedin as an adult in 1880 on the *Oamaru*, along with her family, who settled in the North East Valley. Ellen Payne, who arrived in New Zealand in 1874 at the age of six, married Thomas Crane, son of Elizabeth and James Crane, in 1888. Mary List left London at the age of nine, arriving in Dunedin with her family in 1874, and in 1882 she married George Palmer. Unlike the male newcomers who arrived in Dunedin during the 1840s and 1850s as single adults, these women travelled with their parents and siblings to New Zealand. Given these strong family ties, their choice of marriage partner was more likely to generate social disapproval. There is little evidence that marriage served to assimilate the women into the Ngāi Tahu community. Apart from George Brown and Helen McNaught, few of these couples lived at Maitapapa for a lengthy period.

It was through marriage that mixed-descent men could make good connections back into Ngāi Tahu. When Caroline Howell's nephew, William Brown, married Margaret Davis in 1879, the union linked the Browns to a number of well-known Ngāi Tahu families of mixed descent, such as the Moss, Dawson, Wixon and Owen families. William Crane's marriage to Charlotte Areta Paipeta of Tuahiwi consolidated community connections, as well as uniting resources and families. Most importantly, such marriages symbolically tied these families to a Ngāi Tahu identity. Interracial marriage did not always represent loss. Instead, it could act to consolidate, confirm and authenticate an individual and their family as Ngāi Tahu, thus helping to strengthen and remake tribal identity, and negating the development of a separate cultural identity based on racial hybridity in southern New Zealand.

· · ·

By the middle of the nineteenth century, Ngāi Tahu were increasingly of mixed descent. Wohlers was certainly correct in identifying a 'new stock' arising out of extensive interracial contact. Marriage alliances undertaken by whalers ensured that the newcomers were embedded in a Ngāi Tahu world, and were bound by affective ties to provide for their family and community. The uneven social and economic success experienced by southern mixed-descent families often depended on class, status and wealth, all of

Helen McNaught and George Brown, the son of Jane Palmer and Robert Brown, were married in 1889. Helen was one of the few European women to marry into the mixed community at Taieri and to settle there. [Photograph courtesy of David Brown]

which could be achieved through a good marriage alliance. John Howell's pastoral wealth was entirely dependent on the marriage alliance he contracted with Kohikohi, because it tied him to a high-ranking Ngāi Tahu family with access to vast resources.

Interracial marriages such as Howell's were conducted as an alliance, but not all were based on trade; many in fact were formed on the basis of 'tender ties'. This is demonstrated in the longevity of the relationships, the willingness of those involved to have their customary marriage sanctified by the Christian church, and their determination in seeking economic and social security for their children during a difficult period when colonisation and land purchases were proceeding apace. Indeed, by 1864, when the tenth and final land purchase of Ngāi Tahu territory was completed by the Crown, the tribal land base was almost entirely eroded.

Marriage remained an assimilatory tool for southern Ngāi Tahu into the 1850s and 1860s. Even at Taieri, newcomers were integrated into the community through marriage. Patterns of migration and assimilation into British settlements and culture did not begin until the 1870s, when large-scale government-assisted immigration began. Nonetheless, as the next two chapters will demonstrate, the permanent settlement of the newcomers on small reserves and the growing mixed-descent population caused some disruption among Ngāi Tahu, who began to appeal for government assistance from the 1860s. This economic distress did not mean, however, that people of mixed descent were excluded from tribal participation; in fact, they were heavily involved in tribal politics, and contributed to the social and cultural life of Ngāi Tahu communities.

The new stock that arose in the 1840s did not become, as Wohlers and others had hoped, an important class in settler society, but affiliated instead with Ngāi Tahu, at least until the latter part of the century. In large part, the first generation of mixed-descent children married within their class, and few became part of the landed southern gentry. A social world connected by a web of kinship, and a shared experience of colonialism, involving economic marginalisation, ensured that mixed-descent families did not develop a distinct community based on a separate ethnic and cultural identity.

Chapter 4. Boundary Crossings

In July 1844 William Wakefield, on behalf of the New Zealand Company, purchased 533,600 acres of land in Otago from twenty-one Ngāi Tahu chiefs and principal men of the tribe, for the sum of £2,400.[1] The transaction, known as the Otago Purchase, was the first phase in a planned colonisation scheme known as New Edinburgh, which was promoted by Scots and envisioned as Scottish in character. Under the terms of the purchase, Ngāi Tahu were left with three small parcels of land for their future maintenance, referred to in the deed as 'native reserves'.

In addition to these three areas, Ngāi Tahu believed that 'tenths' reserves were to be made within the boundaries of the Otago Purchase. In theory, the New Zealand Company policy to set aside a tenth of the available rural and urban sections for Māori occupation was designed to 'promote social alliances with settlers and amalgamation through living in close proximity'.[2] At the time of the purchase, both Wakefield and John Symonds, the government representative, expected that such reserves would subsequently be made by Governor Robert FitzRoy. Both noted that tenths reserves were discussed with Ngāi Tahu, that these reserves were to be situated within the boundary of the purchase block, and that Ngāi Tahu preferred to retain control over those lands.[3]

Nonetheless, tenths reserves were not provided for in the Crown Grant of 1846, despite Lord Stanley's instructions that land not already reserved by Symonds for Ngāi Tahu 'out of the tract included in the deed of sale' be included in the grant.[4] In 1845 William Cargill, leader of the New Edinburgh

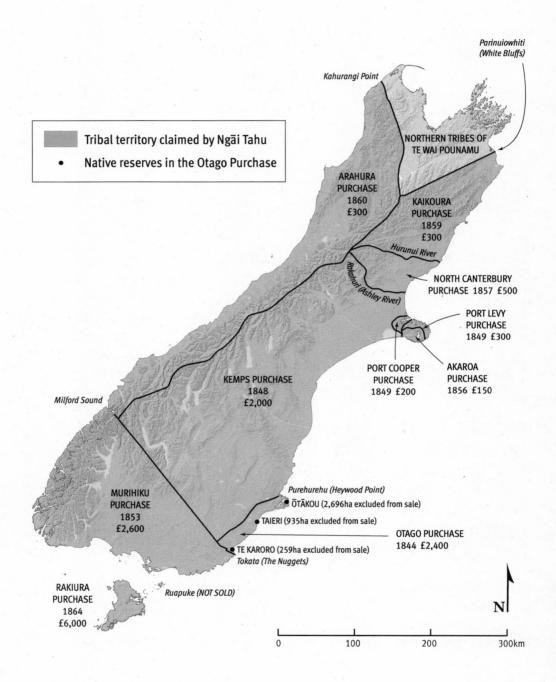

Map of Crown purchases, 1844–1864, showing the location of native reserves at Taieri, Ōtākou and Te Karoro.

Association, explained to the secretary of the New Zealand Company why the tenths policy had been abandoned. In his view, applying the policy in Otago would constitute the establishment of uninhabited waste lands, and thereby hinder the progress of British colonisation.[5] By 1848 Ngāi Tahu retained control over the exempted lands only.

In numerous colonial societies during the nineteenth century, native reserves represented the power of the colonial state to capture and contain indigenous populations. In New Zealand, native reserves were, broadly speaking, geographically bounded 'native spaces', designed to be distinct and separate from European settlements.[6] But no matter how much colonial surveyors and government agents attempted to draw physical boundaries, the lines did not separate, but were in fact quite porous in nature.[7] A boundary line did not negate or halt interracial contact, especially when interracial couples and mixed-descent families were already an established part of southern New Zealand. Native reserves were rarely the distinct sites of occupation that cartographers attempted to create. Instead, the continuation of interracial marriage during the period of systematic settlement exposes native reserves as a 'middle ground' of economic and cross-cultural exchange.[8] At Taieri, for example, the boundaries of the native reserve were crossed as interracial marriage continued after the whaling era. Through marriage, the reserve was settled, occupied and cultivated by male newcomers, whose presence challenged official attempts to delineate between indigenous and settler sites of occupation.

From the outset, it was not clear whether interracial families and people of mixed descent could occupy these reserves. Most people of mixed descent lived within or close to Māori communities during this period. But the formal colonisation of New Zealand, involving the large-scale purchase of Māori land from the 1840s, raised the question of where interracial families lived, and who was economically responsible for them, as the available land became more limited. Ngāi Tahu leaders and government officials engaged in public debate about such matters during the 1860s. This suggests that while interracial marriage may have been welcomed by Ngāi Tahu, smooth integration and acceptance did not always follow. In a context of inadequate reserves and limited resources, interracial marriages generated conflict within communities, reframing the ways in which individuals and families interacted.

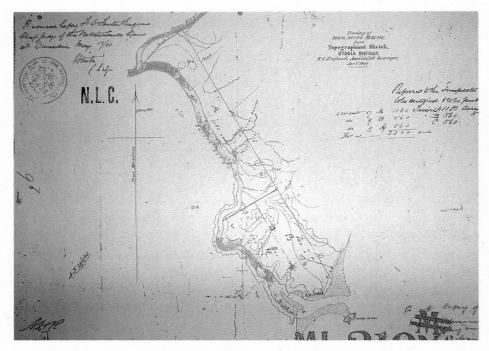

Topographical Sketch Map of Taieri Native Reserve, 1860, as amended in 1868. As required under section 38 of the 1865 Native Lands Act, a survey map with marked boundary lines, paid for by the applicant, had to be submitted to the Court for approval before the awarding of titles could be finalised. Under section 25, survey maps presented before the Native Land Court were required to include information pertaining to boundaries, both physical and artificial. Ngāi Tahu boundary marking included reference to traditional sites of occupation and named landmarks. The Act made no provision for including Ngāi Tahu boundary-marking processes in the surveying of native reserves. The 1860 survey map, produced before the Native Land Court sitting in 1868, and with the proposed block divisions added later, recorded few traditional locations; the only features named are Takitui swamp and the Taieri River. While the map shows topographical features such as bush, the river (which acts as a reserve boundary), and the coastline, there is little indication of the steepness of the terrain, or the small area of flat land available for occupation and cultivation. MacLeod's 1868 map included a greater range of traditional place names, and presented the topographical features in more detail. The new internal boundaries were also marked, and within these, sections were laid off. [ML210, Land Information New Zealand]

Colonisation and the associated practices of cartography, surveying and land dispossession were to take their toll on the Ngāi Tahu community at Taieri, restricting the people both geographically and legally. The world of the Taieri families was already bounded by cultural protocols and customs, particularly whakapapa. But once the organised British settlement of Otago began in 1848, that world was increasingly tied to a geographical space as well. Surveying would play a central role in the delineation of boundaries,

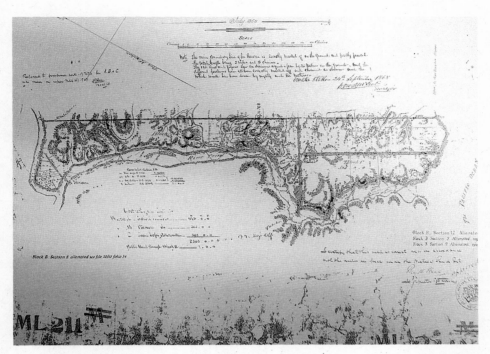

MacLeod's Survey Map of the Taieri Native Reserve, 1868. [ML211, Land Information New Zealand]

particularly in the Native Land Court, where from 1868 it enabled the division of reserve land into blocks, and then sections, for individual occupation and cultivation.

Creating boundaries

From 1844 the Taieri Native Reserve was mapped, named and subdivided, initially by New Zealand Company surveyors, then by Crown surveyors, and finally by the Native Land Court and its officials. In the four years between the Otago Purchase and the arrival of the first Scottish settlers in 1848, the New Zealand Company initially experienced difficulties in getting its title to the land recognised by the British Parliament. As a result, the colonisation of Otago was threatened and the survey of the Otago Block was suspended. Responsibility for promoting the colony was subsequently taken over by the Lay Association of Members of the Free Church of Scotland (known as the Otago Association), who acted quickly to save the project in 1845.[9] The following year a new British ministry and a more sympathetic

Secretary of State for the Colonies, in the form of Earl Grey, saw the revival of the New Zealand Company scheme to settle Otago. In February of that year, Charles Kettle arrived to lay out the town of Dunedin and survey suburban and rural lands within the Otago Block. The requirements of the Otago Association included provision for religion and education, and the availability of land for agricultural development. The fertile lands of the Taieri Plains were ideally situated to meet these requirements.

When the sale of the Otago Block was negotiated, the Ngāi Tahu chiefs requested that certain lands be exempted from purchase. Consequently three areas, totalling 9,615 acres, were set aside, one of them being at Taieri, the others at Ōtākou and Te Karoro. Before the deed was signed, a survey took place to identify the exempted areas. The official survey party comprised the Crown representative, John Symonds, the Sub-Protector of Aborigines, George Clarke (junior), New Zealand Company surveyor, Frederick Tuckett, and the New Zealand Company representative, Daniel Wakefield. Also in the party were six unnamed Ngāi Tahu chiefs, who identified landmarks of spiritual and cultural significance which formed the boundary of the purchase, and chose the lands they wished to retain. The 'unsold' lands at Taieri were described in the Deed of Purchase as being 'bounded on the North by a line drawn from Onumia on the sea shore in a west north-west direction, till it strikes the Taieri River at Maitapapa; on the West and South by the Taieri River; and on the East by the sea shore'.[10] This description, however, gives little indication of how Ngāi Tahu understood and marked the boundaries of the Taieri, nor the significance of the area to them.

Ngāi Tahu leaders chose to retain the Taieri for a number of reasons. The block was situated near inland lakes and a large swamp rich in food sources. In the immediate vicinity of the reserve were lakes Tatawai, Potaka and Marama Te Taha, as well as numerous other eeling sites such as Kaokaoiroroa (near Waihola township), Owiti (near Clarendon) and Kawhakatuatea (north of Waihola).[11] In addition, the area encompassed a traditional burial ground. So important was this land that the Ōtākou chief Korako Karetai stated that 'at Taiari is a burying ground the name of that land is kaikatearorao I will leave it to my five children and their descendants after them'.[12]

Samuel Edwy Green's watercolour of Lake Waihola, dated to the 1860s or 1870s. It reveals the vastness of the lake, which together with Lakes Marama Te Taha, Potaka and Tatawai formed a wetland of immense richness and diversity. In the mid nineteenth century, settlers were beginning to debate the draining of the wetland. [B-116-013, Alexander Turnbull Library, National Library of New Zealand/Te Puna Mātauranga o Aotearoa]

Settlement patterns in the region were also an important factor in its reservation. Ngāi Tahu migration traditions point to the existence of a number of pā in the lower Taieri, located at the north end of Lake Waihola, at the mouth of the Taieri River, on the hill behind Maitapapa, and upriver at Te Amoka.[13] Villages were also located on pockets of flat land along the northern and southern banks of the Taieri River, the most important being the fishing village of Te Au Kukume and the largest settlement, Maitapapa.[14] In his traverse of the Otago Block in 1844, Tuckett found that the land along the northern bank of the Taieri River was occupied and under cultivation. Many traditional place names, however, did not make it onto the surveyors' maps.

Despite being referred to in the Deed of Purchase as 'reserves', the three blocks set aside under the Otago Purchase were not in fact reserved land; they were exemptions from purchase, or unsold land. In Otago, Ngāi Tahu and the New Zealand Company agreed on the lands to be excluded from purchase; these were denoted 'reserves', but were not included in the Crown Grant to the New Zealand Company. However, the policy on native reserves was soon to change. In May 1848 Governor Grey, in his dispatch to Earl Grey, explicitly stated that reserves were to be included within the boundary of a purchase block, thereby extinguishing native title to that land.[15] Hence in 1848 there were two categories of 'native reserves' in New Zealand: those included in, and those exempted from, a purchase block. The key difference between them was that lands exempted from purchase did not have native title extinguished, and therefore remained under customary ownership. This category applies to Taieri specifically, and Otago generally.

Exempted lands generated some anxiety among colonial officials, primarily because they were neither legally designated reserves, nor land that had been purchased by the Crown for that purpose.[16] Because customary title had not been extinguished, these lands constituted the few areas initially remaining under Ngāi Tahu control and management. Hence, while the external boundary of the Taieri reserve was described in the Deed of Purchase, Ngāi Tahu remained in control of the reserve land and its use.[17] However, with the establishment of the colonial state, the external boundary of the reserve was soon to be transgressed by colonial officials.

From 1856, a series of laws relating to the management of native reserves were enacted by the new Parliament. Under the Native Reserves Act 1856, Commissioners of Native Reserves were appointed in each province, in panels of three.[18] Section 14 of the Act defined a reserve as land where customary title had been extinguished, and thus the management of reserves by Native Commissioners did not extend to exempted lands.[19] Under the 1856 Act, unsold lands could be classified as reserves with the consent of Māori; but Ngāi Tahu rarely vested the management of their Otago lands in Native Commissioners, preferring to maintain customary title.[20] As a consequence, the Commissioner of Crown Lands for Otago, W. H. Cutten, stated that 'unless the Natives consent to extinguish their original title and accept a title from the Crown, the Commissioners have no power to deal with the land'.[21]

Native Land Court processes for determining title, together with native lands legislation, established the conditions whereby Ngāi Tahu control over their reserve lands was undermined. It was up to the Native Land Court to establish the owners of customary land, to extinguish customary ownership of that land through the issue of Crown title, and to regulate succession to land held under individual title.[22] Under the Native Lands Act of 1867, the Land Court could investigate the title to exempted lands, and such lands could also come under the Court's jurisdiction through the authority of the Governor, without the owners' consent. In effect, land under customary ownership could be referred to the Land Court, where certificates of title would be awarded and customary title extinguished.[23] The jurisdiction of the Native Land Court to determine title was now extended to all land under Māori ownership, including the Taieri Native Reserve.

While the internal boundaries of the Taieri Native Reserve were steadily encroached upon and redefined under the processes of the Native Land Court, the external boundary was also under pressure by other means. British settlement of the lower Taieri further restricted local Ngāi Tahu to their reserve. Geographically, townships such as Taieri Ferry and Otokia were located on the margins of the reserve and along the banks of the river. Seeking further development, Charles Kettle had travelled to Taieri reserve in 1850 to persuade residents to sell portions of their land to enable townships to be surveyed and encourage the closer settlement of British colonists. Kettle described the residents as engaged in a subsistence and seasonal way of life, and noted their lack of energy and ambition, 'which characterises all the natives who live together in large bodies'; their 'ideas of doing anything for themselves scarcely extend beyond the cultivation of a few potatoes for their own consumption'.[24] The sale of land, Kettle argued, would enable the residents to invest in stock, 'by which their reserve would then become really useful to them', and to gain the advantages of a 'body of Europeans [living] near them'. Despite his efforts, 'they unhesitatingly declined to sell any portion of their land, affirming that money to them was like the dew upon the grass which is soaked up by the sun as soon as he rises'.[25]

British settlement in the Taieri also influenced economic development within the reserve. Based on subsistence agriculture, and a continued reliance on traditional food sources such as ducks, eels and fish, the reserve economy was increasingly supplemented by engagement with the cash economy through local markets, such as the one operating at Taieri Ferry in the early 1860s.[26] Nonetheless, the families were described in 1868 as living in 'eight or ten dilapidated huts' with only a few acres under cultivation. The remainder of the reserve consisted of 'steep hillsides, and broken ground, only adapted for grazing'.[27] By the 1860s, the Taieri families were confined within the boundaries of the reserve, with insufficient land to earn a livelihood from pastoral farming, and few alternatives for employment, either on the reserve or beyond.

Contesting boundaries

Government officials used evidence of uneconomic reserves to promote the individualisation of communal lands for the 'improvement' of Ngāi Tahu. In an 1863 report on the condition of South Island Māori, James Mackay (junior) concluded that 'the natives have been confined to their reserves'; not only were they hemmed in by settlers, but their cultivations were constantly trespassed upon. Mackay encouraged the move to individual titles, arguing that:

> [the] sub-division and apportionment of these reserves among the occupants would be one of the best measures which could be adopted for promoting the welfare of the Native inhabitants of the Middle Island, and would assist more than any other in placing them on the same footing as the Europeans.[28]

Five years later, when the Native Land Court sat in the South Island for the first time, one of the chief aims of the hearings was to prepare reserves for individualisation by determining the ownership of such lands so that Crown grants could be issued.[29] Through this process, individuals could obtain title, then apply for blocks to be partitioned and subdivided into sections. The sittings of the Native Land Court in Christchurch and Dunedin during April and May 1868 were the result of a promise by Governor Grey, on a visit to the South Island in 1867, 'that [the Natives'] claims to reserves in the south should be investigated and Crown titles issued', together with a desire for subdivision already expressed by officials.[30]

Ngāi Tahu had also pushed for the Court to sit in their territory. Multiple, competing claims to the Taieri Native Reserve had been made to officials in

Tiaki Kona, also known as John Conner, was one of the most politically active members of the Taieri community. A favourite informant of ethnographer Herries Beattie, Kona was born on Stewart Island in 1840 and raised by the French whaler Nicholas Robelia and Romatiki. In 1865 Kona settled at Maitapapa, where he had kinship ties: already living there were his half-sister Ani and her husband Robert Sherburd, his uncles Tuarea and Te Uraura, and his grandfather, Samuel Te Makahi. Being of mixed descent did not absolve Kona of his duties to Ngāi Tahu, and he took on the leadership responsibilities required of someone with his connections. This photograph, reproduced from the *Otago Witness*, shows Kona attending a Native Land Court meeting at Puketeraki in 1905. [E5316/44a, Hocken Collections/Uare Taoka o Hākena]

the years prior to the 1868 hearings, based on whakapapa, occupation and use.[31] In 1867 the Ōtākou chief, Korako, and his family wanted 'a portion of it back for themselves, excluding some Kaiapoi natives at present living at Taiari'.[32] Many were looking for clarification on the issue of access and other rights in the context of limited land. In an 1867 letter, Tiaki Kona, a leading member of the reserve community, informed authorities of the 'ancestry of present occupiers of their Reserve', as did John (Te One) Topi Patuki of Foveaux Strait, the successor to Ngāi Tahu paramount chief Tūhawaiki.

Among those who communicated with the Native Affairs Department in the same year were Rawiri Te Uraura and Wi Naihira.[33] Te Uraura was the successor to the chief Te Raki, who had bequeathed the Taieri reserve land to him on his death in 1862. This led to conflict within the community, and Te Uraura was now applying to the Native Land Court to clarify owner-ship of the reserve. However, by resorting to the Court to resolve internal disputes, Te Uraura and those he represented brought the reserve under the authority of the Court, with its imperatives of extinguishing native title and individualising reserve land through the granting of certificates of title.

The Native Land Court sat on 20 May 1868 to hear Te Uraura's claim and to decide the ownership of the Taieri Native Reserve. An arrangement to share the reserve, devised by the counter-claimants, 'the Natives residing at Otago Heads', had already been suggested independently of the Court. At an earlier meeting of the two groups:

> All the people of the Taieri and Otakou were present, and with the exception of the half-castes at the Taieri, all agreed to the arrangement. The arrangement had been proposed by the Otakou Natives, who said that if the Taieri Natives refused, they would not have any land at all.[34]

At the hearing of the Native Land Court, the agreement to share the reserve was approved by Chief Judge Fenton. The claimants and counter-claimants 'had agreed that the Taieri Natives should have half of the reserve; the Otakou Natives a quarter; and Te One Topi's descendants the remain-ing quarter'.[35] In accordance with the judgment, certificates of title were issued to the three claimant groups. An area of 1,173 acres, designated as Block A, was awarded to eight trustees for the current residents. Block B, comprising 565 acres, was granted to representatives of the Ōtākou group. Block C, also of 565 acres, was awarded to nine individuals with kinship ties to Foveaux Strait.

Wereta Tuarea, who had lived at Taieri for thirty-seven years ('ever since I came from Kaiapoi'), objected to the arrangement because the people of Ōtākou 'have no title'.[36] Understandably, those who had lived on the reserve and cultivated the land since the 1830s felt that their unbroken occupation gave them a clear right to the land. Tiaki Kona later described 1868 as the year in which 'half of the reserve was taken away by other natives of other parts'.[37] He was correct in this claim: the Court decision reduced the land available to the families residing there from 2,310 acres to the 68-acre vil-lage and the steep and inaccessible terrain of Block A.

Wereta Tuarea was the brother of Rawiri Te Uraura, the man who succeeded Te Raki as leader of the Taieri community in 1862. Two other brothers, Rimene Tira and Teoti Te Korihi (who worked on Craigie's farm at Taieri Ferry), also lived at Maitapapa. It is believed that Tuarea died at Maitapapa in 1888, at the age of 100, having lived there for fifty-seven years as a 'refugee' from Kaiapoi. [PA2-2293, Alexander Turnbull Library, National Library of New Zealand/Te Puna Mātauranga o Aotearoa]

Interracial families in 'native spaces'

A central part of the native reserve policy as it was finally implemented in Otago was to establish a clear distinction between Māori sites of occupancy and those of British settlers, and these boundaries were not to be crossed.[38] But interracial marriage disrupted imposed physical boundaries, and collapsed social distance. By 1868, fifty-eight Ngāi Tahu were residing at Taieri, while eighteen 'half-caste children [were] living with their parents at a distance from the pah'.[39] The growing mixed-descent population added to the complexity of debates over land. Evidence presented before the Native Land Court in 1868 indicates that four groups, not three, claimed an interest in the Taieri Native Reserve: those from Ōtākou, the group with links to Foveaux Strait, the 'refugees' from Kaiapoi who had lived at the reserve since the 1830s, and their 'half-caste' kin. It was this last group that opposed the independent solution reached in 1868.

Interracial marriage was of particular concern to Ngāi Tahu leaders because it increased fears of land loss through the establishment of 'half-caste' lands, as well as creating competition for land in already small reserves. During the 1850s and the 1860s, people of mixed descent were increasingly perceived as a problem, disrupting the economic, political and social life of Ngāi Tahu. Nowhere was this more evident than in the question of land rights. From the 1860s Ngāi Tahu leaders pushed for the government to take responsibility for mixed-descent children in the absence of their Pākehā fathers. Frustrated by a lack of official interest, H. K. Taiaroa, the member for Southern Māori, asked Parliament in 1876 that

> [something] be done for these half-castes, because their fathers had not taken notice of them, and had not provided for them. During all these years they had been living with, and had been brought up by, their Native mothers. Some of them had obtained land, but, on the contrary, others were simply squatting on what belonged to the Maoris.[40]

Taiaroa alleged that 'half-caste' children had been the sole responsibility of Ngāi Tahu women and their communities, and an impediment to the smooth functioning of the Ngāi Tahu land rights system. Further, the presence of a mixed-descent population placed added pressure on inadequate

View of the Taieri Native Reserve from Taieri Ferry, c. 1860s. A few houses can be seen in the distance, located on the only significant area of flat land on the reserve, which was also low-lying and prone to flooding. [S09-333b, Hocken Collections/Uare Taoka o Hākena]

reserves and an imposed system of land allocation. In cases where a father could not provide for his children, or had abandoned them, Ngāi Tahu leaders believed the government should fill that role.

Meanwhile, disputes over the internal boundaries of the Taieri reserve continued as David MacLeod, the Native Land Court surveyor, embarked on the land division in June 1868. Local Ngāi Tahu had a measure of control over his activities and monitored his work closely, often walking the ground with him. After completing the survey of individual sections in July 1868, MacLeod reported that:

> ... almost all the Natives in connection with the Reserve attended the survey ... it was unanimously agreed amongst them to mark a division of the land and get it marked off at once. I accordingly got them all out on the ground and made them put in all their pegs and cut their lines as shown on the maps.[41]

MacLeod's report confirms that the work of the surveyor in 'native settlements' was carried out with the active co-operation of residents.

At that time there were fifty-eight Ngāi Tahu living on the reserve, and eighteen people of mixed descent, bringing the total population to seventy-six. Each adult was allocated, on average, 39 acres.[42] The inclusion of eleven people of mixed descent in the allocation effectively reduced the average interest in Block A. Interracial families were granted lands on the margins of the reserve, which were notoriously inaccessible and uneconomic, rather than the more favourable sections on the flat.

Some mixed-descent residents questioned the awarding of the best land to leading people of the village. In a letter to the Native Minister, dated June 1868, the Palmer family expressed their distress over the allocation:

> This is our talk to you about the portion of land of the Taieri People which is left. The Surveyors work is greatly interrupted. The good lands are being taken away by Rawiri o hapu Te Uraura for themselves alone. The bad pieces are being offered to us by some of those people who are living on their land – but the whole of the land has been subdivided by the Surveyor and the Runanga have agreed about the other portions. The portion that is disputed is 130 acres … Hariata wants to be at the gate of the fence [so] that she may get some portion of the good land to build a house upon [and] that Nane Sherburd should have 12 chains of the good land and herself three chains. This is a good arrangement but the decision is with you. Write quickly that this dispute may cease.[43]

This suggests that some residents colluded with the surveyor in the division and allocation of land at the reserve, and that those of mixed descent were not part of the process.

Nane (Ann) Sherburd wrote on a similar matter to the Native Minister 'about my piece of land at Taieri the size of the land is 100 acres for myself, my child and husband'.[44] Apart from Nane and her Australian-born husband, Robert Sherburd, a number of Ngāi Tahu or mixed-descent women living on the reserve in September 1868 were married to European men. They included Eliza Brown, married to William Neil; Eliza's aunt, Sarah Brown, married to former whaler Ned Palmer; and Hannah Parera/Ann Holmes, married to former whaler William Palmer. William's 'half-caste' daughters were all married to Pākehā men: Betty to James Crane, Mere to William Bryant, and Hannah to Peter Campbell (junior). Six Pākehā men had access to reserve land through their mixed-descent wives. The creation of 'half-caste lands' out of reserve land was thus a reality, and the presence of newcomers, married to women of mixed descent, further exacerbated fears of land loss.[45]

These events illustrate the disruption caused to Ngāi Tahu communities by the presence of people of mixed descent, especially in the area of customary land rights. In the context of limited resources, reserve land allocations to 'half-castes' were an important issue in the 1860s. Land scarcity has also been identified as a key concern surrounding the development of the mixed-descent population in the South Island from the 1870s, and would result in a series of 'half-caste' land claims.[46]

·   ·   ·

In the mid nineteenth century, a range of official policies restricted Ngāi Tahu in the region to the confines of the Taieri Native Reserve. They include assimilation, the individualisation and subdivision of reserve land, and Native Land Court processes for title determination. The community's increasing confinement was based on a range of cultural encounters, beginning with the whaling industry and followed by the systematic pastoral settlement of the Taieri Plain. But it was the decision to abandon the 'tenths' policy within the Otago Block that effectively turned land exempt from purchase into 'native spaces'. The creation of native reserves as sites of occupation, separate from European settlement, was consolidated by the work of New Zealand Company and Crown surveyors, and later through the title determination processes of the Native Land Court. At the same time, this system effectively eroded Ngāi Tahu ownership of the Taieri reserve through a system of individualisation designed to promote the 'civilisation' and assimilation of its residents.

Interracial marriage proves that reserve land was not spatially separate from sites of British occupation, while the resulting mixed-descent population at Taieri undermined the pretence of separate living spaces in the district. Furthermore, interracial marriage instituted a process whereby the external and internal boundaries of the reserve were contested and continually negotiated. These conflicts were centred on land rights, and were played out in the physical space of the reserve, in the surveying of the land, and through the Native Land Court. Significantly, the disputes over land, both at Taieri and before the Court, suggest that the imposed system of reserve allocation disrupted the economic, rather than the cultural, integration of people of mixed descent into Ngāi Tahu communities.

Chapter 5. Fears and Anxieties

In the mid to late nineteenth century, Ngāi Tahu anxieties about the impact of interracial marriage on land ownership, the rights of mixed-descent children, and the economic burden this growing population placed on small reserves were paralleled by official concerns about interracial relationships. Interracial marriage was never legally prohibited in New Zealand. In fact, it was encouraged as a biological component of the state's racial amalgamation policy, the object being the economic, cultural and physical integration of Māori into British colonial society. However, the tolerance of colonial authorities did not extend to immoral or illegitimate relationships. In the first decades of colonial government, officials were keenly interested in regulating, monitoring and policing interracial intimacy. Official acceptance of interracial marriage also gave rise to complicated legal issues surrounding the property rights of Māori women, which had material implications for the white men they married, as well as their mixed-descent children.

Colonial authorities targeted certain groups of men involved in such relationships. Routinely described as having 'gone native', these men were a source of anxiety in numerous settler colonies during the late nineteenth century.[1] In North America they were known as 'squaw men', living on reservations and attracting scorn from settlers and officials, who viewed them as dissolute, debased and corrupt. 'Squaw men' were also regarded as traitors to white masculinity, because they were implicated, as political agitators, in working against the colonial project.[2] Worse, they were seen as benefiting economically from reservation life.[3] 'Squaw men' were accused of engaging in interracial relationships not for love, but in order to gain access to land. In the Pacific, such men were known as 'beachcombers'. In New Zealand, the term 'Pākehā-Māori' was commonly used to describe men who had given up their racial status in favour of 'going native'.[4] Like their North American counterparts, the traders, whalers and early settlers who lived with Māori women were considered to have degraded their race and undermined white masculinity. Having abandoned European society and its values, they were acting as disruptive political and economic forces within indigenous communities. With their economic and affective ties to such communities, such men were highly problematic figures who had to be dealt with so that colonisation could proceed smoothly. Seen as corrupt and manipulative, these men could not be trusted with the civilising project; they had to be controlled.

Interracial marriage was welcomed by Māori, especially in the South Island, to gain access to trade and wealth, and to repair the damage done to their populations by intertribal wars. After 1840, however, colonial officials sought to legally define such relationships, not through prohibition but by encouraging their legitimacy. The motives of traders and whalers who aligned themselves with Māori women may have attracted suspicion, but colonial authorities rewarded those who entered into a legal, Christian marriage. Unlike the situation in North America, where 'squaw men' were socially marginal figures and disliked by authorities, officials in New Zealand hoped to generate loyalty among these pre-1840 settlers, who could prove useful as translators, mediators, spies and cultural intermediaries. Their loyalty was cultivated through land grants, as evidenced by the passage of colonial ordinances and statutes relating to interracial marriage in the latter half of the nineteenth century. In part, these preserved the men's economic power, assisted in establishing a mixed-descent elite, and furthered racial amalgamation. As in British Columbia during the same period, colonial legislation passed in New Zealand 'did not reject, but rather reinforced, the power accorded white men in a colonial and patriarchal society'.[5]

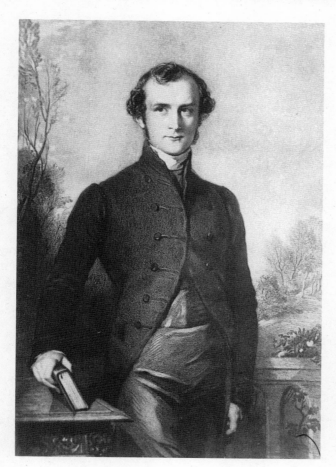

Bishop George Selwyn took an active role in advocating for the rights of mixed-descent children during the 1850s. He saw land, held in trust, as a way to guarantee the economic and social futures of such children, especially when their fathers were absent. Land grants also won the government the loyalty of interracial families, especially as cultural intermediaries in times of trouble. [S06-262a, Hocken Collections/ Uare Taoka o Hākena]

Marriage and racial amalgamation policy

On the eve of the signing of the Treaty of Waitangi, around two thousand newcomers, comprising whalers, traders, early settlers and missionaries, were resident in New Zealand. With the establishment of British authority and law in the decades that followed, the question of interracial marriage and the rights of white men came up for debate. In 1842 Willoughby Shortland, Administrator and Colonial Secretary of New Zealand, 'recommended to the Home Authorities that some provision be made suitable to the circumstance of those who may have formed connexion with Maoris legally', adding that 'the legal intermarriage of Europeans with the Aboriginal subjects of Her Majesty is highly worthy of every just encouragement'.[6] The policy of 'amalgamation', which dominated the relationship between Māori and the Crown during the nineteenth century, was designed to bring Māori under the control of British law, and was predicated on a belief in the superiority of British institutions.[7]

Amalgamation encompassed not only legal and social infrastructure, but also, in the form of interracial marriage, a biological component.

For amalgamation to be successful, interracial marriage had to be legalised, the legitimacy of mixed-descent children established, and the uncertain land rights of white men resolved. The latter was especially important, because kinship ties could motivate such men to work against official interests and act as a powerful force for indigenous autonomy. Shortland was not the only one to recommend the encouragement of legal unions. The naturalist Ernst Dieffenbach, writing in 1843, noted that 'a great many unions have taken place between Europeans and Native women, and a number of half-caste children exist', and argued that the land rights of the mothers, who 'have often received a quantity of land as a dowry from their fathers, or as being their property by birthright', should therefore be recognised under British law. He believed that a system of 'protecting and gradually civilizing the natives' had to include the purchase of waste land and the security 'of the property of the children of Europeans by natives'.[8] Governor George Grey's opening address to the Legislative Council in October 1846 entreated members to 'devise some means by which you will prevent European fathers from abandoning and leaving in a state of destitution and misery, families of children whom they may have had by native mothers'.[9]

The broader ramifications of interracial relationships and the rights of mixed-descent children had been recognised early on by colonial officials who travelled through southern New Zealand assessing its potential for settlement. In 1844, Frederick Tuckett suggested setting aside land for the support of mixed-descent children at Moeraki.[10] Four years later, when Walter Mantell visited the settlement to set the boundaries of a reserve, he noted the wretched position of 'half-castes' living there:

> For the half-castes living in such a community as that which I have broken up at Moeraki I see no future but vice and misery for the half-caste when scattered among the general population [but] with means of education and in a better state of Society, a less bad example from their Parents with provision too against want from lands properly administered for their benefit I anticipated that good standing among us which their general natural intelligence entitles them to occupy.[11]

Walter Mantell surveying the Moeraki reserve in November 1848 (detail), sketched by Francis Edward Nairn. [E-333-084-3, Alexander Turnbull Library, National Library of New Zealand/Te Puna Mātauranga o Aotearoa]

Preventing abandoned and illegitimate mixed-descent children from becoming a burden on the state required that the state redeem and reward those who entered into legal marriage with Māori women. Such rewards came in the form of land grants, which also ensured the economic security and welfare of mixed-descent children.

'Half-castes' required attention because of uncertainty about their loyalty to the government and to British cultural values. The board of inquiry appointed to investigate the state of native affairs in New Zealand reported in 1856 that:

> [The] half-caste race, occupying as they do an intermediate station between the European and native, have neither the advantages of the one, nor the other, and [their] future destiny may, by proper management, be directed in the well being of the Colony, or by neglect be turned in a contrary course. They are

objects of great solicitude to their native relatives, as well as to their European fathers, who desire to secure them sufficient portions of land for their mainte-nance, and when such is the case there is every reason for the co-operation of the Government. The Board would therefore recommend, provided the native title is in the first place extinguished, that Crown grants should be issued in their favour in trust to some public functionary.[12]

The board identified land rights as a priority, in order to secure the loyalty of mixed-descent children – and their parents – to the Crown. In evidence before the board, Bishop Selwyn advocated the case of half-caste children: 'I think they especially should be attended to – their interests strictly guarded – for they are growing up to be a very important class of settlers in several parts of New Zealand'.[13] For this reason, he argued, their land rights should be protected and guarded by reliable trustees, such as religious bodies, because 'the fathers of some are dead, and the fathers of others are drunkards. It is necessary therefore that the lands given them should be under some control'.[14] He also remarked that in the South Island a number of newcomers married to Māori women had secured Crown grants, 'but many of them have been overlooked especially in the Foveaux Straits, Stewart's Island, Ruapuke, the Bluff &c. I should like to see them placed in a proper position'.[15] Mr Black, a settler at Matata, agreed with Selwyn, but warned the board of inquiry that 'great care should be taken' in the man-agement of such children.[16] Most importantly, government intervention was required to encourage legitimate unions in the future. While all should now be cared for alike, Selwyn emphasised, 'in future I would make a distinction lest promiscuous intercourse between the two races should be still further encouraged by the prospect of maintenance for the illegitimate children'.[17]

The proposed trusteeship arrangements meant that Grey's fears about the abandonment of mixed-descent children could be allayed, and their land rights ensured. Missionaries giving evidence before the board of inquiry also supported the concept. The Reverend John Whitely, of the Wesleyan Mission at Kawhia, proposed that 'there should be a difference made between the half-caste children born in wedlock and the illegitimate children. In giving Crown Grants to half-caste children, I think the parents should be required to marry'.[18] Some missionaries agreed that land grants could be used to induce newcomers to legitimate their relationships, and thus to eradicate immorality. The Anglican missionary at Opotiki took a different line, arguing that no distinction ought to be made between 'those children born in wedlock and otherwise', because in 'the eye of the Maori law all these half-castes are legitimate'.[19] The Aborigines Protection Society also supported interracial marriage as part of a wider programme of racial amalgamation, and supported a policy of legitimising the land rights of interracial couples and their children.[20]

Political debate and legislative activity in the 1840s and 1850s prove that officials, in part, tried to regulate, license and control interracial marriage, but not to outlaw it.[21] Interracial marriage was a reality in New Zealand, and an official response was required. In his 1859 book *The Story of New Zealand*, A. S. Thomson celebrated interracial marriage as a positive force in the 'union of the races'. This union, he argued, should be promoted in New Zealand law with regard to inheritance, because as the 'law now stands, concubinage is indirectly encouraged, and legal unions between European males and native females are discouraged'.[22] Thomson's wish was soon to be realised, in the form of the Half-Caste Disability Removal Act 1860.

The Act fostered racial amalgamation by encouraging regular, moral and legitimate interracial relationships. As long as the marriages were legal, interracial relationships were not obstructed by officials.[23] Children born to interracial couples prior to 1860 were legitimised under the Act, along with their inheritance rights. These provisions were designed to ensure that white fathers retained their racial status, by removing the taint of immorality attached to these relationships. The fact that Māori women's property rights were retained after marriage to a white man also encouraged legitimate interracial unions, thus removing the 'official premium' on concubinage. But the 1860 Act targeted a certain class of people: the children of mixed descent who had 'wealthy fathers, or those whose father had secured property to his name', and who therefore suffered a legal disability in regards to inheritance.[24] Through the 1860 Act, white fathers secured social and economic status for their children. The Act seemed to be concerned with Māori women's property rights, but in fact it retained economic status for the white men who had co-habited and entered into marriage with Māori women. Interracial marriage was not prohibited in colonial New Zealand partly because sanctions against the practice would have undermined the claims to respectability of male newcomers and, by extension, settler society.

During the 1850s, colonial politicians had debated how to deal with interracial marriage, especially as it pertained to inheritance of property. Some believed that any Māori woman married to a European man was subject to common marriage law, thus bringing her property under her husband's control. Interracial marriage, therefore, was 'on occasions used by the colonial administration as a subtle way of enlarging the holdings of Crown land'.[25] Certainly, economics and property rights underpinned debates leading up to the passage of the 1860 Act. The wish of Māori women to maintain separate property rights was seen as encouraging immoral inter-racial relationships. Fears of an increase in illicit relationships ensured the passing of the Act, as did fears that, without formal marriages, the Crown could not gain access to Māori land: if a Māori woman should 'merely live in concubinage with a European, all the powers in New Zealand cannot touch one acre of [her] land'.[26]

Promises and petitions

Anxieties about the rights of white men and of mixed-descent children were shared by the fathers of those children. Fearing for the status and economic well-being of their families, many looked to the colonial government for assistance, or at least recognition under British law to ensure the property rights of their wives and children.[27] Unlike many Pākehā-Māori, who were highly mobile in search of work, these men were settlers wanting to raise families. In some ways, this made them more problematic to the colonial authorities, because the legitimacy of their marriages, children and property rights were now in question.

White men's property rights were investigated as part of the Old Land Claims Commissions held in the 1840s and 1850s. Commissioners dealt with pre-Treaty land sales between Māori and private individuals, and waivers of the Crown right of pre-emption in the late 1840s, which allowed the private purchase of Māori land. As part of these investigations a number of 'half-caste' claims came to light, the majority of them relating to the Bay of Islands, Auckland and Tauranga. All such cases involved claims by white men on behalf of their mixed-descent children to gifts of land, made over to them on marriage by their wife's Māori relatives, for any future children of the relationship. Fathers applied to have these marriage gifts formally acknowledged in a Crown Grant in their name as a trustee for the children.

The Land Claims Settlement Act 1856 and the Land Claims Settlement Extension Act 1858 were the legal mechanisms whereby grants were made to the fathers of mixed-descent children. Not everyone who applied secured land under these Acts, resulting in landlessness for some, and prompting letters and petitions to authorities into the late nineteenth century. Such appeals for assistance constitute an important archive on white masculinity in the colonial era. In her examination of the relationship between marriage, the law and colonialism in Queensland, Ann McGrath discovered an archive consisting of letters from white men requesting consent to marry. These requests brought interracial couples into the ambit of the court system and the Aboriginal Protectorate, and also made claims to 'respectability' and 'responsibility'.[28] McGrath demonstrates that the rights of white men were at stake under Queensland law. If found to be engaged in an illicit and therefore illegal relationship, a man could lose his Aboriginal partner to 'removal', and officials could break up the family. Claims to respectability, which centred on evidence of economic independence, were paramount in gaining consent to marry, as well as in retaining family life.

Similar claims to 'respectability' were made in colonial New Zealand by white men applying for land grants on behalf of their mixed-descent children. Petitioners and those who assessed their claims wrote extensively about their worth as settlers and as family men. Surveyor William Searancke, himself the father of mixed-descent children, wrote to Chief Land Commissioner and Native Secretary Donald McLean in 1858, describing Thomas Uppadine Cook of the Wairarapa as a man who was 'engaged in business and generally respected by the Natives and Europeans and has a large and increasing family of seven children'.[29] In his claim, John Marmon emphasised his lawful marriage to his Māori wife. Moreover, he was 'a poor man', who had 'been struggling very hard for many years to get my living', and had purchased his land 'with the savings of my hard earnings'. Marmon had lived on his property for twenty-eight years, but feared he might be 'turned off my land' unless he could gain a Crown grant.[30]

Many petitioners and letter-writers lived in the South Island, and a significant number of them had arrived in New Zealand between 1829 and 1850 as shore whalers. From the late 1840s, those with mixed-descent children made claims to colonial authorities for economic aid, offering evidence of respectability and their commitment to stable family life.[31] One result of these petitions was the Stewart Island Grants Act 1873, which secured land grants to a handful of early settlers, pioneers in the southern regions. The respectability thus gained was reinforced by applications from descendants of early interracial unions in the 1870s and 1880s who, citing poverty, applied for land grants based on the long residence of their fathers.[32]

Requests for assistance from former whalers did not derive solely from Old Land Claims. Some were based on promises made by Walter Mantell while completing the purchase of Ngāi Tahu territory for the Crown in 1848 ('Kemp's Purchase'), and the Murihiku Purchase of 1853. Mantell promised the white men living within the boundaries of these purchase blocks that their Māori wives and mixed-descent children would be provided with land under Crown title. In evidence before an 1869 inquiry into these promises, Mantell stated that:

> [In 1848] there were resident a number of families of halfcastes, whose fathers it was naturally supposed might, unless reassured [as] to their prospects after the cession of the land to government, throw obstacles in the way of its acquisition: so when I was sent in August to persuade or compel those natives who had not joined in Kemp's deed to acknowledge that their land was sold to the Crown, and with the rest to permit the survey of Reserves within the Block, I was instructed to promise these people, that when the land belonged to the Crown provision in land under Crown Title would be made for their wives and children. To have included this provision within the Native Reserves would have, it was held, subjected the Natives therein to undue domination on the part of the Whites and half-castes of their families.[33]

Mantell's comments about the 'Whites' demonstrates that these men were considered a threat, firstly to the successful completion of the purchase, and secondly to the distinction between white and 'native' spaces. Mantell feared that these Pākehā-Māori, like the 'squaw men', would incite discontent among Ngāi Tahu by dominating their communities, both politically and economically. His job was to keep them off the native reserves, and to prevent further discontent by promising them land grants.

Very soon after the completion of the purchases, Mantell received letters from men requesting the fulfilment of his promises. In May 1852 he recommended to the Colonial Secretary that grants be made 'in favour of those who had wives and families', of which 'many applications have been sent to me'.[34] Despite his earlier comments about the 'bad example' set by parents of mixed-descent families at Moeraki,[35] Mantell now recast himself as the champion of white fathers, seeking official support for this 'class of poor yet deserving individuals, the pioneers of civilisation'.[36] He regularly endorsed their applications for land grants, on the grounds of poverty, old age or large families. In May 1868, for example, he informed the Colonial Secretary that Thomas Chaseland was a 'poor man [who] has a wife, an elderly halfcaste from Kaiapoi, and five or six children, the eldest about fourteen years old'.[37] In 1863 Joseph Donaldson, already in possession of 10 acres for his children, submitted a 'begging application' for further land at Moeraki, 'for the five extra children that my wife Pokiri has born to me'.[38] This second claim was rejected.

Mantell struggled to gather support for legitimising the land rights of interracial couples. Writing to the Colonial Secretary in 1854, he pressed for the matter to be released from the control of local authorities, in this case the Commissioner of Crown Lands of Otago. He claimed that the latter's powers would 'be productive of the most serious detriment to the Public welfare on such cases as those under comment' because 'their claims to a provision for their declining years for their wives and children [are subject] to the caprice of a Gentleman ignorant of their merits'.[39] Numerous applicants did not receive a land grant for decades. Henry Wixon, promised a section of land at Hawksbury, near Waikouaiti, wrote to Mantell several times requesting recognition of his claim. Mantell had granted him 42 acres in 1854, but eight years later Wixon reported that:

> *I have been to Mr Cutten for the deed and he told me that he did not know what principle it was granted on. I purchased a map at the printing office and my section is in it and I showed it to Mr Cutten but for all that he should not permit me to live upon it and I am living upon the natives land at Waimate bush and other people are living on the land that you gave to my children and they have built 2 houses upon it.*[40]

Six months later, in desperation, Wixon again pressed Mantell for assistance:

> *I am only a poor man with a Family of 10 children and I am living in Waimate Bush at present on the Native Reserve and the Natives are very kind to me and my children but I should like for the children to live on there own land if it is possible before all the timber is taken off.*[41]

While officials wished to secure the rights of white men who were legally married to Māori women, they remained suspicious of the motives of those who engaged in such relationships. Grants were awarded, but anxiety focused on how this land was to be secured for mixed-descent children, the fear being that the white father coveted the land and would dispose of it as though it were his own. Alexander Mackay, Commissioner of Native Reserves in the South Island, expressed his concern to Harry Atkinson, Minister of Crown Lands, in March 1875:

> *[The] plan of granting land to the European fathers of half-caste families instead of to the person who it is intended to benefit is a disadvantageous one to the persons concerned, especially if the Grant is silent respecting the object for which the land is apportioned. There is one instance of the injustice that may be done in this way in the case of the Haberfield family. In this case according to the terms of the Grant, the Father holds the land for his life. The result of this is, that he can do what he pleases with it as far as occupancy is concerned. Since the death of his first wife, a half-caste, named Meriana Tete, he has married a European woman and has farmed away all the children of the former marriage, thereby preventing them from deriving any benefit from the land that was given in the first place as a maintenance for them.*[42]

William Isaac Haberfield, born in Bristol in 1815, took up shore whaling at Moeraki in 1836 under the direction of John Hughes. Like many other whalers in the southern regions, Haberfield entered into a customary marriage with a Ngāi Tahu woman, Merianna Teitei. After her death he married Akari, the former partner of Banks Peninsula whaler Joseph Price, and their relationship was formalised in a Christian marriage ceremony. In 1875 Alexander Mackay believed Haberfield had deprived his children of their land. There is no evidence to support Mackay's claim. [E1796/5, Hocken Collections/Uare Taoka o Hākena]

Such cases merely reinforced official mistrust of men who had 'gone native'. Their motive for engaging in interracial marriage was understood to be economic gain, and it was assumed that land grants would be followed by abandonment. How to protect the rights of Māori women and their mixed-descent children, particularly if the interracial relationship subsequently failed, was a question that officials struggled to resolve from the 1840s.[43]

The economic implications of interracial marriage were explicit in the mid nineteenth century. Legislation was enacted to preserve the economic rights of former whalers in the lower South Island who had married Māori women. Provincial Waste Land Boards, for example, were given power to set aside land for interracial couples and their children under the Waste Lands Act 1862. This Act was needed because local officials had resisted separate grants of land being made to interracial couples. In 1856, Otago Land Commissioner Peter Proudfoot suggested that interracial families be provided for out of the 'numerous Native Reserves'.[44] Proudfoot had little sympathy for landless 'half-caste' families, nor for the rights of Māori women within interracial marriage: 'I do not apprehend that the mothers having married a European, invalidates her right or interest in what [she] would have been entitled to under other circumstances, that is, if she had remained with or had married one of her own Tribe'. He argued that:

> ... unless the granting of land in the manner and for the purpose alluded to has been a stipulation by the Natives in the sale of the land to the Government, or is in fulfilment of a promise made by the Government to the Natives or to the Half-castes I can see no reason for making grants in this way at all.[45]

By ignoring interracial families and their claims, Proudfoot ensured that they became an economic burden to Ngāi Tahu living on native reserves.

The recognition of Māori women's land rights was crucial to land being set aside for mixed-descent children, especially if their white fathers had 'disappeared'. Government officials understood this, even if local authorities were less than sympathetic. 'Being the daughter of a Maori woman and another being my stepmother', Mary Ann Tandy claimed, 'I am entitled to their land as it was bequeathed to me by them before they died. I have made no inquiry into this matter as I left the Maoris when my father was lost, and have been among European people ever since.'[46] With no father to make an application on her behalf, Mary Ann, and others like her, were left out of the system of land grants established under the Land Claims Settlement Act 1856. Ironically, the Act secured the rights of white men rather than those of Māori women – even if the men's claims were based on the status and land rights of their wife.

'Half-Caste' Land Grants

The 1856 Act and its 1858 amendment held little meaning for South Islanders of mixed descent whose claims to land were based on Mantell's promises and on provisions made for 'half-castes' in the Rakiura Purchase of 1864. Under the terms of the purchase, mixed-descent families were to be provided with land at The Neck, on Stewart Island, 'in order to save the descendants of the early white settlers from eviction and poverty'.[47] For the first time, government officials paid specific attention to the growing mixed-descent community in the far south. Prior to 1864, the land purchases in Canterbury, Otago and Southland had been made with no concern for mixed-descent children, nor any thought for their future needs.[48]

Giving effect to the terms of the Rakiura Purchase took some time. It was Andrew Thompson's petition for land on behalf of his 'half-caste' wife and children in 1869 that set in train a series of official investigations into the plight of the mixed-descent population of southern New Zealand. A select committee reporting on Thompson's petition in August of that year found that the Crown was obliged to set aside land within the purchase blocks 'for the half-caste families resident thereon at the time of cession'.[49] Native Reserves Commissioner Alexander Mackay was instructed to investigate, and reported to the Native Department in October. He recommended that large blocks of Crown land, separate from reserves, be set aside for the families, who were to be allocated individual sections to 'prevent quarrelling amongst them in time to come'.[50] Petitions were received from Andrew Moore, Elisha Apes, Joseph Crocome, George Newton, Henry McCoy, Nathaniel Bates, John Kelly, George Printz, John McShane, James Leader, Jose Antonio, Thomas Leach, John Paulin, John Howell, Richard Sizemore, Henry Wixon, William Smith, William Low, James Crane, Edward Edwards,

English-born Joseph Crocome (1811–74) was a trained surgeon, who worked on whaling ships for several years before landing in Sydney in 1838. He then moved to Otago as an employee of the Weller brothers, and by 1839 was living at Waikouaiti. Crocome married Raureka/Arabella in 1844 and they had two children together, who were raised by their mother's kin. Crocome did not abandon them economically, but fought to have their land rights acknowledged through the offices of Walter Mantell. In 1869 Crocome wrote to the authorities, requesting recognition of the land title '[of which] I was put in possession by Mr Mantell on behalf of my half-caste children'.[51]
[S06-189L, Hocken Collections/Uare Taoka o Hākena]

Thomas Hardy and Patrick Gilroy. Eventually the weight of petitions, combined with pressure from Ngāi Tahu leaders, who 'required something to be done for these half-castes, because their fathers had not taken notice of them, and had not provided for them',[52] resulted in legislation designed to provide South Island 'half-castes' with an economic base and fulfil promises made under the Rakiura Purchase. By then, Mackay had made it clear that those promises were to be extended to 'half-castes' who were not born on Stewart Island, but were deemed equally entitled to land because of their mixed-descent status.[53] The statutes were the Middle Island Half-Caste Crown Grants Acts of 1877, 1883, 1885 and 1888.

The four Acts claimed to fulfil promises to provide 'half-caste' people with land in the 'Middle Island' (i.e., the South Island), through the awarding of Crown grants of 10 acres for men and 8 acres for women. Grants were awarded to 'half-castes' only, and were issued with restrictions on alienation. Trusteeship continued to be a central premise on which land grants were awarded. As in contemporary native land legislation, any owner who wished to sell had to apply to the Native Land Court to have the restrictions removed. Consent was given only if 'the Natives possessed other lands' for their support.[54] Restrictions on alienation sought to ensure that sellers were left with sufficient lands for their maintenance, and to prevent 'half-castes' becoming dependent on the state.[55]

Under the 1877 Act, individuals were to be provided with 'portions of the waste lands of the Crown situate within the Provincial Districts of Canterbury and Otago'.[56] An amendment was passed in 1883 to include 'half-castes' who were entitled to grants under the 1877 Act but who had been omitted 'by accident', and to provide for those added to the schedule to be issued with Crown grants. Several places in Otago were designated as 'half-caste' land: Hawksbury, North Harbour, Blueskin, Clarendon (south of the Taieri River) and Moeraki. But the majority of land grants were in Southland, where the mixed-descent population was concentrated: at Longwood, Paterson Inlet, Anglem, Jacob's River Hundred, Pourakino, the Invercargill Hundred, Fortrose Town and the Otara District. Many of these lands were located near native reserves, resulting in the demarcation of separate but adjoining spaces. This situation is clearly illustrated at Moeraki, where Mackay's 'preference for Block I Moeraki is on acct. of sec 23 being adjacent to the Native Reserve'.[57] Mackay's solution to the plight of mixed-descent families relied on the willingness of local authorities to remove the land from settlement. In 1878, the Otago Land Board refused Mackay's application to have certain waste lands set aside for such families. It was the only suitable land in the vicinity, and applicants were 'highly pleased at the probability of securing land within easy distance of the Native settlements'; but the board would not agree, even though the Commissioner of Crown Lands supported the applications.[58]

At Maitapapa, a small group of men and women were provided with land under the Half-Caste Crown Grants Acts, this land being spatially distinct from the native reserve. The Clarendon Block at Taieri was set aside under the 1877 Act for Elizabeth Crane, Robert Brown, Jack Connor (Tiaki Kona), Sarah Palmer, Ann Williams, James Williams, Mary Kui, Ann Owen, Jenny Palmer and Hannah Palmer. However, it did not take long for the allocation of sections to become the subject of complaints. Two years later, in 1879, a dissatisfied Tiaki Kona asked Mackay to 'try and get the ground I was speaking about for the children of the Tairei' [sic].[59] The 1883 Amendment to the Act allowed the granting of larger sections to individuals within their original blocks as listed under the 1877 Act, in recognition that those lands were of 'inferior quality' and 'not sufficient for their support'.[60] Yet the problems at Clarendon continued. Kona wrote to his local Member of the House of Representatives in 1885, claiming that 'if we had got [the other section] at the First we Would have some Benefit of it'.[61] The following year he complained to the Native Department that 'the piece that Mr McKie blocked of for us is no good at all I wish we could have it in some other place'.[62]

The Middle Island Half-Caste Crown Grants Act 1885 was designed to remedy errors and omissions made under the 1877 and 1883 Acts. In particular, officials had experienced difficulties in defining or understanding the term 'half-caste', and who should be included in this category. The problems with issuing Crown grants, it was claimed, were due to the difficulty of tracing the individuals concerned. This is evidence that the 'half-castes' did not consistently occupy either the Ngāi Tahu or the settler world.[63]

The Chief Draughtsman claimed in 1885 that:

> ... *the Schedule of Titles for Halfcaste claims was commenced long since but could not be completed on account of the difficulty in identifying the names given in the Act with those furnished by the Surveyor arising probably from changing their names and marriage. There are two lists of the Clarendon claim sent in by the Surveyor at different times which do not agree with each other. The Surveyor Mr. Mackenzie is again instructed to take copies of these and ascertain which is correct.*[64]

Difficulties were still being experienced in 1893, when Robert Brown requested that the Crown grants be issued for the land awarded to him and his wife Jane at Clarendon.[65] In the 1950s, when the current owners agreed to the sale of the Clarendon Block for a scenic reserve, officials discovered that only five of the eleven original owners had been granted title.[66]

The last Act in the series was passed in 1888, after a government commission two years earlier had investigated the cases of people excluded from the provisions of the earlier legislation.[67] Taken together, the four Acts suggest that a great deal of activity went into providing for the 'half-caste' population in the South Island. However, the parliamentary debate on the legislation undermines this view. The slow pace of implementing the grants made under these Acts reflects wider government lethargy in fulfilling promises made to Ngāi Tahu in respect of Crown land purchases between 1844 and 1864, as outlined in the report of the Smith-Nairn Commission of 1879–80 and the 1886 Report of the Royal Commission into Middle Island Claims.

· · ·

The fate of mixed-descent children whose parents' relationship was not recognised as legitimate caused a great deal of anxiety for both parents and officials. However, interracial relationships did not absolve Māori communities of responsibility for the welfare of mixed-descent children. Indeed, many interracial families lived on Māori land and within Māori communities. But as British laws and institutions were established in New Zealand from 1840, white fathers sought to ensure their children's property rights and economic security. To prove themselves worthy of government support, they were prepared to embrace monogamy, respectability and a settled agricultural life. In response, colonial authorities introduced a range of mechanisms to encourage newcomers to formalise their relationships in legal Christian marriage, the most important being the recognition of land rights of mixed-descent children. Gaining the necessary Crown grants was not easy, and many children were excluded from the system, particularly those who were not recognised, or were abandoned, by their white father. The special circumstances of a large and growing mixed-descent population were formally acknowledged in 1864, in the context of the Rakiura Purchase. Yet despite consequent legislation designed to provide mixed-descent families with an economic base, the state was unable or unwilling to resolve the matter quickly. Families fought for recognition for decades, often with no success, leaving many of them impoverished and reliant on kinship networks for support.

Chapter 6. Racial Categories and Lived Identities

From the mid nineteenth century, the colonial government attempted to measure the extent of cultural and physical assimilation of Māori into mainstream New Zealand, and commented on the success of this policy in Native Department and census reports. The modern perception of Ngāi Tahu as 'the white tribe'[1] has its origins in a history of sustained interracial marriage, but it was a view consolidated by colonial population counts undertaken from the 1840s. By the 1890s, government officials and politicians were using the evidence from the census to proclaim Ngāi Tahu the most 'European' of the Māori tribes, based on genetics, 'way of living', and use of English, as well as dress and physical appearance.

The national census was crucial in shaping perceptions of Ngāi Tahu identity as it employed a 'language of fractions' to classify the population, at a time when social scientists were keenly interested in the implications of crossing the 'races'.[2] Significantly, that language of fractions – 'three-quarter-caste', 'half-caste', 'quarter-caste', 'one-eighth-caste' – was first applied to Ngāi Tahu in 1890, but did not enter the official lexicon of the national census until 1926. Census-taking embedded racial categories and classifications in the public and official consciousness, together with a view of Ngāi Tahu as 'white'. But while these categories were used to define a population, the census statistics that emerged did not reflect the everyday reality of the people concerned.

The census and categories of 'race'

Census reports were one of the key sites where official views and anxieties about 'race' were articulated. Melissa Nobles argues that the national census has played a major role in 'the formation and perpetuation of racial politics'.[3] In the nineteenth and early twentieth centuries, the national census was a racially informed document and census enumerators were active participants in the formation of racial ideas and the construction of racial categories.

Generally speaking, the classifications employed in a census were fluid, reflecting not only a changing demographic but also the interests of racial science. In the United States, for example, the category of 'mulatto' was introduced in the 1850 census at a time when social scientists were seeking evidence for the theory of polygenism – that is, the notion that different 'races' have different origins.[4] In 1890 the terms 'quadroon' and 'octoroon' were added to the US census, but by 1930 officials were favouring the 'one-drop rule', in which anyone with 'black blood' was legally defined as black.[5] In Latin America, a very different view of interracial mixing arose. Instead of associating racial hybrids with degeneration, Brazilians looked to interracial marriage as a source of racial strength, arguing that miscegenation offered a way for Europeans to survive in the tropics. The social elites and intelligentsia of Brazil favoured 'constructive miscegenation', whereby human bodies – and, by extension, the nation – would gradually 'whiten'.[6] As in New Zealand, the success of this approach was monitored in the national census.

The first nationwide census of the Māori population was undertaken in 1874. While regional censuses had been taken prior to that date, this census set the pattern for the enumeration of Māori on a national basis. Notably, the census was held separately from that of the non-Māori population, and was not comprehensive, with officials initially preferring estimates rather than precise numbers.[7] Carried out by sub-enumerators, who reported on their district to the Native Department, the four-yearly (later five-yearly) census was framed by instructions issued by the Registrar-General. Information was requested on the state and welfare of the Māori population, the size of the population, any increase or decrease in 'half-castes', and whether the

Taieri Ferry, *c.* 1860s. [S09-333a, Hocken Collections/Uare Taoka o Hākena]

latter were 'living as Maori' or 'living as European'.[8] District native officers also reported to the Native Department on the nature of the Māori population in their area, providing similar information to that gathered by the enumerators, but on an annual basis.

In 1916 a separate section on 'race' was added to the national census, but racial terms and classifications had been utilised in the census since 1874. The only term used in that year was 'half-caste', but in 1926 graduated 'blood' categories, including 'three-quarter-caste' and 'quarter-caste', were introduced to describe the Māori and mixed-descent populations. In that year Māori filled out an individual census form for the first time, but it was not until 1951 that the Māori and general census were merged and everyone answered the same census questions. Prior to 1916, enumerators were required to categorise those of mixed descent either as 'half-castes living as European' or 'half-castes living as Maori', the former being included in the general census, and the latter in the Māori census. However, these categories were unevenly applied by census officials, who often based their decision on an individual's living conditions and visual appearance. Moreover, they often changed the way in which 'half-castes' were to be categorised. In 1891, for example, the enumerator in Otago decided that people of mixed descent were not 'living as members of a Maori tribe'; he therefore omitted them from the Māori census and included them in the general schedule instead.[9] In the 1906 census report it was noted that, 'as a rule, the sub-enumerators show no discretion in separating the half-castes who are living as members of Native tribes from those who are, to all intents and purposes, living on exactly the same footing as the Pakeha'.[10] Moreover, it was 'quite impossible to check their work in this respect'.[11] By 1921, however, 'census practice included the classing of all those nearer in blood to European than half-caste as full-blooded European, and vice versa, as Maoris'.[12] The classification of 'half-castes' according to mode of living was discontinued in 1936 because of confusion.

Despite these difficulties, from the early twentieth century politicians and government agents used census results as evidence of successful assimilation policy. Physical and cultural absorption was regarded as the key to Māori survival, and progress in this area was measured in terms of interracial marriage and the production of a mixed-descent population.[13] The 1901 census, reporting on the fate of the Māori population, linked their future place in New Zealand to physical and cultural hybridity: '[Their] ultimate destiny must remain a matter of speculation. The pessimist sees a remnant of beggars wandering over the land their ancestors once possessed, while the optimist looks forward to a complete fusion of the two races.'[14] Five years later the Registrar-General commented on the widely held belief that the 'ultimate fate of the Maori race is to become absorbed in the European', and emphasised that any tendency in this direction 'must be gathered from the increase or decrease in the number of half-castes'.[15] In 1916 the Minister for Native Affairs, William Herries, stated that the 'policy of the Government has been to encourage the blending of the two races'.[16] Māori 'will become extinct', predicted one commentator, 'but not in the sense of dying out, but by reason of amalgamation with our people'.[17]

Ngāi Tahu and the census process

Ngāi Tahu were very familiar with the census-taking process, even before the first national census of Māori in 1874. Their population had been counted, and interracial marriages commented on, from the time the first missionaries and colonial officials arrived in the South Island. In 1843 and 1844, while visiting the 'east coast of the Middle Island, from Banks Peninsula to Foveaux Strait',[18] Edward Shortland recorded the numbers living in each settlement and commented on the mixed-descent population. He found 'no sufficient reason to anticipate the extinction of the Maori race, except by the possible means of its becoming blended with the European stock'.[19] Walter Mantell conducted a census of the Ngāi Tahu population of Canterbury in 1848, and of the Murihiku (Southland) population in 1853. These occurred immediately after the systematic colonisation of these regions by British settlers, and were undertaken in order to mark out native reserves at a time when colonial officials were eager to gain access to Ngāi Tahu land. In the years that followed, population counts of Ngāi Tahu were made by Alfred Chetham Strode, Otago's resident magistrate, and Alexander Mackay, in addition to Francis Dart Fenton's nationwide, and imprecise, 1858 census.[20] In all these surveys, the term 'half-caste' was used to describe people of mixed descent.

In 1890 a Royal Commission, commonly known as the Middle Island Native Land Claims Commission, investigated the adequacy of reserves set aside for Ngāi Tahu as a result of land purchases between 1844 and 1864. As head of the Commission, Mackay visited all Ngāi Tahu settlements to take evidence. He was also instructed to obtain a correct list of residents, and the land owned by them, in order to assess its sufficiency for their maintenance and support. Mackay did not find this an easy task. Ngāi Tahu leaders viewed the Commission and its investigations as yet another government tactic to delay the investigation of the South Island purchases and the settlement of the Ngāi Tahu Claim relating to land grievances.

In every community, much suspicion was attached to the process of 'periodical counting'. Past censuses had failed to include all members of the tribal population, and leaders everywhere commented on the material implications of inaccurate census-taking, linking it explicitly with their economic survival. In his 1848 census of Canterbury Ngāi Tahu, Mantell had failed to account for those who were absent for seasonal food-gathering or visiting relatives in Otago and Southland.[21] Statistics reflect this erasure, and the consequent loss experienced by Ngāi Tahu. On the basis of his 1848 census Mantell set aside 10 acres per person; but 843 people were omitted from that census, representing a loss of 8,430 acres.[22] The census-taking process was thus implicated in the landlessness experienced by 90 per cent of Ngāi Tahu in 1890, and played a crucial role in the setting aside of reserves that were inadequate for their social, cultural and economic survival.[23]

What is most interesting about Mackay's Commission, and the list of residents it generated, is the application of graduated racial categories to tribal members. The inquiry was designed to obtain information on Ngāi Tahu land holdings by compiling a 'list of names of all the Native population, inclusive of half-castes and quarter-castes residing amongst the Europeans'.[24] Mackay's aim in including all people of mixed descent, regardless of where they were living, 'was to make the return as full as possible'.[25] Ironically, Mackay hoped that this census could assist in rectifying earlier erasures. The outcome of the Commission was a thirty-page list of naming all 2,212 individuals of Ngāi Tahu descent.[26] This 'return' was different from previous population counts in two important respects. It was the first time that the categories 'three-quarter-caste', 'quarter-caste' and 'one-eighth-caste' had been used in a census in New Zealand, at a time when colonial officials in other countries were increasingly employing the census to classify and measure indigenous populations.[27] And because it included all Ngāi Tahu descendants, whether living as European or as Māori, it was far more thorough than the Māori census, where inclusion was theoretically based on residence in Māori settlements.

Mackay did not use graduated racial categories to advance racial science, but to offer a much more inclusive view of tribal identity and participation, and one that reflected Ngāi Tahu structures and processes. As such, his report was in marked contrast to official views embodied in the national census. Mackay was critical of the recent national Māori census, claiming that it did not 'exhibit all the population, inclusive of persons descended from Natives'.[28] While the purpose of the 1890 list was not to define Ngāi

Robert, William and Jack Palmer (date unknown). Like many people of mixed descent, the Palmer brothers understood the material effects of the term 'half-caste'. When petitioning the government they used the racial language of the era, knowing that this gained them some advantages at a time when the economic plight of the southern mixed-descent population was under investigation. Land set aside for such people was often marginal, and even more uneconomic than native reserves, or situated at a distance from family. Requests for government assistance on the basis of 'half-caste' status was common during the late nineteenth century, signalling that responsibility for the economic welfare of these people did not rest with Ngāi Tahu alone. [Photograph courtesy of E. M. Palmer]

Tahu racially, the application of racial 'fractions' to each individual served nonetheless to reinforce an official view that Ngāi Tahu were 'white'.

The 1890 return makes a powerful statement about the complicity of the census-taking process in erasures of people from place. Mackay's list of 2,212 names, embracing 'all the Native population together with their descendants irrespective of the degree of consanguinity',[29] contrasts with the official figure of 1,231 Ngāi Tahu in the national census of the same year. Mackay arrived at the larger figure because he followed Ngāi Tahu views of identity, as demonstrated by his process. At each settlement, he 'requested the parties to furnish a list of names of the present residents'.[30] Despite the initial reluctance of many leaders, a committee was formed at each settlement to prepare the list of residents, which was then read out to 'afford an opportunity for any persons who were omitted to apply to have their names included'.[31] To ensure accuracy, and thus prevent the problems encountered by Mantell, 'each head of family present was questioned whether all names were included'.[32] This approach was taken at all settlements, although many had to be convinced. The residents at Moeraki, for example, initially refused to make a list because such information 'had been frequently furnished, and nothing had come of it'.[33] Communities themselves decided who was Ngāi Tahu, and based that decision on residence, tribal participation, and descent. People of mixed descent – many of them less than 'half-caste', and therefore not Māori in official and legislative terms – were named and claimed as Ngāi Tahu by tribal leaders. The result was a list of names that followed Ngāi Tahu custom, using whakapapa as the basic criterion for Ngāi Tahu membership.

As Mackay's list demonstrates, a person's identity was not necessarily bound to a single place. Some names appear twice, reflecting rights and kinship ties to multiple sites, even if the person did not reside there. Louisa Barrett, for example, is listed at the settlement of Taieri, where she was born, and also at Kaiapoi, where she lived. Mackay attempted to resolve this by reading out all the names at the final sitting of the inquiry at Kaiapoi, 'to enable them to be identified, with a view to prevent the names being duplicated'.[34] But because the list included residents in each settlement as well as 'relatives at a distance', some duplication was inevitable.[35]

Ngāi Tahu also employed other means to defy attempts to categorise and 'fix' the population to one place. By the late nineteenth century, surnames of European origin had become widespread among Ngāi Tahu, and communities used these names and their Māori transliterations to disrupt the census process. Multiple names translated into multiple representations in the census figures. Importantly, this multiplicity of names disrupted any interpretation of the 1890 list as a meaningful guide to the success of assimilation policy. The Palmers, for example, were a large and prominent mixed-descent family living at Taieri in the 1890s. In Mackay's list, family members are listed as Palmer, but also as Paama. The success of such strategies to increase access to land, and to rectify, to some extent, Mantell's erasures, depended on the complicity of the community, and Mackay's lack of familiarity with Ngāi Tahu kinship ties. The 1890 list points to the ability of Māori, especially those of mixed descent, to disrupt the census-taking process. They did so because land rights were a fraught issue among Ngāi Tahu, at a time when the tribe was grappling with the inadequacy of reserved lands to accommodate a growing mixed-descent population.

Interpreting identity

By the 1870s, as Māori became increasingly subject to national census enumeration, Ngāi Tahu were regarded as the most 'European' of the Māori tribes. James West Stack, district native officer for Canterbury, reported in 1877 that in 'dress, food, and house accommodation, there is very little to distinguish the Maoris in the South Island from their European neighbours'.[36] In 1886, it was claimed that Ngāi Tahu in the towns of Geraldine and Waimate had 'adopted the European mode of living, dress in the same manner, eat the same food, and live in cottages not very unlike those occupied by their white neighbours of the labouring class'.[37] Census enumerators and district native officers attested to this transition. In the 1906 national census report, the living conditions of Ngāi Tahu were described as 'particularly European in manner': the people had largely 'separate holdings and separate homes, although the areas they hold and cultivate are much smaller than are usually owned by Europeans'.[38] Education levels and physical appearance reinforced the belief that southern Māori 'now live in European fashion', a situation commonly attributed to early and widespread interracial marriage.[39]

The 'assimilation' of Ngāi Tahu culminated in their inclusion in the general census from 1921.[40] In practice, however, this assimilation was not as complete as the statistics and census reports indicated. Māori politicians understood the complexities of identity, and the inability of a census to represent it accurately. Āpirana Ngata, the long-serving representative for Eastern Māori, had a much more sophisticated view of the cultural affiliations and identity of Ngāi Tahu than many government officials. In 1929, when he was Minister of Native Affairs, Ngata noted that while 'a large proportion [of Ngāi Tahu] are half-caste, and midway between half-caste and full European, still, in their outlook and spirit and physical characteristics they are very much Maori'.[41]

When dealing with government officials, people of mixed descent were well aware of the significance of the term 'half-caste' in colonial society. Throughout the 1870s and 1880s, numerous people of Ngāi Tahu descent asserted their 'half-caste' status in petitions and letters to the Native Department, at a time when the government was investigating 'half-caste' land claims in the South Island. Some, like the families at Awarua in Southland, signed their letters: 'From us, the half-castes in this District'.[42] Others rejected the term, preferring to identify themselves as 'tangata' (person), 'Māori', 'wahine' (woman) and 'Native'.[43]

Statistics are problematic: they not only fail to capture this complexity of identity, but are also devoid of social and cultural context. Indeed, it has been argued that:

> ... census categorisations were so arbitrary and random that they provide little help in deciphering how these people [of mixed descent] saw themselves, what community or communities they belonged to and how their cultural or physical lives functioned.[44]

The everyday lives of mixed-descent people undermined any statistical claims to a clear separation between 'half-caste' and Māori. Identity cannot be captured through fractions alone. Taieri, for example, had 140 residents in 1890, 25 per cent of whom were recorded as 'Maori'. Taieri was one of the most intermarried Ngāi Tahu communities, and marriages between

Members of Ngāi Tahu attending a Native Land Court hearing at Puketeraki in September 1905. While individuals claiming their land interests before the Court identified themselves as Ngāi Tahu by presenting their whakapapa, the outcome of Court attendance, for the Taieri people as for Māori elsewhere, was the erosion of their interests in the reserve through the process of succession. [S08-140d, Hocken Collections/Uare Taoka o Hākena]

'half-caste' and European had taken place on a larger scale than in any other settlement, producing a largely 'quarter-caste' population. In the 1891 official census, 57 per cent of the Taieri population were identified as 'half-caste'. That proportion increased steadily to 59 per cent in 1896, 63 per cent in 1901, and 75 per cent in 1906, reaching a peak of 93 per cent in 1911.[45] With the exception of 1891 and 1896, these figures are higher than those for Ngāi Tahu in general, which peaked at 77 per cent in 1896, dropping to 63 per cent in 1906.[46]

Yet none of these statistical findings reflects the reality of a vibrant community of people who expressed Ngāi Tahu identity. In many respects, the experiences of the mixed-descent families at Taieri in the late nineteenth and early twentieth centuries reflect the wider Ngāi Tahu experience of the impact of colonial encounter. These intersections with a larger Ngāi Tahu narrative centred on land dispossession, poverty and social marginalisation, as well as vigorous efforts to retain cultural values and resource rights.

In many respects, daily life in the Taieri community undermined the official racial categories that identified its population as 'European'. By the late nineteenth century, an annual economic cycle had been established at the settlement. In spring and summer, the families engaged in shearing and the harvesting of wheat. In October and November they went whitebaiting, and in summer they fished. In the autumn, potatoes were harvested. In the winter, families went rabbiting, duck shooting, and muttonbirding.[47] Other winter work consisted of labouring on local farms, such as erecting and maintaining fences. Families supported themselves through a mix of subsistence agriculture and wage labour. While William Brown kept sheep on the reserve, there was also 'plenty of fish and game in the river and swamplands'.[48] Traditional food sources provided sustenance throughout a period marked by poverty and population growth.

Land and politics

Identity was expressed in a number of social and cultural forms, and none was more important than connection to land and participation in tribal politics. In the 1890s, land remained the dominant issue for the Taieri families, and for Ngāi Tahu generally. As the Ngāi Tahu population grew and placed greater pressure on the land, concern was expressed about the size of reserves. Evidence presented by Ngāi Tahu leaders before the Middle Island Native Land Claims Commission of 1890 emphasised the inadequacy of existing reserve land for their sustenance and economic survival. In every community, Mackay heard accounts of poverty and hardship, of the poor quality of reserve land, and of families having to depend on seasonal employment. The Taieri families were no exception. In his evidence, Tiaki Kona described their inability to make a living from the land because of its small size and poor quality.[49] In 1886 Taieri had been claimed as 'one of the poorest reserves on the South Island', where 'there is not enough land for all the people that is there'.[50] Illness and old age had curtailed the working lives of a number of the men; Martin Korako and Tom Brown were unable to work, while 'others were just able to live and that was all'.[51]

Thomas Brown, son of William Brown and Margaret Davis, was born at Maitapapa in 1885. With George Wellman, he joined the Pioneer Māori Battalion and fought in Europe during World War I. Thomas left behind a valuable record in the form of his unpublished memoirs. He remembers growing up in a thriving, politically engaged and culturally active community, despite its marginal economic position. [Photograph courtesy of David Brown]

Adding to the pressure on reserve land was the erosion of land interests resulting from the practices of the Native Land Court. The Court never sat at Taieri, so vigilance was required to maintain the title and succession to land. This meant that a family representative had to travel to Kaiapoi, Waikouaiti, Puketeraki or Invercargill to attend Court sessions. In cases where a deceased person left no will, the Native Land Court generally divided their interests equally among all surviving children, effectively rendering the land uneconomic and more difficult to use.[52] After the death in 1898 of Robert Brown, for example, his land at Maitapapa was awarded to his six surviving children, Thomas, Robert, Eliza, William, George and Elizabeth, and his granddaughter Mabel.[53] As a result, the six-acre block was divided into seven interests, which were to be further eroded through the practice of succession on the death of Robert's children, many of whom had large families. Robert Brown had in fact made a will, in which he recognised the role of the Native Land Court in alienating land: 'All the lands in Taieri must not be sold or mortgaged but may be leased'; moreover, these lands 'are for the descendants of Paraone [Brown] only'. The will ended with a warning: 'let not you or any of you [illegible] the Native Land Court [go] against any of the words which I have written in this my will'.[54] Making a will could counteract the effects of equal succession on a holding by naming specific successors or by placing restrictions on the lease or sale of the land in question. But Robert Brown's will was never presented before the Native Land Court, so equality of succession was applied.

Engaging with Ngāi Tahu politics and identity was not limited to giving evidence before commissions and government inquiries. Such engagement extended to participation in major hui (tribal gatherings) where the everyday difficulties of the families were expressed. During a hui at Ōtākou in December 1892, Tiaki Kona told the Native Minister, A. J. Cadman:

> I am from the Taieri river. The Taieri people unfortunately, are unable to come here to see you; they have gone abroad to seek work for themselves … The reason I came was this – that I thought you would be unable to go to the Taieri. There are a number of people who are in trouble there, who are living without adequate sustenance. There are a number of men and also children who are without sufficient means.[55]

The Taieri families placed their faith in Ngāi Tahu leaders to resolve the situation, or at least to gain them some relief. Yet they too were active in tribal matters, establishing a runanga (committee) in the 1890s as a formal structure through which to engage in Ngāi Tahu politics. Through the runanga, families contributed money to Te Kereme (The Claim), a fighting fund established in 1879 to press for an investigation into Ngāi Tahu land grievances.[56]

In 1893, with a population of 170 living on a reserve of 2,310 acres, of which only 68 acres were economically viable, many families were struggling to survive.[57] In that year, the Matene, Tuarea, Bryant and Sherburd families were receiving relief aid from the government.[58] During the 1890s, agricultural labouring was the staple form of employment. Among those resident at Maitapapa were Robert, William, George and John Brown, Tiaki

Harriet Overton, the daughter of William Palmer and Ann Holmes, with her son George (date unknown). Harriet married William Brandon Overton in 1865, and after his death in 1890 had to raise a family of ten with little financial support. To supplement the small income from their farm, Harriet worked as a cleaner at the Henley School, while her eldest son, Benjamin, took up labouring work with the Bruce County Council. Nonetheless, at her death in 1913, Harriet's children were all well educated, married, and socially successful. George became Inspector of Schools in Otago, and later in Nelson. [Photograph courtesy of E. M. Palmer]

Kona, Robert Sherburd, William Bryant, Henry Palmer and James Smith, all of whom were farm labourers.[59] Thomas Brown, son of William Brown and Margaret Davis, remembered his father 'was working hard [in] those early days, contract work, and was often away shearing'.[60] William's father, Robert Brown, was a first-class pit-sawyer, shearer and carpenter, as well as a skilled blacksmith.[61] Those who had no trades, such as the Wellman family, did their best to farm their 6 acres of land at the reserve. Members of the Brown family worked as shearers on the Salisbury estate in North Otago. Others, such as the Bryants, worked on local farms.[62] While the men were 'abroad', engaged in seasonal work, the women managed the homes and properties, with the children labouring on the family farm. They supplemented their income by 'milking a few cows', and selling the milk to the local dairy company.[63]

In times of seasonal employment, Maitapapa was essentially a community led by women with large families, living in poverty. Widows suffered particular hardship. The experiences of Mere Kui, Harriet Overton, Ani Sherburd and Ani Williams illustrate the importance of marriage and remarriage for survival. In the late nineteenth century, widowhood was characterised by economic and social uncertainty.[64] Widows at Maitapapa, with large families to care for, were driven to appeal for government assistance. Mere Kui requested that her rights to land at Otago and Canterbury be investigated and acknowledged, as 'she looks to the Government to allow her some land for herself and family'.[65] Tiaki Kona, writing to the Native Minister on Harriet Overton's behalf, presented her situation as desperately in need of investigation:

> [She] is a widow with five young children, who are not able to do anything for themselves, and are entirely dependent upon her ... If under the circumstances you could grant her some relief, or induce the Government to give her assistance, you would be doing an act of justice.[66]

Meanwhile, Ani Sherburd, 'a widow with four children', was living on land at Taieri that was 'gifted' to them when they arrived from Kaiapoi in the 1860s.[67] Remarriage was one way to alleviate the poverty of widowhood. Ani Sherburd, for instance, would eventually remarry in 1894, to Abraham Starkey.

Joe and Rihi Joss and their three children in 1900, at Lowry's Beach, The Neck, Stewart Island. The Joss family raised several foster children, including George Brown, who was introduced to muttonbirding while resident on the island. [S08-542g, MS-1416/045, Maida Barlow Papers, Hocken Collections/Uare Taoka o Hākena]

Waterways and mahinga kai

Maintaining access rights to mahinga kai (food-gathering sites) for tuna (eels), īnanga (whitebait) and tīti (muttonbirds) became increasingly important during hard economic times. But the significance of these traditional sites went much deeper. Rights to the Titi Islands in Foveaux Strait, for example, have been described as 'a most important cultural, social and political facet of Ngāi Tahu tribal identity'.[68] During annual seasonal migrations to the islands, 'sometimes the kaik [village] would be deserted'.[69] Thomas and George Brown often stayed with Walter Joss at Rakiura for the muttonbird season. During those four weeks on the islands they were taught to catch, clean, slate and cure the birds, and to make the flax baskets in which to preserve and transport them.[70] On their return, the preserved birds formed a key part of the Ngāi Tahu food exchange network.[71] Muttonbirds brought back to Taieri were given to local tradespeople to pay debts, and sent on to kin elsewhere.[72] Muttonbirding was not just a food-gathering exercise but a major social, economic and cultural enterprise, one that was crucial to reinforcing kinship links, maintaining access rights to resources, and preserving cultural knowledge.

With its accessible lakes and river system, Taieri was itself an important fishing area and source of traditional foods. Families made regular trips to the inland lakes to gather food and raw materials essential to cultural practices. Mere Kui and her children would often camp near Tatawai and Waihola to fish for pātiki (flounder) and eels.[73] In the early twentieth century, eels and whitebait were a staple part of the local diet. Eels strung on the tree outside Tiaki Kona's house for drying were a common sight.[74] Before restrictions on nets were introduced, families would set their whitebait nets in the river permanently.[75] According to Kath Hislop, 'most kaik people did this', as well as fishing for flounder.[76] When work on local farms was scarce, 'the Kaik people would often go to the lakes to spear eels' and catch trout and game.[77] Attempts by local councils and central government from the 1890s to drain the inland waterways triggered a long struggle by local Ngāi Tahu to maintain access to traditional food sources, similar to that experienced by many Māori communities from the late nineteenth century.

From the time of British colonisation, the landscape of the lower Taieri had been physically transformed by the introduction of agricultural practices. Central to this process was the drainage of the large inland wetland, which resulted in the loss of three shallow lakes. Originally the Taieri Plain was a wetland that extended from Wingatui in the north to Waihola in the south, with the river and its major tributaries providing natural drainage.[78] The wetland included three further inland lakes, Potaka, Tatawai and Marama Te Taha (Lake Ascog), 'formerly a famous eeling place'.[79] The draining of the wetland began in the 1860s, and by 1867 around 28,000 acres were under cultivation, growing wheat, barley, oats, grasses and potatoes, while sheep farming and dairying were also becoming significant in the area.[80] As the gold-rushes brought greater settlement and industry, the processes of mining, sluicing, deforestation and cultivation caused the lakes to become increasingly filled with silt, thus reducing the depth of the water.[81]

For the Taieri families, maintaining access to the inland waterway system was essential to their economic and cultural survival.[82] Not only did the Taieri River and the inland lakes provide abundant food,[83] but the Taieri Plain contained the only large swamps south of the Waitaki River that grew both harakeke (flax) and raupo, which drew local and migratory Ngāi Tahu families into economic activities based on their harvesting and processing.[84] The loss of Lake Tatawai was of particular concern. In 1891, Tiaki Kona requested that:

> ... a portion of land inland from Hapua [be] given to us for the purpose of cultivation because the Europeans are always running after persons who go there to grow food. I request that the 'mana' over this portion of land be given to us. The name of this portion is Tatawai.[85]

His request came six years after an initial petition seeking the return of Tatawai (also known as Waihoropunga).[86] In evidence presented before the Middle Island Native Land Claims Commission, Tiaki Kona stated that access to cultivations was restricted by the encroachment of farm holdings and the stocking of the river with trout, which prevented his people from catching eels.[87] These complaints were not only about being denied sustenance, but also about the loss of an important cultural tradition. Drainage practices at Taieri eventually led to the loss of Potaka as well as Tatawai. Marama Te Taha was also drained, despite a request for its reservation in 1901.[88] Taieri's waterways may have been a key site of interracial encounter in the early decades of contact, but by the late nineteenth century they had become a source of conflict between Ngāi Tahu, settlers, local authorities and the state, triggering a clash of cultures in the 'contact zone'.

The Taieri was not the only wetland environment under threat from drainage projects and measures for flood control.[89] The drainage of wetlands was a key to successful colonisation, as it enabled the creation of agricultural land for settlers.[90] It was also in the national interest, in order to turn 'unproductive' land into 'productive' land for the burgeoning meat industry. From the late nineteenth century, the government supported this process by introducing legislation, which continued into the twentieth century in the form of the Hauraki Plains Act 1908 and the Rangitaiki Land Drainage Act 1910.[91] The loss of Tatawai by 1920 is part of a national story of the loss of wetland environments by many Māori communities.

'Descendants of Ngai Tahu tribe at the Taieri River mouth with Amos McKegg, 1913'. The photographer, James McDonald, did not record the names of the women and children portrayed here, apparently on a picnic. However, by referring to other photographs of the Maitapapa families, it is possible to identify a few of them. To the right of Amos McKegg (standing) is Helen Brown, formerly McNaught. On the far right is Hinehou Martin. Reclining in front of Helen is Olive Martin, Hinehou's granddaughter. [B.13137, Museum of New Zealand Te Papa Tongarewa]

Family and community life

Despite the erosion of land ownership and the loss of traditional food sources, the community at Taieri grew in strength throughout the late nineteenth century. Interracial marriage continued into the early twentieth century, consolidating Taieri as a mixed-descent community and bringing newcomers into the nexus of social and economic obligations. The pattern of mixed-descent men and women marrying the daughters and sons of local settlers continued, reinforcing links with the Pākehā community as well. James Smith and William Bryant married Emma Robson and Fanny Horne respectively, both young women being the daughters of well-known Taieri Ferry families. Marriages increasingly took place outside the confines of the reserve, reflecting the pull of employment opportunities and kinship ties

The opening of Te Waipounamu Hall at Maitapapa attracted Ngāi Tahu from across the southern regions for week-long celebrations, and merited several pages of photographs in the April 1901 edition of the *Otago Witness*. [S08-153a, Hocken Collections/Uare Taoka o Hākena]

to settlements beyond the lower Taieri district. Alfred Palmer, for example, was married at Leeston, where his sister Beatrice lived with her husband, local fisherman Charles Johnson.[92] There were also additions to the reserve community, including William Robertson, who married Sarah Sherburd in 1897, and Thomas Garth, who married Lizzie Brown the following year. By 1894 Frederick Cook, who was married to Mere Smith, daughter of Mere Kui, was also living at Maitapapa (now known as Henley).[93] In 1896 there were twenty-eight Europeans – thirteen men and fifteen women – living on the reserve.[94]

Large gatherings associated with important social and cultural events were a feature of life on the reserve. Thomas Brown, who grew up at Maitapapa in the 1890s, remembered that his grandparents, Robert and Jane, 'always had visitors from other pah' at their home.[95] Such visits were one of many ways in which to maintain kinship links and access to resources. A space was needed to host visitors, as well as community events, religious meetings and political gatherings, and in 1900 residents began to plan for a hall. This was a significant step in the community's history, and the culmination of two decades of population growth. The selection of a site and the collection of subscriptions were undertaken by the 'Committee for the Native Hall', established in June 1900.[96] The committee included two European men, Thomas Garth and James Tanner, both married to mixed-descent women, which demonstrates that marriage continued to be an integrative process involving responsibilities to family and community.

Although women were rarely involved in the organising committee, they played a key role in the hall's opening, hosting visitors for the weeklong celebrations and managing the catering. Led by Rebecca Matene, they also made the flag bearing the name of the hall, which was hoisted at the opening ceremony.[97] And reflecting the pattern of early interracial marriage, in which Ngāi Tahu women married male newcomers, it was the matriarchs who represented their families and Ngāi Tahu identity at the opening. A number of Ngāi Tahu leaders were also in attendance, among them Tame Parata, parliamentary representative for Southern Māori, and representatives of the Ngāi Tahu settlements of Ōtākou, Arowhenua, Molyneux, Waikouaiti and Waihou.[98] The presence of these leaders reflected Taieri's position as a widely recognised Ngāi Tahu community.

Built by local subscription, the hall was used for religious services on Sundays and other meetings during the week, for example to organise politically to protect fishing rights to Lake Tatawai. The community thus became 'independent in the way of a meeting house'.[99] The hall also hosted a range of social activities, with regular dances and concerts attended by reserve families and local settlers. Weddings were also held there, including that of Miss Parsons, the daughter of a prominent local settler, in June 1912.[100] John Wellman and Sarah McIntosh were married at the hall in 1904, as were Betsy Brown and Alexander Smith in 1909. At these weddings, members of the Crane, Brown and Wellman families provided the entertainment.[101] Betsy Brown ran a regular culture class for local children in the hall, teaching singing and dancing, and how to make and use poi.[102]

Tame Parata (centre) at the official opening of Te Waipounamu Hall, with Ihaia Potiki (standing, far left) and Rawiri Te Maire (standing, far right). Others in the photograph are unidentified. [E5316/44a, Hocken Collections/Uare Taoka o Hākena]

Among those living at the reserve in the final decades of the nineteenth century were the Wellman, Brown, Garth, Drummond, Hanna, Tanner, Matene and Sherburd families. In noting that there were 'quite a few there then', former Taieri resident Kath Hislop indicates that the strength of the community lay in its families, whose leaders were confident and able, and who were aligned with the Ngāi Tahu polity.[103]

. . .

By the late nineteenth century, the development in the South Island of an increasingly mixed-descent tribal population had economic and cultural implications for both Ngāi Tahu and colonial officials. In their ability to cross boundaries of identity, individuals of mixed descent challenged widely understood colonial categories and hierarchies of race. One way in which the state attempted to manage the mixed-descent population was through census enumeration, which enabled the success of interracial marriage as an assimilation tool to be monitored and commented on. But census categories were arbitrary and imprecise, and their application subject to the whim of enumerators. As a result, the 'half-caste' defied classification, occupying an unstable position in the national census and remaining outside the boundary of state control. Mackay's 1890 inventory of Ngāi Tahu settlements illustrates the extent to which people of mixed descent disrupted colonial categories of race, in the same way that interracial relationships undermined racial theories and hierarchies throughout the nineteenth century colonial world.[104] As the case of Ngāi Tahu illustrates, despite a long history of interracial marriage, and statistical claims of assimilation, identification with Māori cultural practices and knowledge persisted, and was intimately tied to tribal politics.

Beyond the abstract notions of census categorisation, the 'language of fractions' played an important role in the lives of mixed-descent people, and had significant implications for identity. But while those categories were central to official definitions of Māori identity, the reality of community life was very different. As the Taieri families demonstrate, people of mixed descent inhabited and straddled two cultural worlds. While the families were largely European by 'blood', the identity articulated by the strong community at Taieri was Ngāi Tahu. This was a time when political organising and social occasions brought the community together, serving to reinforce its Ngāi Tahu identity to the wider tribe and to outsiders, and demonstrating how one community accommodated and negotiated colonial categories of race.

Chapter 7. Migration Stories

By the 1890s, the families of the largely mixed-descent community at Taieri were heavily immersed in Ngāi Tahu culture and politics. They used the Māori language when communicating with the government, and were politically united with other Ngāi Tahu communities in dealing with the impact of colonisation, especially land alienation, and the erosion of access to significant economic and cultural resources. European surnames predominated, among them Garth, Overton, Crane, Sherburd, Brown, Smith, Bryant, Tanner and Wellman; but many were used in their transliterated forms, such as Paraone (Brown), Onira (O'Neil) and Kipi (Gibb). European men who married into the community prior to 1890 integrated into a Ngāi Tahu world; but that world was becoming fragmented, and would physically disintegrate as the population dispersed into urban areas over the next half century.

Moving away

A generation of mixed-descent children from large families reached adulthood in the first decades of the twentieth century, and many left the Taieri community in search of new social and economic opportunities. Outward migration was rapid, often permanent, and largely complete by the mid 1930s. While Elizabeth Garth, William Brown, and Betsy and Doug Dawson stayed at the settlement, few of the others returned to Taieri to live. Jessie Hanna returned from Dunedin on the death of her mother in 1920, and shifted into the old homestead with her young family, but the Drummond

This photograph of the Martin family was taken at the opening of Te Waipounamu Hall in April 1901, and printed in the *Otago Witness*. The Martin (Matene) family had lived at Taieri since 1843. Korako Matene Wera had worked at several whaling stations in southern New Zealand, including Tautuku. He married Mere Hinehou of Moeraki, and they had four children together: two of them, Walter and Victoria, died young. Korako himself died in 1896. Here Hinehou is flanked by her surviving children, Henry and George. Henry married Ripeka Karetai in 1893, and their daughter Olive is standing next to Hinehou. George never married. By 1918 Hinehou, George, Henry, Ripeka and Olive were living at Tuahiwi. [E6875/14, Hocken Collections/Uare Taoka o Hākena]

and Martin homes were empty.[1] The Martin family were living at Maitapapa in February 1915, but by 1918 they were at Tuahiwi, near Kaiapoi, where Herries Beattie found them residing in a 'comfortable house'.[2] When their mother's estate was probated in 1918, the Wellman children were already dispersed: John was a fishmonger and poulterer in Dunedin, William was working as a rabbit agent at Balclutha, Charles was a sawmill hand at Paeroa, and George was employed as a fitter in Dunedin.[3] Only their sister Elizabeth and her labourer husband John Drummond were still at Maitapapa. When the interests in section A13 of the reserve were sold to Harriet Crossan for £90 in 1928, the former owners were living in Timaru, Invercargill, Pukekohe and Feilding.[4]

The settlement patterns of men were influenced by the availability of land and access to material resources. George Palmer worked as a labourer at Allanton in East Taieri, before farming a property at Edendale in Southland, one of the large estates broken up by the Liberal government between 1892 and 1912.[5] Thomas Crane was an engine driver at Waihola before moving around the turn of the century to Lochiel, where he farmed a property. William Bryant moved to Otokia, where he engaged in farming, was an elder in the Brethren church, and in 1902 was appointed secretary and treasurer of the Henley School Committee.[6] James Palmer married into a local farming family, the Reids, worked as a storekeeper in Outram, and then as a carpenter in Dannevirke, where he died in 1903.[7] This outward migration from Maitapapa in pursuit of economic opportunity reflects the reduced importance of farming in people's lives as urbanisation took hold in New Zealand.

Agricultural employment remained an important catalyst for migration, however. James Smith, who married Emma Robson at Taieri Ferry in 1891, farmed a property at Barnego, in south Otago, from 1905.[8] Previously he had worked as a labourer on local estates in the lower Taieri. Joseph and Jane Crane farmed a property at Otokia before settling at Waitahuna in 1915 and raising a family of eleven children.[9] John Wellman, who married Ann Campbell in 1898, worked as a shearer on back-country stations such as Mt Somers in mid Canterbury.[10] William Wellman worked on stations in Lumsden, where he was a blade shearer.

Women too moved away to find employment. Many went to Dunedin to work in factories or to train in traditional female occupations such as nursing. Eliza and Emma Brown both trained as nurses at Dunedin Hospital, and went on to become matrons of the Wellington and Auckland hospitals respectively.[11] Ngahui Brown moved to Dunedin 'to obtain employment as a member of the domestic staff in several of the homes of prominent citizens'.[12] After her marriage to David Connell in 1920, she moved to his family farm at Owaka, in south Otago, where she ran a confectionery and hairdressing business in the 1930s.[13] Martha Reid was raised in south Dunedin, and worked there initially as a bookkeeper before spending four and a half years at Sandringham's Cake Shop in Caversham.[14]

Table 3: Ngāi Tahu and Mixed-descent Women of Maitapapa, Marriages: 1901–1940

NAME OF BRIDE	NAME OF GROOM	OCCUPATION OF GROOM	BIRTHPLACE OF GROOM	YEAR OF MARRIAGE	PLACE
Ann Bishop	Percival Thomson	Compositor	Waipawa	1902	Wellington
Harriet Overton	Richard Crossan	Storeman	Milton	1903	Henley
Elizabeth Wellman	John Drummond	Labourer	Outram	1903	Henley
Jessie Tanner	Harold Hanna	Boilermaker	Invercargill	1907	Dunedin
Mary Brown	John Walker	Labourer	Dunedin	1907	Henley
Elizabeth Tanner	James Cushnie	Farmer	Wyndham	1907	Invercargill
Hannah Palmer	Fred Crane*	Farmer	Waihola	1908	Seaward Downs
Betsy Brown	Alex Smith	Engineer	Dunedin	1909	Henley
Alma Palmer	John Russell	Labourer	Taieri Mouth	1911	Taieri Mouth
Jessie Bishop	John Horn			1912	Hawera
Caroline Flutey	August Annis	Labourer	Waihola	1912	Milton
Ngahui Brown	David Connell	Labourer	Owaka	1920	Dunedin
Mary Smith	John Cunningham	Farmer	Hillend	1921	Barnego
Dorothy Wellman	David Wilson	Woolsorter	Wakanui	1921	Ashburton
Betsy Smith	Walter Dawson*	Labourer	Stewart Island	1922	Dunedin
Eliza Crane	James Smith	Labourer	Waihola	1923	Waihola
Dora Stevenson	Leonard Lopdell	Comm. Traveller	Invercargill	1923	Invercargill
Ani Sherburd	Thomas Garth	NZR Inspector	Dunedin	1925	Invercargill
Emma Brown	William Harte			1925	Christchurch
Mary Ann Bryant	Duncan MacKay	Radiographer	Moeraki	1928	Dunedin
Margaret Wellman	Sherwin Garner	Factory Hand	Ashburton	1928	Ashburton
Nancy Yorston	Sam Gutsell	Labourer	Chaslands	1930	Balclutha
Ida Milward	Richard Sparnon	Electrician	Tasmania	1933	Dunedin
Caroline Annis	Charles Archbold			1934	Christchurch
Ivy Robinson	John Campbell			1936	Henley
Eileen Milward	James Reid	Labourer	Scotland	1939	Dunedin

* Ngāi Tahu Descent
Source: Registered Marriage Certificates, Department of Internal Affairs.

Table 4: Ngāi Tahu and Mixed-descent Men of Maitapapa, Marriages: 1901–1940

NAME OF GROOM	NAME OF BRIDE	OCCUPATION OF BRIDE	BIRTHPLACE OF BRIDE	YEAR OF MARRIAGE	PLACE
Robert Bryant	Pani Potiki*		Balclutha	1902	Dunedin
William Wellman	Sarah McIntosh		Winton	1904	Henley
John Palmer	Minnie Carter			1904	Wellington
Charles Overton	Margaret Chalmers		Milton	1907	Milton
William Crane	Rawinia Ruben*			1908	Tuahiwi
John Palmer	Cora Flint			1912	Dunedin
George Overton	Lucy Eggers		Waituna	1913	Raurimu
James Liddell	Ellen Higgie			1914	Taieri Beach
Alfred Palmer	Kare Manihera†			1914	Featherston
Thomas Overton	Eva Carson		Auckland	1916	Dunedin
Ernest Sherburd	Isabella Mackie		Mosgiel	1916	Mosgiel
Joseph Campbell	Evelyn Corsan		Rimu	1919	Hokitika
George Wellman	Ethel Smith		Scotland	1919	Abbotsford
Thomas Bryant	Mary Ann Bates*		Waikouaiti	1920	Dunedin
Benjamin Palmer	Helen Wilson			1920	Seaward Downs
George Brown	Brenda Farmer		Sydney	1921	Sydney
William Wellman	Elsie Rendall		Lumsden	1921	Lumsden
Oliver Palmer	Mabel Sinclair	Wool Mill Hand	Waihola	1922	Waihola
Arthur Dickson	Margaret Shaw		Naseby	1923	Dunedin
William Crane	Ellen Ryan		Waitahuna	1923	Waitahuna
J. A. Crane	Mary Lenz		Waitahuna	1923	Waitahuna
John Sherburd	Madeline Adie			1925	Dunedin
George Bryant	Janet Meek			1926	Dunedin
James Dickson	Agnes Reid		Otokia	1927	Dunedin
James Brown	Dorothy Parker		Mangatainoka	1927	Napier
Robert Stevenson	Alice Moore		Geraldine	1928	Timaru
Donald Wellman	Doris Tait			1928	Ashburton
James Wellman	Janet Quartley		England	1928	Wellington
Ben Palmer	Helen Wilson			1930	Seaward Downs
James Crane	Margaret Chalmers			1933	Lochiel
Wm. Drummond	Agnes Collins			1933	Ashburton
John Sherburd	Barbara Adie		Nevis	1936	Dunedin
Travis Brown	Mary O'Reilly		Waikaia	1937	Gore
Alex Cushnie	Muriel Spittle			1937	Gore
Walter Brown	Isabella Williams		Dunedin	1938	Dunedin
Alex Bryant	Edna Livingstone	Nurse	Blenheim	1939	Balclutha
Ian Stevenson	Lillian Wood			1939	Dunedin
Herbert Crane	Olive Cook			1939	Dunedin
Charles Bryant	Thelma Pay			1940	Dunedin
John Sherburd	Joyce Campbell		Dunedin	1940	Dunedin
William Wellman	Louise Grimmett		Dunedin	1940	Dunedin

* Ngāi Tahu Descent
† Māori (iwi unknown)
Source: Registered Marriage Certificates, Department of Internal Affairs.

In the majority of cases, however, it was interracial marriage that drew women away from the community. Mary Brown left Maitapapa to follow John Walker's career with New Zealand Railways; the couple later settled on a property at Katea, in south Otago, where John was secretary of the Fairfield Dairy Company.[15] Sarah Sherburd married William Robertson in 1897; a few years later they moved from Momona to Fairlie, where William farmed a small property.[16] Marriage also drew sisters Elizabeth and Jessie Tanner from the community: Elizabeth followed her husband James Cushnie to Invercargill, and Jessie lived in Caversham with her husband Harold Hanna. Although the settlement broke up for economic reasons after World War I, outward interracial marriage contributed to the population decline. This process was assisted by a ready supply of educated mixed-descent women and men who were Pākehā in appearance.[17]

Those who stayed in the Taieri region tended to marry into local farming families. Such marriages, like that of James Stuart Dickson, grandson of Sarah Brown and Ned Palmer, to Agnes Reid in 1927, consolidated kinship ties between people of Ngāi Tahu descent and European settlers.[18] Through land ownership, the Dickson and Palmer families were able to maintain a presence in the lower Taieri, if not at Maitapapa. But their landholdings were small, requiring a mixed economy to ensure economic survival. James Dickson milked cows, and cleared manuka to sell as firewood, alongside rabbiting and whitebaiting.[19] Some families moved to where they had kin and land interests, especially Tuahiwi and Taumutu in Canterbury. William Crane spent his married life as a farmer at Tuahiwi, near his sister Amelia, who married Tare Paruti (Charles Flutey).[20] The strength of ties to Taumutu was demonstrated at the turn of the century by the permanent settlement there of John Brown and Mabel Smith.[21]

The migration away from Maitapapa that began during the 1890s became a rapid, wholesale desertion from the 1920s. According to the 1916 census, just three Māori people were living at Taieri, coinciding with the lowest Ngāi Tahu population recorded since the 1874 national census.[22] Local Māori sub-enumerators were replaced by Pākehā enumerators in 1916, which explains the low numbers recorded across all communities in that year's census.[23] In 1921 there were thirty Māori living at Taieri.[24]

This photograph was probably taken in 1907, when Mary Brown (seated) married John Walker; or in 1912, when Lena Koruarua (standing) married William Joss. The Koruaruas were one of the leading families of Taumutu, a Ngāi Tahu settlement at the southern tip of Lake Ellesmere (Waihora). The Koruarua and Brown families are connected through the marriage of Eliza Brown, Mary's aunt, to Teone Paka Koruarua. Teone and Eliza had no children, but raised Eliza's nephew Teone Wiwi Paraone. They also raised Eliza's grandchildren, Lena and Leah Koruarua and Moana Sermous. [Photograph courtesy of David Brown]

By 1926, only seven Māori resided at Maitapapa.[25] Thomas Brown, writing in the 1930s, described Maitapapa as 'deserted': 'The cottages are empty and nothing remains of those old days. The descendants are scattered afar and so few left.'[26] In 1942 Herries Beattie's cousin, William Adam, claimed that 'the Maori element was very scarce at the Kaik'.[27] By this time the permanent migration of families into new regions, towns and cities was complete. Only a handful of families remained at Maitapapa, farming the land and attempting to maintain customary fishing rights and practices.[28]

The loss was felt not only in population terms, but also culturally. Sarah Stevenson, writing to the registrar of the Native Land Court in 1919, requested that because 'I am unable to read Maori, would you please send an English copy [of the form]?'[29] Sarah Stevenson was the daughter of Sarah Palmer, described in 1897 as 'a Native or three-quarter Native [who] speaks English',[30] who had moved to Dunedin in 1910. The leader of the Taieri community, Tiaki Kona, was described in 1922 as speaking 'English better than Maori'.[31] By the 1920s, decades of education in the English language had contributed to the gradual loss of the Māori language among the mixed-descent families. Gaining social status completed and reinforced ethnic transformation. Encouraging children to succeed in the Pākehā world led to the erosion of culture and language. Parents refused to teach their children Māori, in order to help them 'fit in' to mainstream society; yet the loss of language positioned those of mixed descent, and by extension Ngāi Tahu, as 'plastic Maoris'.[32] Because they lacked the requisite language skills or cultural knowledge they were not considered authentically Māori, and because of their dual heritage they were not completely accepted as Pākehā.

Migration also had consequences for land ownership. Partition applications, 'an integral part of the alienation process', had already effectively divided the land in the 1870s,[33] while the succession practices of the Native Land Court had further eroded land interests. After the passage of the Native Land Act 1909, however, succession orders formed 'the overwhelming bulk' of the Native Land Court's work'.[34] Section 207 of the Act removed all existing restrictions on the alienation of Māori land, in order to facilitate its lease, mortgage or sale; this also made the retention of land more difficult, especially at a time when families were dispersed. Landowners

Lena Teihoka, Waitai Brown and Mere Teihoka at Taumutu in the early 1930s. A number of Maitapapa families migrated to Taumutu. Teone Wiwi Paraone (John Brown), born at Maitapapa but raised by his aunt Eliza Brown (Koruarua) at Taumutu, returned to Taieri to marry Mabel Smith in 1900. He and his new wife moved to Taumutu in 1902, and raised a large family. Waitai Brown (1920–86), the author's grandmother, was their last-born child. Beatrice Palmer, the daughter of William Palmer and Ann Holmes, married Cornelius Johnson, a fisherman, at Ellesmere in 1889. The Johnson and Teihoka families were connected by marriage, and the Browns and Teihokas by kinship. Eliza Brown's granddaughter, Moana Sermous, married Hohepa Teihoka of Tuahiwi, and Lena and Mere are their daughters. [Photograph courtesy of Maraea Johnson]

with an interest in the Taieri Native Reserve took the opportunity to alienate their shares, as provided for under the Act. In 1907, for example, Sarah Palmer mortgaged her interest in the 86-acre section C1a in the reserve to the Government Advances Corporation for £200.[35] It was explained that she and her husband Ned 'need the money it would fetch to live on … Their desire is to buy a small cottage near Dunedin where they would be near several of their children.'[36]

Growing migration thus coincided with increased land alienation, as native land legislation multiplied the ways in which land loss could be facilitated. In times of hardship, many absentee owners chose to sell their interests in the reserve to repay debts or buy necessities. In 1940, Hakita Hutika Huria of Tuahiwi sold her interest in section 8 of the Taieri Native Reserve because 'I am in urgent need of winter clothing'.[37] Alice Hariata Uru sold her interests to Walter and Bessie Dawson, in order to renovate and repair her home and make it 'clean and comfortable'.[38] In 1937 Teone Wiwi Paraone, now living at Taumutu, requested that his interests from the sale of reserve sections A7 and A11 be released to him, as he had 'been unable to work and has had to live on the charity of others and is urgently in need of some money to keep him going until he recovers his health again'.[39] By 1939 the remaining Wellman brothers, both domiciled in Ashburton, were seeking to dispose of their interests in the Waitutu Block because they were 'living in poverty'.[40]

As the migration of families to Tuahiwi and Taumutu demonstrates, connections to land elsewhere played a role in the exodus from Maitapapa. The Yorston and Gutsell families moved to the Balclutha region because land was available there. A further attraction was their traditional association with the site, where previous generations had been born, raised, and buried. The family chose to settle at Makati, near Chaslands, where Marna Dunn's mother and grandmother held interests in Māori land.[41] Their hut was superseded in the 1920s by a wooden house, symbolising the permanence of the migration from Maitapapa to Waihola, then to south Otago, and finally to Makati. But families who exchanged life at Maitapapa for settlement elsewhere did not outrun poverty. Like many other Ngāi Tahu, the Gutsell and Yorston families had to rely on seasonal work to survive. Marna recalls that the family turned to the bush and the sea for their food, including pigs, pigeons, mullet, flounder, trout, pipi, paua and cod.[42]

The outward migration that took place between 1890 and 1940 was the culmination of decades of interracial marriage in the lower Taieri region. Between 1850 and 1940, 116 residents and former residents of Maitapapa entered into formal marriages. All but one of them were of mixed descent, and ninety-nine of them married European partners. Interracial marriage shaped the demographic character of the community, and was generally followed by a pattern of migration; this had implications for identity, which

Muttonbirders in 1910. An important cultural tradition, the annual expedition to the Titi Islands in April and May also provided an essential source of sustenance as Ngāi Tahu became economically marginalised. [S07-053a, Hocken Collections/Te Uare o Hākena]

was much harder to sustain in the city. By the 1940s, Maitapapa was bereft of families. The only visible remnants of the once thriving Ngāi Tahu community were the burial ground and the empty houses.

Urban worlds

Māori migration to the cities began after World War II and reached its height in the 1960s.[43] In the post-war years, Māori were the most visible minority in New Zealand cities at a time of immense economic, social, and cultural shifts. Less well known in this story of urban migration are the people of mixed descent who had settled in the suburbs before World War II. By 1926, over one-third of New Zealand's non-Māori population were living in the four main cities of Auckland, Wellington, Christchurch and Dunedin, and nearly half of that population lived in towns.[44] Ngāi Tahu had lived in New Zealand cities from the turn of the century, but were 'hiding in plain view', to borrow the phrase of historian Susan Sleeper-Smith.[45] Many of these migrant families developed a range of strategies for city living, and supposedly 'disappeared' into the suburbs. Yet although they may have looked little different from their neighbours, mixed-descent families were rarely 'invisible' in the city.

The Taieri families migrated to the southern cities of Christchurch and Invercargill, as well as to towns such as Ashburton. Others moved to rural settlements like Waitahuna, while those employed by New Zealand Railways moved further afield, to Auckland and Hamilton. A large group of families went to Dunedin, where many of them clustered in the southern suburbs of Caversham and St Kilda. From 1919 George Christie Wellman and his Pākehā wife Barbara lived in Caversham, where he was employed as a cabinetmaker. William Sherburd, a railway guard, and his wife Sarah lived in Kensington from 1902. By the late 1930s, James Henry Crane was employed as a contractor in south Dunedin. Jane and Joseph Bryant, both of mixed descent, lived in Caversham from 1893; Joseph's brother Thomas, who resided with them, was a platelayer. In 1911 Herbert and Alice Bryant, and Herbert's cousin Robert Drummond, lived in Dunedin's southern suburbs, as did Joseph and Maretta Bryant. Members of the Bryant family were attracted to south Dunedin because that was 'where the industry was'.[46] South Dunedin drew a number of Taieri families to its job opportunities, particularly the Hillside railway workshops, where they were employed as boilermakers, japanners and iron-turners.

The integration of mixed-descent families into New Zealand cities was relatively successful in the period 1890 to 1940. Very few people in southern Dunedin, for example, identified themselves as Māori during this period, with only twenty-one doing so in the 1936 census.[47] Education, dress and physical appearance, together with the material trappings of financial success helped people of mixed descent to 'disappear' into mainstream society. The families who assimilated culturally into mainstream urban life are the group that are truly invisible in this migration history, and are difficult to trace through traditional historical sources. Others maintained a cultural presence in the city, even if they appeared little different from their neighbours. While on the surface these families 'disappeared', they in fact retained their identity in new places of settlement.

This migratory phase coincided with a great deal of official pressure for Māori to assimilate to British cultural values and institutions. In the first half of the twentieth century, the government measured the success of assimilation in a number of ways, the most important being education and the speaking of English. It was for their children's education that a number of Taieri families moved to Dunedin. Joseph and Jane Crane sent their daughters to Otago Girls' High School. Charles and Allen Bryant attended Otago Boys' High School and King Edward Technical College in Dunedin, Charles later becoming an engineer and Allen a doctor.[48] Other former residents of Maitapapa also achieved a measure of educational and professional success. Both Ian Stevenson and William Overton trained as solicitors; George Overton was Inspector of Schools in Dunedin and Nelson; and Eliza Brown was matron of Wellington Hospital and editor of the *New Zealand Nursing Journal*. People of mixed descent certainly wanted to 'get on' in life; but, as oral histories demonstrate, 'getting on' was dependent on 'fitting in'.

Invisibility was assisted by physical appearance and clothing. Looking European, and dressing to respectable standards, were key factors in being accepted into mainstream society. Many descendants of Taieri families remember respectability being of paramount importance to their parents or grandparents. William Wellman's daughter fondly remembers that he was always well dressed, never going out without a hat and waistcoat.[49] A person's clothing reflected their civilised status. For those of mixed descent, clothing also masked ethnic difference and facilitated assimilation.

Physical appearance was one of the standards used to monitor the process of assimilation. The state, in measuring physical and cultural changes through census reports, noted with favour the impact of interracial marriage in the South Island. Ngāi Tahu were regarded as the model of successful assimilation because 'only a very small percentage of half-castes in the South Island can be truly said to be living as members of Maori tribes'.[50] The colonial processes of erasure, at work in the national census, led to Ngāi Tahu being 'assimilated' into the general census on the basis of their similarity to their European counterparts. Yet this scenario is undermined by oral histories, which demonstrate that 'invisibility' was a strategy of survival, and that it was only ever partial.

Like many Maitapapa families, the Drummonds migrated in pursuit of economic opportunities in the 1930s, settling in Ashburton. John Drummond married Elizabeth Wellman, the daughter of Englishman John Wellman and Ani Williams, in 1903. Ani was the daughter of William Williams, who is believed to have been African-American, and his Ngāi Tahu partner, Auwahine. Several former Taieri families clustered in Ashburton, including branches of the Brown and Garth families. [Photograph courtesy of Shirley Tindall]

In the shift from native reserve to towns, suburbs and cities, families renegotiated their identities, maintaining some aspects of Ngāi Tahu culture, while others were eroded. An extensive kinship network was brought into the urban environment. This is particularly evident in Ashburton, where the Wellman and Drummond families worked in the Alford Forest Mill, and all lived on Alford Forest Road.[51] In the suburbs of Dunedin, the continuation of women's traditional hosting role played an important part in maintaining family connections. Caroline (formerly Bryant) and George Milward lived in south Dunedin for over fifty years; that is where their children, nieces and nephews were born, and where significant social events took place. Numerous members of the Bryant and Crane families, who were connected by kinship ties, also moved into southern Dunedin, often living in the same street and working alongside each other in the same occupations.

The maintenance of kin networks in urban spaces did serve to retain some traditional knowledge. Much of this knowledge – about resources, their importance and their correct use – was attached to the vast wetland and river system of the Taieri Plain. William Richard Wellman did not speak Māori, but 'he had a lot to do with Henley', often rowing his children down the river and showing them how to make whistles with flax to call birds.[52] Marna Dunn, who was raised by her grandmother in Balclutha, was taught the correct plants to use as remedies for minor ailments, while George Drummond passed on his knowledge of traditional fishing nets to his children.[53]

Despite their urbanisation, some families maintained their links to the Taieri. Descendants remember talk of 'going down to Henley'.[54] Allan was born and raised in Dunedin and went to Henley often as a child, 'but did not understand Mother wanting to go there all the time'.[55] Charles Drummond regularly visited Henley, where he maintained a small house beside the river.[56] Elizabeth also recalls regular visits to the settlement before her family moved to Nelson in 1941; after that, 'we never ever got back to Henley or the Taieri'.[57] For Hazel, the granddaughter of Joseph and Jane Bryant, Maitapapa was a place the family passed through on their way to Waitahuna, which was recognised as the 'family base'.[58] From its former status as a place of permanent occupation and cultural significance, Maitapapa was reduced, for many, to a holiday site and playground.

Not surprisingly, oral histories also point to the generational erasure of cultural links to Taieri. The lack of remembered conversations or personal memories of Taieri reflects the erosion not only of family connections but also of cultural ties to Ngāi Tahu. Many descendants of the generation who moved away from Maitapapa remember very little discussion about the settlement when they were children. Given that his father did not acknowledge his Ngāi Tahu links, Ian remembers there being little mention of Taieri in the household in which he was raised.[59] Taieri was a 'closed topic' when Elizabeth was young. She and her siblings knew only that their grandfather, William Wellman, 'came from the south'.[60] Hazel recalls that Taieri was mentioned in relation to the hardships created by flooding, rather than to her family's Ngāi Tahu connections to the area.[61] Hazel's parents 'shared

Waitahuna experiences and people rather than Henley [ones]', but when the aunts and uncles got together 'talk of Henley came up'.[62]

From the 1930s, there was a deliberate denial in many families of any Ngāi Tahu ancestry. Some descendants recall their relatives maintaining a silence when questions were asked about Taieri, Ngāi Tahu ancestry, and their land interests.[63] Allan's mother never spoke of the family's connections to Ngāi Tahu until much later in her life. Others grew up in households in which Taieri was never mentioned.[64] During the heyday of assimilation policy, a great deal of shame was attached to being of mixed descent. Urban migrants who retained cultural ties to the Taieri were careful to hide their connections. A number, for example, inherited important taonga (treasures) such as woven baskets and mats, and carved objects; but these were kept out of sight in the home, and rarely placed on display.

The visual record

Most traditional historical records portray mixed-descent families in the South Island as having been successfully assimilated, primarily because these people are difficult to trace in census material, electoral rolls, and birth, death and marriage certificates. The census in particular served to make people of mixed descent invisible through its role in reporting on the progress of assimilation. In the colonial era, art and photography were also implicated in the dual processes of in/visibility.

In the mid nineteenth century, people of mixed descent were highly visible in the colonial landscape and much discussed in intellectual and political circles. Missionaries and colonial officials commented on their bodies, noting the beauty of 'half-caste' women. In 1854 a Dr Menzies claimed that:

> ... half-castes are generally handsome and good looking, often having Italian features and complexion, and soft melodious voices. One family, the Browns, are strikingly handsome; Mrs Howell and Thomas are models ... the latter might sit for a figure of Apollo; both are fair enough to pass for Britons. Their other brother and sister are also good looking, but have the Maori complexion.[65]

A few years earlier, Johannes Wohlers had described mixed-descent children as 'all very pretty', and added:

> ... *it might well happen, that in ten years time Foveaux Strait will be famous because of its beautiful girls. The reason for the beauty of the children might be that the local Europeans have selected without exception very beautiful Maori girls as their wives. If these women were to be painted, their portraits could compete with the pictures of the beauties of Europe.*[66]

Mixed-descent people were almost a colonial obsession.[67] Officials took copious notes and wrote reports on the 'half-castes' and their particular implications for colonial policy. This keen interest was reflected in the sketches and paintings of notable colonial artists such as George Angas and Richard Oliver. Many of these images and descriptions appeared in colonial propaganda and travel publications. The fascination of artists and travellers attests to the fact that living as mixed descent was a highly visible experience in the nineteenth century. In the twentieth century, however, living as mixed descent entailed a process of becoming 'invisible', particularly for Ngāi Tahu. As sustained interracial marriage continued among the Taieri families, that process became easier as physical appearance was transformed.

By the 1890s, as the Taieri families were beginning to move into towns and cities, government officials no longer viewed the mixed-descent population in the South Island as problematic, as they had done earlier in the century. Instead, census enumerators and district native officers celebrated the ability of racially mixed people to embrace British culture and values. By the turn of the century, the 'whitening process' commented on in census reports was regarded as succeeding, and mixed-descent people were no longer as 'visible' as they were in the colonial period; indeed, many claimed they had assimilated both biologically and culturally. But the Taieri families who lived 'in-between', in urban spaces, demonstrate the tensions and contradictions in this view. These tensions are clearly reflected in the family photograph album, as we shall see.

As Edward Said has pointed out, colonialism and its interpretations involve 'images and imaginings'.[68] Leonard Bell describes the photograph, with its multiple meanings and representations, as a 'metaphor for dualities,

This photograph of former whaler William Palmer, published in the *Otago Witness* in 1902, has entered into family collections. In that shift, the way in which the image can be interpreted has also changed. As an archival item, it merely records Palmer's existence. Historians can use his clothing and other material objects to interpret his class status, and infer something about his background. As a family photograph, it is 'read' quite differently by Palmer's descendants, as they engage actively with the content, trace family resemblances, and construct a history for the subject which is linked to family memory. [F402/12, Hocken Collections/Uare Taoka o Hākena]

ambivalences and sheer oddities that could characterize [colonial] relations'.[69] It is commonly claimed that photography was employed by colonial
officials to document the success of assimilation.[70] Photography was crucial
to racial classification, and was an essential tool for investigating, measuring and, most importantly, representing 'race'. Ethnographic photographs
of 'racial types' were common in the late nineteenth century: the names of
the subjects did not matter, only the objectified image. Like cartography,
photography is implicated in colonial practices of erasure. Individuals were
reconstructed as racial types, to be consumed by the scientific community,
and displayed in a range of texts marketed to the public.[71] In the colonial
era, the commodification of indigenous peoples – in the form of postcards,
for example – made them a public text, which was 'used to tell or illustrate
any number of stories'.[72]

The responses of indigenous people to photography, and their engagement in the process, show that they were not always being objectified.
Nonetheless, the visibility and cultural 'otherness' of Māori made them a
popular subject of early photography, particularly for the postcard trade.[73]
As the new sciences of ethnography and anthropology bolstered the popular view of Māori as the 'dying race', photography was employed to document this demise and thus 'preserve' Māori culture for future generations.
The Burton brothers were notable photographers of Māori, both on their
travels around the country and in their Dunedin studio, from the 1860s.[74]
James McDonald was employed by the Dominion Museum in the early
1900s, and his photographs of Māori life were used by the state for propaganda purposes, often accompanying the annual report of the Education
Department to document the success of assimilation policy through the
native schools system.[75]

The family photograph is a very different entity from the ethnographic
representation of 'racial types' or the professional image used for commercial
or propaganda purposes. Family photographs provide an insight into the
tensions and contradictions of living as mixed descent, and the processes
of in/visibility that this entailed. At one level, such images show successful assimilation; but at another, they point to resistance, and the visibility
of difference. Indeed, photographs can be read in a variety of ways, and it

is this ambiguity that makes images, especially those that lack captions or stories, subject to a range of interpretations, and to potential manipulation. In this context, 'interpreting family pictures poses a series of challenges to different pasts, as memory interweaves with private fantasy and public history'.[76] The family album and the images it contains are full of ambiguities, complexities and contradictions. The images may be conventional in subject, but the format is intimately connected to the process of in/visibility. Albums, for example, can omit and disinherit people: absence is part of the format, and its meanings are varied. Thus 'family albums are about forgetting as well as remembering'.[77]

At the same time, family photographs can be a source of strength, a way to reclaim long-lost links and reassert identity.[78] Photographic archives form part of collective memory. This is certainly the case for descendants of the Maitapapa families, many of whose photographs record significant personal and social events, especially weddings. Many public photographs, particularly from newspapers and institutional archives, have been integrated into family albums, and become part of family stories and oral traditions. This transfer of images from public archive to private collection transforms their meaning. A photograph in the *Otago Witness* of William Palmer, a former Taieri whaler and patriarch of a large mixed-descent family who died in 1903, has become a prized item in the family photograph albums of multiple descendants.

Such photographs are a key resource through which descendants of the Taieri families have sought to establish kinship ties, and to overcome a history of dispersal and loss. For the current generation, the family photograph album has become a way to engage with and interpret family history, and to reassert their Ngāi Tahu identity. The photographs it contains provide a tangible link to a past from which many have long been disconnected.

Photographs thus live multiple lives, through a process of ongoing consumption within families, in official collections, and in museums and archives.[79] In each context, the meaning of a photograph changes. Through these ongoing interactions, photographs can lose their original purpose. Newspaper photographs designed for wide public consumption become private images, used by families to tell very different stories. In their new

This 1869 studio portrait of Tiori (seated), with William Adam, was taken at the Burton Brothers studio in Dunedin, and reproduced in Herries Beattie's 1954 book, *Our Southernmost Maoris*. [E4055/36, Hocken Collections/Uare Taoka o Hākena]

setting, the images 'whisper their secrets most loudly to those who already know what they are', acting as storytelling mechanisms that are 'very significant in filling the empty pages of [the] family album'.[80]

The oral context of photographs has been recognised in other colonial settings. In an attempt to capture aboriginal children's experience of residential schooling in Canada, Jim Miller turned to photography and oral history sources, regarding them as 'vital components in a multidisciplinary research strategy'.[81] Oral histories help to transform photographs of the 'nameless into ancestors', and provide a powerful way to interrogate the impact of colonialism. In combination, photography and oral histories reveal the presence of indigenous peoples in a variety of places and spaces. Moreover, when used by indigenous peoples, photographs can challenge scientific discourses about race and racial inferiority, and proclaim a 'presence in the face of spectacular erasures'. In this way, they constitute an important 'counter-archive'.[82]

Back in New Zealand, Tiori was the first person of Ngāi Tahu descent from Taieri to be photographed. In 1869 he accompanied William Adam, a Taieri farmer and uncle of ethnographer Herries Beattie, to the Burton Brothers studio. From the 1890s, many mixed-descent families at Taieri decided to have their photographs taken in studios. This interest in the formal portrait was not unusual. The records of studio photographers from the 1890s reveal that 'Maoris were actively commissioning pictures for their own, for family and for ceremonial use'.[83] The formal studio portrait stands as a record of how the subject wished to be perceived by outsiders, and was designed to be placed on display. Numerous photographs in the family albums of Taieri descendants are formal in nature, and represent the achievement of respectability. The studio portrait thus acts as another 'fitting in' strategy, alongside the speaking of English and the wearing of European dress. Their significance is reflected in the donation of some portraits, such as that of Mere Kui Tanner, to the Otago Settler Museum's Portrait Gallery, where images of the region's early British settlers are housed and displayed.

Family photographs conceal more than they reveal. Poverty and living conditions of families are invisible in studio portraits, where subjects are dressed in their best formal attire. Scholars of colonialism have used

Mary Tanner, also known as Mere Kui, was born in 1843 to Titi and William Palmer. She is the matriarch of the Smith, Bryant and Tanner families. With her first husband, James Smith, she had two children, Mary and James. Her second husband was William Bryant, an Englishman, with whom she had five children. Four of the Bryant children married into local settler families, with the sons achieving a measure of social standing in the district as farmers. Mere's last marriage was to Irishman James Cleland Tanner. She outlived him, dying in 1920 at Henley. [Otago Settlers Museum]

photography to examine the extent to which racial identity was masked by physical appearance and clothing, and the successful 'assimilation' of racially mixed people into mainstream society. In her investigation of five founding families of Victoria, British Columbia, Sylvia Van Kirk identified the family photograph or portrait as a central resource for illuminating the process of acculturation and examining social networks and family aspirations.[84] She found that a lack of portraits among some families indicated social failure or unsuccessful assimilation to 'British material culture'. Anne Maxwell argues that the formal studio portrait was adopted by indigenous peoples around the turn of the twentieth century to illustrate their 'ability to master the codes of social dress and behaviour that characterized civility'.[85] In taking up the studio portrait, the mixed-descent families of Taieri were recording their successful integration and, by extension, the 'transformations brought about by colonialism'.[86]

Robert Brown had this formal studio photograph taken as part of celebrations for the marriage of his son George to Helen McNaught in 1889. Such photographs often portray the person as they wished to be perceived. Certainly, this one gives little indication of the poverty in which the family lived in that period. The existence of such photographs signals the engagement of mixed-descent families in mainstream social conventions, in order to assert their similarity to their settler neighbours.
[Photograph courtesy of David Brown]

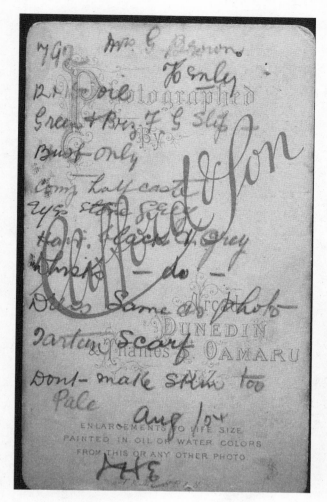

On the reverse of the photograph of Robert Brown are instructions to produce an enlarged colour portrait based on the image (see back cover). In the nineteenth and early twentieth centuries, photographers often employed a colourist for the purpose of tinting photographs or making enlargements. Mrs George Brown, Robert's daughter-in-law, ordered the portrait in August 1904, six years after his death. What is most interesting is the direction to give Robert a 'half-caste' complexion, and to avoid making the 'skin too pale'. [Photograph courtesy of David Brown]

Many studio photographs were later made into portraits for family use, and served to illustrate their similarity to local settlers. As such, they played a role in the representation and transformation of ethnic identity. The image of Robert Brown is one example of a studio photograph taken for the family album but subsequently transformed into a painted and framed portrait for the living-room wall. On the back of the original black-and-white photograph were directions for the painter, who was asked to give Robert a 'half-caste' complexion, but not 'too pale'; his hair and beard were to be a distinguished 'black and grey', and his eyes were to be 'stone grey' (their actual colour).

Formal photography was not the only medium that locates mixed-descent families within urban settings. The *Otago Witness*, which published

The Drummond family, at the homestead near Henley, after a good day's fishing (undated).
From left: Charlie (holding Rona), Nellie, Billie, Jean, Elizabeth and John Drummond.
[Photograph courtesy of Elizabeth Rangi]

One of several photographs of the Bellett-Printz wedding, published in the April 1902 edition of the *Otago Witness*. [S08-256a, Hocken Collections/Uare Taoka o Hākena]

weekly pictorial supplements, made Māori and mixed-descent families visible not only as city dwellers but also to a wider public. While some of these images took stereotypical forms, others served to challenge those stereotypes. As the white wedding evolved into a significant social institution and a marker of class, status and respectability, wedding photos became a visual feature of the *Otago Witness*. Interracial marriages, once private affairs, were now displayed for public consumption in pictorial supplements. In April 1902, for example, when Miss Bellett and William Printz were married at South Dunedin, the celebration was recorded in the pages of the *Otago Witness*.[87]

As photographic technology improved, the nature of images in the family album changed, along with their content. Photographs recording customary practices emerge from the 1930s, along with increasingly informal snapshots. The Drummond family were now living in Ashburton, but made regular fishing trips to the Taieri in order to maintain their resource rights, and to enable the younger generation to forge links with Ngāi Tahu culture. Photographs also provide an insight into family formation, but without oral histories the complex family structures behind images are often unknown. The formal photograph of Elizabeth Garth and her two sons, for example, reveals an unconventional family. Elizabeth was 'half-caste', her son Teone was illegitimate, and her youngest son Thomas was European and adopted. The absence of a patriarch is notable, but unsurprising. The gap in the photograph underscores the fact that these children were without such an important figure in their lives. The answer to this absence is located in family stories and memory.

. . .

Assimilation is only one possible reading of the family photograph. Other less formal images point to a different history. When used alongside oral history, these images provide a counter-agent to the colonial process of erasure. While the memories of descendants dwell on loss, the very act of remembering challenges a past that is entwined with state assimilation policy and community disintegration. The very process of descendants collecting images to put into the family album points to the resonance of community history, and represents an attempt to overcome a loss that was enacted through dispersal and invisibility. Images of people at home, in photographer's studios, at weddings, and at work illustrate untold stories. Photographs are an important text, because they are about visibility: they are the key to reclaiming community history and family stories.

The cultural identity of the Maitapapa community has survived: it still exists today in images, in memory, and in family narratives. In this respect, community can exist beyond a spatial boundary, and well beyond its physical loss. As Anne Else has noted, photography has the 'power to make available to ordinary people long-lasting, portable depictions of absent people and places closely connected to them'.[88] Today, descendants of the Taieri families use photographs to tell stories, and to make visible those who supposedly 'disappeared' into the towns and cities of New Zealand during the first half of the twentieth century.

Chapter 8. In/visible Sight

The Maitapapa families' experience of colonialism and colonisation was, in many respects, very similar to the pathways of numerous Ngāi Tahu families over the nineteenth and early twentieth centuries. These similarities centre on land alienation, the erosion of mahinga kai, poor quality reserve land, poverty, mobility and cultural loss. However, their experience is also characterised by a sustained pattern of interracial marriage which may have contributed to the 'disappearance' of the community, thus distinguishing the history of Maitapapa and its mixed-descent families from the general trajectory of Ngāi Tahu histories. Interracial marriage not only shaped culture contact at Maitapapa, and in southern New Zealand more broadly, it was also an essential part of the lived experience of families and individuals.

As a result of interracial marriage, Ngāi Tahu experienced transformations of various kinds over the nineteenth and early twentieth centuries. Physical transformation took place as interracial families emerged out of the contact era; new identities and cultural affiliations followed, as communities, alliances and kinship networks were forged out of intimate encounters. Physical 'disappearance', an outcome strongly associated with interracial marriage, was traced by state mechanisms such as the national census. From 1874, the census was informed by racial beliefs, which defined racial categories and boundaries. Interracial marriage was regarded as a tool of assimilation, and officials used the census to monitor and comment on its success. That 'success' was dependent on racial categorisation, but in many cases the census categories were arbitrary and imprecise.

Quite often, census-takers relied on physical features, style of dress, and living conditions, rather than 'blood quantum', in deciding whether to categorise people of mixed descent as Māori or 'European'.

Despite official claims of successful assimilation, the reality experienced by interracial families was very different. In the latter half of the late nineteenth century, the growing mixed-descent population in southern New Zealand was accommodated within Ngāi Tahu tribal identity. Participation at hui and Native Land Court hearings, and the maintenance of important customary activities such as muttonbirding, are evidence of this identity, alongside the contribution of money to the Ngāi Tahu Claim/Te Kereme from the 1890s. Paradoxically, while interracial marriage contributed to the development at Taieri of a mixed-descent population that identified as Ngāi Tahu, it also contributed to the eventual loss of community and an erosion of cultural ties to Maitapapa and to Ngāi Tahu. The result was the dispersal of families in search of better economic opportunities, and their assimilation into mainstream New Zealand society.

By the first decade of the twentieth century, the Maitapapa families were overwhelmingly 'quarter-caste' or less. As the photographs in this book illustrate, physical appearance was important to those living as mixed descent. As 'quarter-castes', many of those who left the village were able to pass as 'white'. While there was little mention of 'passing' in the oral histories used in this book, informants did indicate that dress and respectability were important to their grandparents. Successful assimilation into local communities is evident in the deliberate attempts by some to deny their Ngāi Tahu ancestry. By 1940, members of the former Taieri families appeared 'European' and had integrated into towns, suburbs and cities.

A history of interracial marriage has given rise to generations for whom mixed-ancestry was a source of shame. This has certainly been the case for the Maitapapa families. For most of the families, assimilation meant the loss of cultural knowledge in the form of language and cultural traditions, the inability to identify with Maitapapa as a site of cultural significance, and the erosion of ties to a Ngāi Tahu identity, at both whānau and tribal level. Cultural poverty did emerge in the oral histories as a strong narrative; it was indeed a function of interracial marriage and migration; and it did contribute to a kind of 'disappearance'. But the evidence shows that the mixed-descent families of Maitapapa never became truly invisible.

In/visible Sight is not really about loss; it is a story of survival. Today, the generation who were born in urban spaces, and often with few physical ties to Maitapapa, are determined to reforge cultural links with Ngāi Tahu. With the hearings of the Ngāi Tahu Claim before the Waitangi Tribunal and its successful settlement in 1998, many people of Ngāi Tahu descent have discarded the shame and even anger associated with their mixed ancestry and have chosen to reclaim their whakapapa. My experience of readily finding these families, and their willingness to tell their stories, demonstrate quite clearly that, despite a history of overwhelming loss and dispersal, the spirit of the community has survived. The informants who contributed to this book shared their personal experience of shame and anger, the culmination of decades of dislocation from Maitapapa and the deliberate denial of Ngāi Tahu ancestry by earlier generations. Significantly, their accounts also demonstrate that cultural identity has survived, and that the Maitapapa community, while no longer bound geographically to the reserve, still exists today.

Endnotes

Abbreviations
AJHR, Appendices to the Journals of the House of Representatives
NZPD, New Zealand Parliamentary Debates

Chapter 1. Intimate Histories

1   Bruce Biggs, *Maori Marriage: An Essay in Reconstruction*, Polynesian Society, Wellington, 1960, p.27.

2   Biggs, *Maori Marriage*, p.27.

3   Biggs, *Maori Marriage*, pp.40–2, 45.

4   Herries Beattie, *Traditional Lifeways of the Southern Maori: The Otago University Museum Ethnological Project*, Atholl Anderson (ed.), Otago University Press, Dunedin, 1994, p.95.

5   Biggs, *Maori Marriage*, p.33.

6   Biggs, *Maori Marriage*, p.83.

7   Biggs, *Maori Marriage*, p.47.

8   Hazel Petrie, *Chiefs of Industry: Māori Tribal Enterprise in Early Colonial New Zealand*, Auckland University Press, Auckland, 2006, p.12.

9   Atholl Anderson was the first scholar to examine the history of interracial marriage and mixed-descent people in southern New Zealand, in *Race Against Time: The Early Maori-Pakeha Families and the Development of the Mixed-race Population in Southern New Zealand*, Hocken Library, Dunedin, 1991.

10 See Atholl Anderson and Te Maire Tau (eds), *Ngāi Tahu: A Migration History. The Carrington Text*, Bridget Williams Books, Wellington, 2008.

11 Paul Monin, *This Is My Place: Hauraki Contested, 1769–1875*, Bridget Williams Books, Wellington, 2001, p.92.

12 Edward Jerningham Wakefield, *Adventure in New Zealand from 1839 to 1844*, Whitcombe & Tombs, Christchurch, 1908, p.27.

13 Anderson, *Race Against Time*, p.4; Trevor Bentley, *Pakeha Maori: The Extraordinary Story of the Europeans who Lived as Maori in Early New Zealand*, Penguin, Auckland, 1999, p.62.

14 Bentley, *Pakeha Maori*, p.197.

15 Petrie, *Chiefs of Industry*, p.48.

16 Michael King, *The Penguin History of New Zealand*, Penguin, Auckland, 2003, pp.122–3.

17 James Belich, *Making Peoples: A History of the New Zealanders from Polynesian Settlement to the End of the Nineteenth Century*, Penguin, Auckland, 1996, pp.152–3.

18 Sylvia Van Kirk, *Many Tender Ties: Women in Fur-trade Society, 1670–1870*, University of Oklahoma Press, Norman, 1980; Jennifer S. H. Brown, *Strangers in Blood: Fur Trade Company Families in Indian Country*, University of British Columbia Press, Vancouver, 1980; Adele Perry, *On the Edge of Empire: Gender, Race and the Making of British Columbia, 1849–1871*, University of Toronto Press, Toronto, 2001.

19 Van Kirk, *Many Tender Ties*, p.4.

20 Van Kirk, *Many Tender Ties*; Susan Sleeper-Smith, *Indian Women and French Men: Rethinking Cultural Encounter in the Western Great Lakes*, University of Massachusetts Press, Amherst, 2001.

21 David Haines, 'In Search of the "Whaheen": Ngai Tahu Women, Shore Whalers, and the Meaning of Sex in Early New Zealand', in Tony Ballantyne and Antoinette Burton (eds), *Moving Subjects: Gender, Mobility, and Intimacy in an Age of Global Empire*, University of Illinois Press, Urbana, 2009, p.50.

22 Haines, 'In Search of the "Whaheen", p.50.

23 Atholl Anderson, *When All the Moa Ovens Grew Cold: Nine Centuries of Changing Fortune for the Southern Maori*, Otago Heritage Books, Dunedin, 1983; Atholl Anderson, *The Welcome of Strangers: An Ethnohistory of Southern Maori, AD 1650–1850*, Otago University Press, Dunedin, 1998; Bill Dacker, *The Pain and the Love – Te Mamae me te Aroha: A History of Kai Tahu Whanui in Otago, 1844–1994*, Otago University Press, Dunedin, 1994; Harry Evison, *Te Wai Pounamu: The Greenstone Island: A History of the Southern Maori during the European Colonization of New Zealand*, Aoraki Press/Ngai Tahu Maori Trust Board, Wellington, 1993; Harry Evison, *The Long Dispute: Maori Land Rights and European Colonisation in Southern New Zealand*, Canterbury University Press, Christchurch, 1997.

24 Dr. Munro, 'Notes of a Journey through a part of the Middle Island of New Zealand', reproduced in Thomas M. Hocken, *Contributions to the Early History of New Zealand (Settlement of Otago)*, Sampson Low, Marston & Company, London, 1898, p.246.

25 Munro, 'Notes of a Journey', p.246.

26 Munro, 'Notes of a Journey', p.245.

27 Jill Hamel, *The Archaeology of Otago*, Department of Conservation, Wellington, 2001, pp.80–81.

28 Thelma Smith, *Tai-ari Ferry and Henley 'Our Native Place'*, Otago Daily Times & Witness Newspapers, Dunedin, 1941; Margaret S. Shaw, *The Taieri Plain: Tales of the Years that are Gone*, Otago Centennial Historical Publications, Dunedin, 1949; Gwen Sutherland, *Coast, Road and River: The Story of Taieri Mouth, Taieri Beach, Glenledi and Akatore*, Clutha Leader Print, Invercargill, 1962; Win Parkes and Kath Hislop, *Taieri Mouth and its Surrounding Districts*, Otago Heritage Books, Dunedin, 1980; Ronald J. Stuart, Henley, *Taieri Ferry and Otokia: A Schools and District History*, Reunion Committee, Outram, 1981.

29 Ann Laura Stoler, *Carnal Knowledge and Imperial Power: Race and the Intimate in Colonial Rule*, University of California Press, Berkeley, 2002; Antoinette Burton, 'Rules of Thumb: British History and "Imperial Culture" in Nineteenth- and Twentieth-century Britain', *Women's History Review*, Vol.3, No.4, 1994, pp.483–501; Antoinette Burton, 'Some Trajectories of "Feminism" and "Imperialism"', *Gender and History*, Vol.10, No.3, 1998, pp.558–68; Antoinette Burton, 'Thinking Beyond the Boundaries: Empire, Feminism and the Domains of History', *Social History*, Vol.26, No.1, 2001, pp.60–71; Robert J. C. Young, *Colonial Desire: Hybridity in Theory, Culture and Race*, Routledge, London, 1995; Claire Midgley (ed.), *Gender and Imperialism*, Manchester University Press, Manchester, 1998; Angela Wollacott, *Gender and Empire*, Palgrave Macmillan, Basingstoke, 2006; Anne McClintock, *Imperial Leather: Race, Gender and Sexuality in the Colonial Conquest*, Routledge, London, 1995; Tony Ballantyne and Antoinette Burton (eds), *Bodies in Contact: Rethinking Colonial Encounters in World History*, Duke University Press, Durham, 2005; Tony Ballantyne and Antoinette Burton (eds), *Moving Subjects: Gender, Mobility and Intimacy in an Age of Empire*, University of Illinois Press, Urbana, 2009.

30 Monin, *This Is My Place*, p.1.

31 Bentley, *Pakeha Maori*, p.207.

32 Barbara Brookes and Margaret Tennant, 'Maori and Pakeha Women: Many Histories, Divergent Pasts', in Barbara Brookes, Charlotte Macdonald, and Margaret Tennant (eds), *Women in History 2*, Bridget Williams Books, Wellington, 1992, p.39.

33 Anderson, *Race against Time*.

34 Anderson, *The Welcome of Strangers*, p.195.

35 Erik Olssen, '"Where to From Here?": Reflections on the Twentieth-century Historiography of Nineteenth-century New Zealand', *New Zealand Journal of History*, Vol.26, No.1, 1992, p.66; Erik Olssen, 'Families and the Gendering of European New Zealand in the Colonial Period, 1840–80', in Caroline Daley and Deborah Montgomerie (eds), *The Gendered Kiwi*, Auckland University Press, Auckland, 1999, p.40. Ann Laura Stoler called for a transnational approach to interrogating the intimacies of empire and colonialism, in Stoler, 'Tense and Tender Ties'. See also Stoler (ed.), *Haunted By Empire*, and Ballantyne and Burton (eds), *Bodies in Contact*.

36 Kate Riddell, 'A "Marriage of the Races"? Aspects of Intermarriage, Ideology and Reproduction on the New Zealand Frontier', MA thesis, Victoria University of Wellington, 1996, p.33. See also Kate Riddell, '"Improving" the Maori: Counting the Ideology of Intermarriage', *New Zealand Journal of History*, Vol.34, No.1, 2000, pp.80–97.

37 See Sleeper-Smith, *Indian Women and French Men: Rethinking Cultural Encounter in the Western Great Lakes*, University of Massachusetts Press, Amherst, 2001, and Jean Barman, *Stanley Park's Secret: The Forgotten Families of Whoi Whoi, Kanaka Ranch and Brockton Point*, Harbour Publishing, Vancouver, 2005.

38 Nancy Cott, *Public Vows: A History of Marriage and the Nation*, Harvard University Press, Cambridge, MA, 2000.

39 Barbara Brookes, 'Taking Private Life Seriously: Marriage and Nationhood', *History Compass*, Vol.1, No.1, November 2003, pp.1–4.

40 See Hana O'Regan, *Ko Tahu, Ko Au*, Horomaka Press, Christchurch, 2001.

41 The phrase 'hiding in plain view' is borrowed from Sleeper Smith, *Indian women and French men*.

42 J.R. Miller, 'Reading Photographs, Reading Voices: Documenting the History of Native Residential Schools', in Jennifer S.H. Brown and Elizabeth Vibert (eds), *Reading Beyond Words: Contexts for Native History*, Broadview Press, Peterborough, 2001, p.466.

Chapter 2. Pātahi's Story

1   William Martin, 'A Pioneer's Reminiscences', p.38, MS-0206, Hocken Library, Dunedin. Martin's memoirs are based on his diary entries (23 April–15 October 1863), MS-0204, Hocken Library, Dunedin.

2   For a discussion of whaling in the New Zealand economy of the late eighteenth and early nineteenth centuries, see Jim McAloon, 'Resource Frontiers, Environment and Settler Capitalism: 1769–1860', in Eric Pawson and Tom Brooking (eds), *Environmental Histories of New Zealand*, Oxford University Press, Oxford, 2002, pp.52–68.

3   Matthew L. Campbell, 'A Preliminary Investigation of the Archaeology of Whaling Stations on the Southern Coast', MA thesis, University of Otago, 1992, pp.203–4.

4   See Peter Coutts, 'Merger or Takeover: A Survey of the Effects of Contact Between European and Maori in the Foveaux Strait Region', *Journal of the Polynesian Society*, Vol.78, No.4, 1969, pp.495–516.

5   Dorothy Harley Eber, *When the Whales Were Up North: Inuit Memories from the Eastern Arctic*, McGill-Queen's University Press, Montreal and Kingston, 1989, p.xii.

6   Edward Shortland, *The Southern Districts of New Zealand: A Journal with Passing Notices of the Customs of the Aborigines*, Longman, Brown, Green and Longmans, London, 1851, p.115.

7   Harwood Journal, 4 December 1838 and 8 January 1839, G. C. Thomson Papers, MS-0438/59, Hocken Library, Dunedin.

8   *Otago Witness*, 26 April 1927, p.76

9   Edward Weller to George Weller, 14 February 1839, G. C. Thomson Papers, MS-0440/05, Hocken Library, Dunedin.

10   Harwood Journal, 8 December 1840 and 9 December 1840, G. C. Thomson Collection Papers, MS-0438/002, Hocken Library, Dunedin.

11   Frederick Tuckett, cited in Atholl Anderson, *The Welcome of Strangers: An Ethnohistory of Southern Māori A.D. 1650–1850*, University of Otago Press, Dunedin, 1998, p.194.

12   Frederick Tuckett, cited in Campbell, 'A Preliminary Investigation', p.48.

13   See T. A. Pybus, *The Maoris of the South Island*, Reed, Wellington, 1954.

14   Gavin McLean, *Moeraki: 150 Years of Net and Plough Share*, Otago Heritage Books, Dunedin, 1986, p.14.

15   David Haines, 'In Search of the "Whaheen": Ngai Tahu Women, Shore Whalers, and the Meaning of Sex in Early New Zealand', in Tony Ballantyne and Antoinette Burton (eds), *Moving Subjects: Gender, Mobility, and Intimacy in an Age of Global Empire*, University of Illinois Press, Urbana, 2009, p.50.

16   Martin, 'A Pioneer's Reminiscences', pp.17–18.

17   Lachy Paterson, *Colonial Discourses: Niupepa Māori, 1855–1863*, Otago University Press, Dunedin, 2006, p.37.

18   Martin, 'A Pioneer's Reminiscences', p.38.

19   Martin, 'A Pioneer's Reminiscences', p.38.

20   Paterson, *Colonial Discourses*, p.30.

21   Paterson, *Colonial Discourses*, pp.31–2.

22   Paterson, *Colonial Discourses*, p.44. See also Jane McRae, '"E Manu, Tena Koe!" "O Bird, Greetings to You": The Oral Tradition in Newspaper Writing', in Jenifer Curnow, Ngapare Hopa and Jane McRae (eds), *Rere Atu, Taku Manu! Discovering History, Language and Politics in the Māori-language Newspapers*, Auckland University Press, Auckland, 2002, pp.42–59.

23   Penny van Toorn suggests that, in texts produced from interracial encounter and cross-cultural exchange, the writing 'cross-dresses', becoming clothed in the ideology, institutions and practices of another culture; it also 'crosses the borders between categories of writing', and sometimes, I would argue, the borders between oral and written language. See Penny Van Toorn, *Writing Never Arrives Naked: Early Aboriginal Cultures of Writing in Australia*, Aboriginal Studies Press, Canberra, 2006.

24   Martin, 'A Pioneer's Reminiscences', p.41.

25   See Coral Beattie Papers, Ms-Papers-4280-008, Alexander Turnbull Library, Wellington.

26   Tony Hanning, 'The Whaler and the Princess': *Irihapeti Patahi and Edwin Palmer*, Tony Hanning, Dunedin, 2000; Alfred Eccles and A. H. Reed, *John Jones of Otago: Whaler, Coloniser, Shipowner and Merchant*, Reed, Wellington, 1949, p.20.

27   Martin, 'A Pioneer's Reminiscences', p.40.

28   The Visitation Book of Reverend Thomas Burns [1848–1858], p.66, Otago Settlers Museum, Dunedin.

29   Edward Shortland, 'Journal Notes Kept While in the Middle Island November 1843 to 21 January 1844. Lists of Various Inhabitants at Various Places', G. C. Thomson Papers, PC-025, Hocken Library, Dunedin.

30 Holy Trinity Anglican Church, Lyttelton, Transcript of Marriage Register, 1851–1861; Transcript of Baptismal Register, 1851–1858, Christchurch City Libraries.

31 Barbara Palmer to Cath Brown, 28 October 2001, Barbara Palmer, Private Collection.

32 Reverend Thomas Burns, Visitation Book, p.103.

33 Barbara Palmer to Cath Brown, 28 October 2001, Barbara Palmer, Private Collection.

34 Trevor Bentley, *Pakeha Maori: The Extraordinary Story of the Europeans who Lived as Maori in Early New Zealand*, Penguin, Auckland, 1999, p.204.

35 Sylvia Van Kirk, *Many Tender Ties: Women in Fur-Trade Society, 1670–1870*, University of Oklahoma Press, Norman, 1980, p.50.

36 Coral Beattie, 'Palmer, William McLeur (1815–1903)', in Jane Thomson (ed.), *Southern People: A Dictionary of Otago Southland Biography*, Dunedin City Council/Longacre Press, Dunedin, 1998, pp.375–6.

37 Martin, 'A Pioneer's Reminiscences', p.41.

38 Pat White, 'Sizemore, Richard (c.1800–1861)', in Thomson (ed.), *Southern People*, p.458.

39 Raewyn Dalziel, 'Men, Women and Wakefield', in Friends of the Turnbull Library, *Edward Gibbon Wakefield and the Colonial Dream: A Reconsideration*, GP Books, Wellington, 1997, pp.77–86.

40 Bruce Biggs, *Maori Marriage: An Essay in Reconstruction*, Polynesian Society, Wellington, 1960, p.25.

41 General Maori Information (Book 3), Herries Beattie Papers, PC-174, Hocken Library, Dunedin.

42 Margaret S. Shaw, *The Taieri Plain: Tales of the Years that are Gone*, Otago Centennial Publications, Dunedin, 1949.

43 William Adam to Margaret Shaw, 13 September 1948, Box 2, Shaw Papers, AG71, Otago Settlers Museum, Dunedin.

44 Thelma Smith to Margaret Shaw, undated, Box 2, Shaw Papers.

45 *Otago Witness*, 3 April 1886, p.17; Will of Edwin Palmer, DAAC/D239/26/1368, Archives New Zealand, Dunedin.

46 Smith to Shaw, undated, Box 2, Shaw Papers.

Chapter 3. Interracial Families and Communities

1 See Atholl Anderson, *Race Against Time: The Early Maori-Pakeha Families and the Development of a Mixed Race Population in Southern New Zealand*, Hocken Library, Dunedin, 1991.

2 Sylvia Van Kirk, *Many Tender Ties: Women in Fur Trade Society, 1670–1870*, University of Oklahoma Press, Norman, 1980, p.2.

3 Van Kirk, *Many Tender Ties*, p.4.

4 Anderson, *Race Against Time*, p.40.

5 Judith Binney, '"In-Between" Lives: Studies from Within a Colonial Society', in Tony Ballantyne and Brian Moloughney (eds), *Disputed Histories: Imagining New Zealand's Pasts*, Otago University Press, Dunedin, 2006, pp.93–118; Kate Stevens, '"Gathering Places": The Mixed Descent Families of Foveaux Strait and Rakiura/Stewart Island, 1824–1864', BA (Hons) research essay, University of Otago, 2008.

6 Work has begun in this direction. On mixed-descent families, see Angela Wanhalla, 'Marrying "In": The Geography of Intermarriage at Taieri, 1830s–1920s', in Tony Ballantyne and Judith A. Bennett (eds), *Landscape/Community: Perspectives from New Zealand History*, Otago University Press, Dunedin, 2005, pp.73–94. On racial categories, see Kate Riddell, '"Improving" the Maori: Counting the Ideology of Intermarriage', *New Zealand Journal of History*, Vol.34, No.1, 2000, pp.80–97. On the relationship between colonial and imperial policies, see Damon Salesa, 'Race Mixing: A Victorian Problem in Britain and New Zealand, 1830s–1870s', DPhil thesis, University of Oxford, 2000. For the most recent research on the relationship between shore whaling and interracial marriage, see Emily V. Owen, 'Intermarriage: Its Role and Importance within Early New Zealand Shore Whaling Stations', MA thesis, Massey University, 2007; and David Haines, 'In Search of the "Whaheen": Ngai Tahu Women, Shore Whalers, and the Meaning of Sex in Early New Zealand', in Tony Ballantyne and Antoinette Burton (eds), *Moving Subjects: Gender, Mobility, and Intimacy in an Age of Global Empire*, University of Illinois Press, Urbana, 2009.

7 Elizabeth W. Durwood, 'The Maori Population of Otago', *Journal of the Polynesian Society*, Vol.42, 1933, pp.49–82.

8   Edward Shortland, *The Southern Districts of New Zealand: A Journal with Passing Notices of the Customs of the Aborigines*, Longman, Brown, Green and Longmans, London, 1851, pp.77–8.

9   Evidence of Joel Samuel Polack, 6 April 1838, Report from the Select Committee of the House of Lords, appointed to Inquire into the Present State of the Islands of New Zealand, *British Parliamentary Papers. Colonies: New Zealand, 1837–40*, Irish University Press, Shannon, 1968, p.81.

10 John Hall-Jones, *The South Explored*, Craig Printing, Invercargill, 1998, p.73.

11 Edward Shortland to Robert FitzRoy, 18 March 1844, in *British Parliamentary Papers. Colonies: New Zealand, 1846–47*, Irish University Press, Shannon, 1968, p.317.

12 Shortland to FitzRoy, 18 March 1844, p.317.

13 Johannes Wohlers, Travel Report, 1 May 1845, Wohlers Papers, 0428-04A, Alexander Turnbull Library, Wellington.

14 Wohlers, Travel Report, 31 December 1845.

15 Wohlers, Travel Report, 31 December 1845.

16 Wohlers, Travel Report, 19 February 1846.

17 Anderson, *Race Against Time*, p.29.

18 Theophilius Heale to Superintendent of Southland, 15 February 1864, in Alexander Mackay, *A Compendium of Official Documents Relative to Native Affairs in the South Island: Volume II*, Government Printer, Wellington, 1872, p.56.

19 Alexander Mackay to Under-Secretary, Native Department, 3 June 1868, in Mackay, *Compendium: Volume II*, p.64.

20 *Results of a Census of the Colony of New Zealand, taken for the Night of the 3rd of April 1881*, Government Printer, Wellington, 1882, p.12; see also John Hall-Jones, *Stewart Island Explored*, Craig Printing, Invercargill, 1994, and Basil Howard, *Rakiura: A History of Stewart Island, New Zealand*, Reed, Dunedin, 1940.

21 Riddell, '"Improving" the Maori', p.88.

22 William Swainson, *New Zealand and its Colonization*, Smith, Elder and Co., London, 1859, p.28.

23 Swainson, *New Zealand and its Colonization*, p.28.

24 *Results of a Census of the Colony of New Zealand, taken for the Night of the 1st of March, 1874*, Government Printer, Wellington, 1875, p.11; *Results of a Census of the Colony of New Zealand, 3rd of April 1881*, p.11.

25 *Results of a Census of the Colony of New Zealand, taken for the Night of the 28th of March, 1886*, Government Printer, Wellington, 1887, pp.8, 359; *Results of a Census for the Colony of New Zealand, taken for the Night of the 5th of April 1891*, Government Printer, Wellington, 1892, pp.8, xlv; *Results of a Census of the Colony of New Zealand, taken for the Night of the 12th of April 1896*, Government Printer, Wellington, 1897, p.7, and Appendix B – Māori Population.

26 This statistic is based on the census figure for the total Māori population of 41,969, and 2,254 'half-castes living as Maori'. In total, the mixed-descent population was 4,212, which equates to 10% of the total Māori population in 1886.

27 See Bill Dacker, *The Pain and the Love – Te Mamae me te Aroha: A History of Kai Tahu Whanui in Otago, 1844–1994*, Otago University Press, Dunedin, 1994; Hana O'Regan, *Ko Tahu, Ko Au*, Horomaka Press, Christchurch, 2001; M. Jocelyn Armstrong, 'Maori Identity in the South Island of New Zealand: Ethnic Identity Development in a Migration Context', *Oceania*, Vol.57, No.3, 1987, pp.195–216; Te Maire Tau, 'Ngāi Tahu – From "Better to be Dead and Out of the Way" to "To be Seen to Belong"', in John Cookson and Graeme Dunstall (eds), *Southern Capital: Christchurch: Towards a City Biography, 1850–2000*, Canterbury University Press, Christchurch, 2000, pp.222–47; Stephanie Kelly, 'Weaving Whakapapa and Narrative in the Management of Contemporary Ngai Tahu Identities', PhD thesis, University of Canterbury, 2002.

28 For detailed information on the background of these men, and their marriage alliances, see Anderson, *Race Against Time*, and Angela Middleton, *Two Hundred Years on Codfish Island (Whenua Hou): From Cultural Encounter to Nature Conservation*, Department of Conservation, Wellington, 2007.

29 Hall-Jones, *Stewart Island Explored*, p.89.

30 *Results of a Census of the Colony of New Zealand, 12th April 1896*, p.137.

31 Wohlers, Travel Report, 1 May 1845.

32 Johannes Wohlers, Ruapuke Report, 2 February 1845, Wohlers Papers, 0428-04A, Alexander Turnbull Library, Wellington.

33 The famous cases in New Zealand involve Thomas Kendall, lay missionary with the Church Missionary Society (CMS); the CMS printer William Colenso, who fathered a son with his Māori servant; and claims of rape against the Wesleyan missionary William White. For a detailed discussion of missionary views of interracial marriage, see Angela Wanhalla, 'The "Natives Uncivilize Me": Missionaries and Interracial Intimacy in Early New Zealand', in Patricia Grimshaw and Andrew May (eds), *Missions, Indigenous Peoples and Cultural Exchange,* Sussex Academic Press, Eastbourne, 2010.

34 Wohlers, Travel Report, 1 May 1845.

35 Wohlers, Travel Report, 19 February 1846.

36 Journal of James Watkin, 8 March 1841, G. C. Thomson Papers, MS-0440/04, Hocken Library.

37 Wohlers, Travel Report, 31 December 1845.

38 Mary Ellen-Kelm, *Colonizing Bodies: Aboriginal Health and Healing in British Columbia, 1900–50,* University of British Columbia Press, Vancouver, 1998, p.15.

39 Wohlers, Travel Report, 30 June – 17 July 1846.

40 Sheila Natusch, *Brother Wohlers: A Biography of J. F. H. Wohlers* (2nd edn), Caxton Press, Christchurch, 1992, p.179.

41 Ernst Dieffenbach, *Travels in New Zealand,* 1845, republished by Capper Press, Christchurch, 1974, p.42.

42 Wohlers, Travel Report, 1 May 1845.

43 Wohlers, Travel Report, 31 December 1845.

44 Stevens, '"Gathering Places"', p.20.

45 Stevens, '"Gathering Places"', p.19.

46 Stevens, '"Gathering Places"', p.21.

47 Linda J. Scott and Finlay P. Bayne, *Nathaniel Bates of Riverton, His Families and Descendants,* Bates Reunion Committee, Christchurch, 1994, p.5.

48 Stevens, '"Gathering Places"', p.23.

49 See Eva Wilson, *Hakoro ki te Iwi: The Story of Captain Howell and his Family,* Eva Wilson, Invercargill, 1976.

50 Wohlers, Travel Report, 19 February 1846.

51 Wohlers, Travel Report, 19 February 1846.

52 Dieffenbach, *Travels in New Zealand,* p.41.

53 All Māori men aged 21 and over gained suffrage in 1867, twelve years before all non-Māori men in New Zealand. In the same year, four Māori electorates (Northern, Eastern, Western and Southern Māori) were established under the Maori Representation Act 1867.

54 Binney, '"In-Between" Lives', p.95.

55 Donald McLean, when Chief Land Purchaser and Colonial Secretary, found employment in the public service for the sons of prominent interracial families. See Ray Fargher, *The Best Man who ever Served the Crown? A Life of Donald McLean,* Victoria University Press, Wellington, 2007.

56 Joan MacIntosh, *A History of Fortrose,* Times Printing, Invercargill, 1975, pp.39–47.

57 Andrew Sinclair, Otago Journal, 23 February 1860, Sinclair Papers, MS-1947, Alexander Turnbull Library, Wellington.

58 Don Grady, *Sealers and Whalers in New Zealand Waters,* Reed, Auckland, 1986, p.186; Geoffrey W. Rice, *Heaton Rhodes of Otahuna: The Illustrated Biography,* Canterbury University Press, Christchurch, 2001, pp.35–6.

59 Janet Holm, *Caught Mapping: The Life and Times of New Zealand's Early Surveyors,* Hazard Press, Christchurch, 2005, p.253.

60 Sinclair, Otago Journal, 16 February 1860.

61 MacIntosh, *A History of Fortrose,* p.392.

62 Anderson, *Race Against Time,* p.9.

63 Acker Family Reunion Committee, *Acker Family, 1834–1984,* Acker Family Reunion Committee, Invercargill, 1984.

64 Scott and Bayne, *Nathaniel Bates of Riverton,* pp.17–20.

65 'Papers relative to the Claims of Half-Castes of the Ngai Tahu Tribe in the South and Stewart Islands', AJHR, G-9, 1876; The Register of Bishop Harper's Country Baptism Book, 1851–1890, Christchurch City Libraries.

66 G. F. Davis, 'Old Identities and New Iniquities: The Taieri Plain in Otago Province 1770–1870', MA thesis, University of Otago, 1974, p.79.

67 *Otago Daily Times,* 6 April 1985.

68 Peter J. Joseph to John Bowie, 15 August 1936, Shaw Papers, AG71, Otago Settlers Museum, Dunedin.

69 Return of Births and Deaths since June 1874 and Half-Castes at each place, MA 23/17, Archives New Zealand, Wellington.

70 *Results of a Census of the Colony of New Zealand, 28th of March, 1886,* pp.10, 369.

71 'Papers relative to the Census of the Maori Population', *AJHR,* G-12, 1886, p.15.

72 Ian Pool, cited in Anderson, *Race Against Time*, p.31.

73 Jennifer S. H. Brown, *Strangers in Blood: Fur Trade Company Families in Indian Country*, University of British Columbia Press, Vancouver, 1980, p.220.

74 John Hanning to John Bowie, 25 March 1938, Shaw Papers, AG71, Otago Settlers Museum, Dunedin.

75 Alice Lees to Kitty Lees, 26 December 1874, cited in Frances Porter and Charlotte Macdonald (eds), *'My Hand Will Write What My Heart Dictates': The Unsettled Lives of Women in Nineteenth-century New Zealand as Revealed to Sisters, Family and Friends*, Auckland University Press/Bridget Williams Books, Auckland, 1996, p.100.

76 'Papers relating to the Census of the Maori Population', *AJHR*, G-2, 1878, p.8.

77 'Papers relating to the Census of the Maori Population, 1881', *AJHR*, G-3, 1881, p.9.

78 *National Census 1881*, p.90.

79 Ken W. Reid, *The Reids of West Taieri*, Ken W. Reid, Mosgiel, 1990, p.42.

80 Margaret D. Jacobs, 'The Eastmans and the Luhans: Interracial Marriage between White Women and Native American Men, 1875–1935', *Frontiers*, Vol.23, No.3, 2002, p.30. See also Katherine Ellinghaus, *Taking Assimilation to Heart: Marriages of White Women and Indigenous Men in the United States and Australia, 1887–1927*, University of Nebraska Press, Lincoln, 2006.

81 Jacobs, 'The Eastmans and the Luhans', p.30.

Chapter 4. Boundary Crossings

1 Waitangi Tribunal, *The Ngai Tahu Report 1991*, Waitangi Tribunal, Wellington, 1991, pp.281–2. The Governor had waived the Crown's right of pre-emption, established under the Treaty of Waitangi, to allow this purchase to take place. It is also important to note that the size of the purchase block was given at the time as 400,000 acres, but it is now known to be much larger.

2 M. P. K. Sorrenson, 'How to Civilize Savages: Some "Answers" from Nineteenth-Century New Zealand', *New Zealand Journal of History*, Vol.9, No.2, 1975, p.104.

3 *Ngai Tahu Report*, pp.311–12.

4 *Ngai Tahu Report*, pp.328–9.

5 *Ngai Tahu Report*, p.330.

6 The term 'native spaces' is borrowed from Cole Harris, *Making Native Space: Colonialism, Resistance, and Reserves in British Columbia*, University of British Columbia Press, Vancouver, 2002.

7 Sheila McManus, *The Line Which Separates: Race, Gender, and the Making of the Alberta-Montana Borderlands*, University of Nebraska Press, Lincoln, 2005.

8 The term 'middle ground' derives from Richard White, *The Middle Ground: Indians, Empires, and Republics in the Great Lakes Region, 1650–1815*, Cambridge University Press, Cambridge, 1991.

9 A. H. McLintock, *The History of Otago: The Origins and Growth of a Wakefield Class Settlement*, Otago Historical Centennial Publications, Dunedin, 1949, p.203.

10 'Crown Grant of the Otakou Block to the New Zealand Company', in Alexander Mackay, *A Compendium of Official Documents Relative to Native Affairs in the South Island: Volume II*, Government Printer, Wellington, 1872, p.374.

11 Folder 1, Box 1, W. A. Taylor Papers, Canterbury Museum.

12 Will of Korako Karetai, Deeds Register Book, Vol.73, Land Information New Zealand, Dunedin.

13 A. H. Carrington, 'Ngaitahu: The Story of the Invasion and Occupation of the South Island of New Zealand by the Descendants of Tahu-potiki', pp.50–8, 74–5, Te Runanga o Ngai Tahu Collection, Macmillan Brown Library, University of Canterbury; Gwen Sutherland, *Coast, Road and River: The Story of Taieri Mouth, Taieri Beach, Glenledi and Akatore*, Clutha Leader Print, Invercargill, 1962, p.8; W. H. S. Roberts, *Maori Nomenclature: Early History of Otago*, Otago Daily Times & Witness Newspapers, Dunedin, 1910, p.6; R. O. Carrick, *Historical Records of New Zealand South prior to 1840*, Otago Daily Times & Witness Newspapers, Dunedin, 1903, p.190; Atholl Anderson, *The Welcome of Strangers*, Otago University Press, Dunedin, 1998, pp.43–5; W. A. Taylor, 'The Taieri', *The Christchurch Press*, 2 February 1939, Newspaper Clippings, No.3, Folder 80, Box 10, W. A. Taylor Papers, Canterbury Museum.

14 Atholl Anderson, *Otakou: Evidence for the Ngai Tahu Claim Before the Waitangi Tribunal* (Wai-27), p.5.

15 George Grey to Earl Grey, 15 May 1848, in *Great Britain Parliamentary Papers. Colonies: New Zealand, 1847–50*, Irish University Press, Shannon, 1968, p.25; Harry C. Evison, *Te Wai Pounamu: The Greenstone Island. A History of the Southern Maori during the European Colonization of New Zealand*, Canterbury University Press, Christchurch, 1993, p.178.

16 Ann Parsonson, *Otago Tenths: Evidence for the Ngai Tahu Claim Before the Waitangi Tribunal* (Wai-27), p.52.

17 In the Deed of Purchase it was stated that Ngái Tahu agreed not to sell or let these lands without the sanction of the Governor; Waitangi Tribunal, *The Ngai Tahu Report 1991*, pp.1975–6.

18 Robert Chapman, 'The South Island Maoris and their Reserved Lands, 1860–1910', MA thesis, University of Canterbury, 1966, p.64; Ralph Johnson, *The Trust Administration of Maori Reserves, 1840–1913*, Waitangi Tribunal, Wellington, 1997, p.29. In 1857 the management of native reserves in Otago was vested in John Cargill, Alfred Chetham Strode, Robert Williams and John Gillies.

19 Johnson, *Trust Administration of Maori Reserves*, p.25.

20 Evison, *Te Wai Pounamu*, p.220; Johnson, *Trust Administration of Maori Reserves*, p.35.

21 W. H. Cutten, 'Commissioner of Crown Lands Report on Native Reserves', in Alexander Mackay, *A Compendium of Official Documents Relative to Native Affairs in the South Island: Volume I*, Government Printer, Wellington, 1872, p.119.

22 David V. Williams, *'Te Kooti Tango Whenua': The Native Land Court, 1864–1909*, Huia Press, Wellington, 1999, p.142.

23 Alexander Mackay to Chief Judge, Native Land Court, 8 August 1884, Cancelled Court Applications (South Island), MLC AccW2218 Box 17, Archives New Zealand, Wellington.

24 Kettle to Cargill, 9 December 1850, Letterbook, William Cargill Papers, MS-0083, Hocken Library.

25 Kettle to Cargill, 9 December 1850.

26 Win Parkes and Kath Hislop, *Taieri Mouth and Its Surrounding Districts*, Otago Heritage Books, Dunedin, 1980, p.19.

27 Alexander Mackay to Native Minister, 7 February 1868, in Mackay, *Compendium: Volume II*, p.148.

28 James Mackay (junior) to Native Secretary, 3 October 1863, in Mackay, *Compendium: Volume II*, pp.138–9.

29 Evidence of Anthony Walzl, *Ngai Tahu Reserves, 1848–1890*, Crown Papers (M14), (Wai-27), p.70; see also 'Report by Mr A. Mackay of the Sittings of the Native Lands Court held at Dunedin', *AJHR*, 1868, A-7.

30 Mackay, *Compendium: Volume 1*, p.23.

31 K. T. Karetai, 26 June 1865, in Jenny Murray, *Archival Material in the Registers of the Native Affairs Department and the Canterbury Provincial Council*, p.32, Canterbury Museum.

32 Korako, 16 February 1867, in Murray, *Archival Material*, p.37.

33 Jack Kona, 28 May 1867; John Topi Patuki, 29 July 1867; R. Te Uraura, 17 August 1867; Wi Naihira, 29 August 1867; in Murray, *Archival Material*, pp.38–40.

34 Mackay, *Compendium: Volume II*, p.234.

35 Mackay, *Compendium: Volume II*, p.234.

36 Mackay, *Compendium: Volume II*, p.234.

37 Tiaki Kona to Native Minister, 11 February 1886, Land Claims of South Island Half-Castes, MA 13/21, 13[c], Archives New Zealand, Wellington.

38 Waitangi Tribunal, *Ngai Tahu Report 1991*, p.303.

39 Census of Native Population of the Provinces of Canterbury, Otago and Southland 1868, Schedule of Native Reserves in the South Island, MA-MT 6/19, Archives New Zealand, Wellington.

40 H. K. Taiaroa, *NZPD*, 12 July 1876, Vol.20, 1876, p.454.

41 David MacLeod to Chief Judge, Native Land Court, 26 September 1868, Taieri Block File, Box 263, Maori Land Court, Christchurch.

42 Bill Dacker, 'Chapters in Nineteenth-Century South Island Maori History', BA (Hons) long essay, University of Otago, 1980, p.17.

43 Hariata Paama, Charlotte Palmer, Jane Paama and Tare Paama to Fenton, 30 June 1868, Cancelled Court Applications (South Island), MLC AccW2218 Box 17, Archives New Zealand, Wellington.

44 Nane to Fenton, 1 July 1868, Cancelled Court Applications (South Island), MLC AccW2218 Box 17, Archives New Zealand, Wellington.

45 See Taieri Block File, Box 263, Maori Land Court, Christchurch.

46 Anderson, *The Welcome of Strangers*, p.28.

Chapter 5. Fears and Anxieties

1 Daniel Thorp, 'Going Native in New Zealand and America: Comparing Pakeha Maori and White Indians', *Journal of Imperial and Commonwealth History*, Vol.31, No.3, 2003, pp.1–23; James Axtell, 'The White Indians of Colonial America', in Peter C. Mancall and James H. Merrell (eds), *American Encounters: Natives and Newcomers from European Contact to Indian Removal*, Routledge, London, 2000, pp.324–50; Linda Colley, 'Going Native, Telling Tales: Captivity, Collaborations and Empire', *Past and Present*, No.168, 2000, pp.170–93.

2 John Mack Faragher, 'The Custom of the Country: Cross-Cultural Marriage in the Far Western Fur Trade', in Lillian Schlissel, Vicki L. Ruiz and Janice Monk (eds), *Western Women: Their Land, Their Lives*, University of New Mexico Press, Albuquerque, 1988, p.208.

3 Faragher, 'The Custom of the Country', p.208.

4 See Trevor Bentley, *Pakeha-Maori: The Extraordinary Story of the Europeans who Lived as Maori in Early New Zealand*, Penguin, Auckland, 1999.

5 Adele Perry, *On the Edge of Empire: Gender, Race and the Making of British Columbia, 1849–1871*, University of Toronto Press, Toronto, 2001, p.47.

6 Willoughby Shortland to F. W. Whittaker, 6 May 1842, Case File: James Berghan, OLC 1/71 OLC 1323, Archives New Zealand, Wellington.

7 Alan Ward, *A Show of Justice: Racial 'Amalgamation' in Nineteenth-century New Zealand*, Auckland University Press, Auckland, 1995, p.36.

8 Ernst Dieffenbach, *Travels in New Zealand*, reprint, Capper Press, Christchurch, 1974, pp.152, 171.

9 Damon Salesa, 'Race Mixing: A Victorian Problem in Britain and New Zealand, 1830s–1870s', DPhil thesis, University of Oxford, 2000, p.128.

10 Gavin McLean, *Moeraki: 150 Years of Net and Plough Share*, Otago Heritage Books, Dunedin, 1986, p.23.

11 Walter Mantell to Colonial Secretary, 17 May 1852, cited in Waitangi Tribunal, *Ngai Tahu Ancillary Claims Report*, 1995, Waitangi Tribunal, Wellington, 1995, p.182.

12 Report of the Board Appointed to Inquire into and Report upon the State of Native Affairs in New Zealand, 1856, *Great Britain Parliamentary Papers. Colonies: New Zealand*, Vol.11, 1860, Irish University Press, Shannon, 1968, p.107.

13 Evidence of Bishop George Selwyn before the Board of Inquiry into Native Affairs in New Zealand, 8 April 1856, G 51/1, Archives New Zealand, Wellington.

14 Evidence of Bishop Selwyn before the Board of Inquiry.

15 Evidence of Bishop Selwyn before the Board of Inquiry.

16 Evidence of Mr Black before the Board of Inquiry, 9 April 1856.

17 Evidence of Bishop Selwyn before the Board of Inquiry.

18 Evidence of John Whitely before the Board of Inquiry, 7 April 1856.

19 Evidence of J. Wilson before the Board of Inquiry, 5 May 1856.

20 Salesa, 'Race Mixing', pp.166, 168.

21 Salesa, 'Race Mixing', p.122. For further information on the Half-Caste Disability Removal Act 1860 see Binney, '"In-between" Lives', and Peter Spiller, Jeremy Finn and Richard Boast, *A New Zealand Legal History*, Brookers, Wellington, 1996, pp.96–7.

22 Arthur S. Thomson, *The Story of New Zealand Past and Present – Savage and Civilised*, Volume II, John Murray, London, 1859, pp.305–6.

23 Salesa, 'Race Mixing', p.139.

24 Salesa, 'Race Mixing', p.266.

25 Bettina Bradbury, 'From Civil Death to Separate Property: Changes in the Legal Rights of Married Women in Nineteenth-century New Zealand', *New Zealand Journal of History*, Vol.29, No.1, 1995, p.45.

26 Hugh Carleton, cited in Bradbury, 'From Civil Death to Separate Property', p.45.

27 See the letters of Joseph Crocome, James Daniells and William Shearer in the Register of Inwards Correspondence to the Civil Secretary, CS 2/1, Archives New Zealand, Wellington. Letters on similar subject matter are listed in the Register of Inwards Correspondence to the Civil Secretary, CS 2/2, the Register of Correspondence to the Maori Affairs Department, 1840–1847, MA 2/1, and the Register of Correspondence to the Governor, 1840–1870, G 22/1, Archives New Zealand, Wellington.

28 Ann McGrath, 'Consent, Marriage and Colonialism: Indigenous Australian Women and Colonizer Marriages', *Journal of Colonialism and Colonial History*, Vol.6, No.3, 2005.

29 William Seranacke to Donald McLean, 16 October 1858, Case File: Thomas Uppadine Cook, OLC 1/71 OLC1374, Archives New Zealand, Wellington.

30 John Marmon to Governor Gore-Browne, 18 August 1856, Case File: John Marmon, OLC 1/317, Archives New Zealand, Wellington.

31 For letters and petitions from white men and their mixed-descent children requesting land grants, as well as documents and schedules of names pertaining to investigations into these claims, see: Land Claims of South Island Half-Castes, MA 13/19 12[a], Part 1, Land Claims of South Island Half-Castes, MA 13/19 12[b], Part 2, Land Claims of South Island Half-Castes, MA 13/19 12[c], Part 3, Land Claims of South Island Half-Castes, MA 13/20, 12[d], Part 4, Archives New Zealand, Wellington.

32 See, for example, Petition from the Stevens family, 4 August 1881, and Alexander Mackay to Land Claims Commissioner, 22 November 1879, Land Claims of South Island Half-Castes, MA 13/19 12[a], Part 1, Archives New Zealand, Wellington. See also investigations into 'half-caste' claims by the Old Land Claims Commission, in OLC 4/20, Archives New Zealand, Wellington.

33 Evidence of Walter Mantell before the Public Petitions Committee, 20 July 1869, Land Claims of South Island Half-Castes, MA 13/20 12[e], Part 5, Archives New Zealand, Wellington.

34 Mantell to Colonial Secretary, 6 April 1854, Correspondence Regarding Promises of Land, LE 1/38 1863/116, Box 31, Archives New Zealand, Wellington.

35 Mantell to Colonial Secretary, 17 May 1852.

36 Mantell to Colonial Secretary, 6 April 1854.

37 Mantell to Colonial Secretary, 22 May 1868, Case File: Thomas Chaseland, OLC 1/72 OLC15a, Archives New Zealand, Wellington.

38 Joseph Donaldson to Walter Mantell, 28 August 1863, Case File: Joseph Donaldson, Otepopo, OLC 1/72 OLC1a, Archives New Zealand, Wellington.

39 Mantell to Colonial Secretary, 6 April 1854.

40 Henry Wixon to Walter Mantell, 19 May 1862, OLC 18a, 20a, 20b, Archives New Zealand, Wellington.

41 Wixon to Mantell, 12 November 1862, OLC 18a, 20a, 20b, Archives New Zealand, Wellington.

42 See Land Claims of South Island Half-Castes, MA 13/20 12[d], Part 4, Archives New Zealand, Wellington.

43 Judith Binney, '"In-Between" Lives: Studies from within a Colonial Society', in Tony Ballantyne and Brian Moloughney (eds), *Disputed Histories: Imagining New Zealand's Pasts*, Otago University Press, Dunedin, 2006, pp.93–118. See also Angela Wanhalla, 'Marrying "In": The Geography of Intermarriage at Taieri, 1830s–1920s', in Tony Ballantyne and Judith A. Bennett (eds), *Landscape/Community: Perspectives from New Zealand History*, Otago University Press, Dunedin, 2005, pp.73–94, and Salesa, 'Race Mixing'.

44 Peter Proudfoot to Colonial Secretary, 21 January 1856, Land Claims of South Island Half-Castes, MA 13/20 12[e] Part 5, Archives New Zealand, Wellington.

45 Peter Proudfoot to Colonial Secretary, 29 January 1856, Correspondence regarding promises of land, LE 1/38 1863/116, Box 31, Archives New Zealand, Wellington.

46 Mary Ann Tandy to Native Minister, 29 October 1884, Land Claims of South Island Half-Castes, MA 13/20 13[a], Archives New Zealand, Wellington.

47 Basil Howard, *Rakiura: A History of Stewart Island, New Zealand*, Reed, Dunedin, 1940, p.167. For a summary of the Rakiura Purchase, see Waitangi Tribunal, *The Ngai Tahu Report 1991*, Waitangi Tribunal, Wellington, 1992.

48 Atholl Anderson, *Race Against Time: The Early Maori-Pakeha Families and the Development of a Mixed Race Population in Southern New Zealand*, Hocken Library, Dunedin, 1991, p.28. For a detailed discussion of the implications of the Rakiura Purchase for interracial families and, in particular, the specific economic provisions contained within the deed of purchase, see Kate Stevens, '"Gathering Places": The Mixed Descent Families of Foveaux Strait and Rakiura/Stewart Island, 1824–1864', BA (Hons) research essay, University of Otago, 2008.

49 'Survey of Native Reserves in the Provinces of Otago and Southland', *AJHR*, D-20, 1870, p.3.

50 *AJHR*, D-20, 1870, p.4.

51 Joseph Crocome to J. T. Thomson, 3 April 1869, OLC 18a, 20a, 20b, Archives New Zealand, Wellington.

52 H. K. Taiaroa, *NZPD*, 12 July 1876, Vol.20, 1876, p.454.

53 Alexander Mackay to Under-Secretary, 5 September 1874, *AJHR*, G-9, 1876, p.1.

54 A. J. Cadman, *NZPD*, 22 July 1892, Vol.76, 1892, p.53.

55 David V. Williams, *'Te Kooti Tango Whenua': The Native Land Court, 1864–1909*, Huia, Wellington, 1999, p.269.

56 *New Zealand Statutes 1877*, p.164.

57 Letter to Mr Lewis, 27 January 1881, Land Claims of South Island Half-Castes, MA 13/19 12[a], Part 1, Archives New Zealand, Wellington; Waitangi Tribunal, *Ngai Tahu Ancillary Claims Report 1995*, p.182.

58 Alexander Mackay to Under-Secretary, Native Department, 21 November 1878, Land Claims of South Island Half-Castes, MA 13/19 12[b], Part 2, Archives New Zealand, Wellington.

59 Tiaki Kona to Alexander Mackay, 7 January 1879, Volume of Papers relating to Native Reserves, MA-MT 6/15, Archives New Zealand, Wellington.

60 *New Zealand Statutes 1883*, p.151.

61 Tiaki Kona to W. J. Stewart, 29 August 1885, Land Claims of South Island Half-Castes, MA 13/20 13[a], Archives New Zealand, Wellington.

62 Tiaki Kona to Native Department, 11 February 1886, Land Claims of South Island Half-Castes, MA 13/21 13[c], Archives New Zealand, Wellington.

63 *NZPD*, Vol.64, 1889, p.160.

64 Chief Draughtsman to the Commissioner of Crown Lands, 18 August 1885, Land Claims of South Island Half-Castes, MA 13/19 12[a], Part 1, Archives New Zealand, Wellington.

65 Robert Brown to Native Minister, 8 May 1893, Letters to Native Minister, MA 1 1892/2250, Archives New Zealand, Wellington.

66 Memo, Department of Lands and Survey to Maori Affairs Department, 7 December 1951, Clarendon Block XI, MA 1/78 5/5/89, Archives New Zealand, Wellington; Waitangi Tribunal, *Ngai Tahu Ancillary Claims Report 1995*, p.219.

67 *New Zealand Statutes 1888*, p.236.

Chapter 6. Racial Categories and Lived Identities

1 See Hana O'Regan, *Ko Tahu, Ko Au*, Horomaka Press, Christchurch, 2001.

2 Benedict Anderson, *Imagined Communities: Reflections on the Origin and Spread of Nationalism*, Verso, London, 1991; Martha Hodes, 'Fractions and Fictions in the United States Census of 1890', in Ann Laura Stoler (ed.), *Haunted by Empire: Geographies of Intimacy in North American History*, Duke University Press, Durham, 2006, pp.240–70.

3 Melissa Nobles, 'Racial Categorization and Censuses', in David I. Kertzer and Dominque Arel (eds), *Census and Identity: The Politics of Race, Ethnicity and Language in National Censuses*, Cambridge University Press, Cambridge, 2002, p.43.

4 Nobles, 'Racial Categorization and Censuses', p.51.

5 Nobles, 'Racial Categorization and Censuses', p.56.

6 Nancy Leys Stepan, *'The Hour of Eugenics': Race, Gender and Nation in Latin America*, Cornell University Press, Ithaca, 1991, pp.145–7.

7 Kate Riddell, '"Improving" the Maori: Counting the Ideology of Intermarriage', *New Zealand Journal of History*, Vol.34, No.1, 2000, p.88.

8 Riddell, '"Improving" the Maori', p.84.

9 'Papers relating to the Census of the Maori Population', *AJHR*, G-2, 1891, p.8.

10 *Results of a Census of the Colony of New Zealand taken for the night of the 31st of March 1906*, Government Printer, Wellington, 1907, p.1v.

11 'Papers relating to the Census of the Maori Population', *AJHR*, H-14a, 1911, p.19.

12 *Results of a Census of the Dominion of New Zealand taken for the night of 17th April 1921*, Government Printer, Wellington, 1922, Appendix A, p.2.

13 M. P. K. Sorrenson, *Maori and European since 1870: A Study in Adaptation and Adjustment*, Heinemann, Auckland, 1967, p.viii.

14 'Census of New Zealand, April 1901, The Maori Population', *AJHR*, H-26b, 1901, p.3.

15 *Results of a Census of the Colony of New Zealand taken for the night of the 31st of March 1906*, Government Printer, Wellington, 1907, p.1v.

16 M. P. K. Sorrenson, *Integration or Identity? Cultural Interaction: New Zealand since 1911*, Heinemann, Auckland, 1977, p.14.

17 Angela Ballara, *Proud to be White? A Survey of Pakeha Prejudice in New Zealand*, Heinemann, Auckland, 1986, p.88.

18 Edward Shortland, *The Southern Districts of New Zealand: A Journal with Passing Notices of the Customs of the Aborigines*, Longman, Brown, Green and Longmans, London, 1851, p.v.

19 Shortland, *The Southern Districts of New Zealand*, pp.77–8.

20 'Return of Natives in the Otago and Southland Provinces 1852, showing those who have died since 1864', in Alexander Mackay, *A Compendium of Official Documents Relative to Native Affairs in the South Island: Volume II*, Government Printer, Wellington, 1873, p.142; 'Aboriginal Native Population of New Zealand, in the year 1857', *Statistics of New Zealand for 1857*, Government Printer, Auckland, 1858; *Statistics of New Zealand for 1867 including the Results of a Census of the Colony taken in December of that year*, Government Printer, Wellington, 1869, Appendix C. See also 'Reports on the State of the Natives of Various Districts at the Time of the Arrival of Sir George Grey', *AJHR*, E-7, 1861, p.38; F. D. Fenton, *Observations on the State of the Aboriginal Inhabitants of New Zealand*, Government Printer, Wellington, 1859.

21 'Further Reports by Mr Commissioner Mackay Relating to Middle Island Native Claims', *AJHR*, G-7a, 1891, p.3.

22 'Further Reports by Mr Commissioner Mackay', *AJHR*, G-7a, 1891, p.3.

23 For a fuller discussion of the material impact of census-taking on Māori, see Angela Wanhalla, 'The Politics of "Periodical Counting": Race, Place and Identity in Southern New Zealand', in Penelope Edmonds and Tracey Banivanua Mar (eds), *Making Space: Settler-colonial Perspectives on Land, Place and Identity*, Palgrave Macmillan, London, 2010.

24 'Middle Island Native Claims, Report by Mr Commissioner Mackay', *AJHR*, G-7, 1891, p.5.

25 'Middle Island Native Claims', *AJHR*, G-7, 1891, p.5.

26 See 'Return of Native Residents in 1891 at the South Island Native Settlements', *AJHR*, G-1, 1892.

27 See Deborah Posel, 'A Mania for Measurement: Statistics and Statecraft in the Transition to Apartheid', in Saul Dubow (ed.), *Science and Society in South Africa*, Manchester University Press, Manchester, 2000, pp.116–42; Renisa Mawani, 'In Between and Out of Place: Mixed-race Identity, Liquor, and the Law in British Columbia, 1850–1913', in Sherene H. Razack (ed.), *Race, Space and the Law: Unmapping a White Society*, Between the Lines, Toronto, 2002, pp.47–70.

28 'Further Reports by Mr Commissioner Mackay', *AJHR*, G-7a, 1891, p.7.

29 'Middle Island Native Claims', *AJHR*, G-7, 1891, p.5.

30 'Middle Island Native Claims', *AJHR*, G-7, 1891, pp.36, 55.

31 'Middle Island Native Claims', *AJHR*, G-7, 1891, p.33.

32 'Middle Island Native Claims', *AJHR*, G-7, 1891, p.33.

33 'Middle Island Native Claims', *AJHR*, G-7, 1891, p.45.

34 'Middle Island Native Claims', *AJHR*, G-7, 1891, p.54.

35 'Middle Island Native Claims', *AJHR*, G-7, 1891, p.55.

36 'Reports from Officers in Native Districts', *AJHR*, G-1, 1877, p.23.

37 'Papers Relating to the Census of the Maori Population', *AJHR*, G-12, 1886, p.14.

38 'Census of the Maori Population', *AJHR*, H-26a, 1906, p.1.

39 'Census of the Maori Population', *AJHR*, H-14a, 1911, p.2.

40 *Results of a Census of the Dominion of New Zealand taken for the night of the 17th April, 1921*, Government Printer, Wellington, 1922, p.60.

41 Āpirana Ngata, cited in Kate Riddell, 'A "Marriage of the Races"? Aspects of Intermarriage, Ideology and Reproduction on the New Zealand Frontier', MA thesis, Victoria University of Wellington, 1996, p.168.

42 Awarua Families to the Native Minister, 10 February 1886, Land Claims of South Island Half-Castes, MA 13/21, 13 [c], Archives New Zealand, Wellington.

43 Robert Brown and others to Native Minister, 1 September 1893, Letters to Native Minister, MA 1 1892/2250, Archives New Zealand, Wellington.

44 Riddell, 'A "Marriage of the Races"?', p.139.

45 These statistics are based on combining the 'half-caste living as Maori' population in the Māori census and the 'half-caste' living as European in the general census: *Results of a Census of the Colony of New Zealand taken for the night of the 5th April 1891*, Government Printer, Wellington, 1892, pp.10, 1ix; *Results of a Census of the Colony of New Zealand taken for the night of the 31st March 1901*, Government Printer, Wellington, 1902, pp.13, 1vii; *Results of a Census of the Dominion of New Zealand taken for the night of the 2nd April 1911*, Government Printer, Wellington, 1912, p.16 and Appendix A.

46 Atholl Anderson, *Race Against Time: The Early Maori-Pakeha Families and the Development of the Mixed-race Population in Southern New Zealand*, Hocken Library, Dunedin, 1991, p.20.

47 Thomas Brown, 'The Life of Thomas Brown (and Memory of Others) 1885–1974', MS, undated, unpaginated, Cecily Parker, Private Collection.

48 Brown, 'The Life of Thomas Brown'.

49 Royal Commission on Middle Island Native Land Claims, Minutes of Evidence, 26 February 1891, MA 72/1, Archives New Zealand, Wellington.

50 Tiaki Kona to Native Department, 8 August 1886, MA 13/21, 13[c], Archives New Zealand, Wellington.

51 Royal Commission on Middle Island Native Land Claims, Minutes of Evidence, 26 February 1891, MA 72/1, Archives New Zealand, Wellington.

52 Tom Bennion and Judy Boyd, *The Maori Land Court and Land Boards, 1909–1952*, Waitangi Tribunal, Wellington, 1997, p.8.

53 21 June 1899, South Island Maori Land Court Minute Book 10, pp.252–3, Macmillan Brown Library, University of Canterbury.

54 Will of Papu Paraone, 19 July 1895, in Alex Smith and Travis Brown (compilers), 'Some Historical Information', David Brown, Private Collection.

55 *Otago Witness*, 15 December 1892, p.15.

56 List of Contributions and Monies Collected from the Taiari Runanga, 27 March 1892, 1450S/53, Box 22, Taiaroa Papers, Canterbury Museum; Arama Pitama Papers, pp.61, 65, 66, 67, 69, Te Maire Tau, Private Collection.

57 Tiaki Kona to Native Minister, 21 March 1893, in Waitangi Tribunal, *Supporting Papers to Evidence of David Armstrong*, Vol.9, Part 1, Crown Papers (Wai-27), Document 14.

58 'Return of Expenditure on Indigent Natives, Middle and Stewart Islands, for the Last Three Years', AJHR, G-5, 1892.

59 *Wise's Directory 1890–91*, p.230.

60 Brown, 'The Life of Thomas Brown'.

61 *Otago Daily Times*, 24 February 1898, p.3.

62 Brown, 'The Life of Thomas Brown'; Interview with Ian, 20 June 2003.

63 Brown, 'The Life of Thomas Brown'.

64 Katie Pickles, 'Locating Widows in Mid-nineteenth-century Pictou County, Nova Scotia', *Journal of Historical Geography*, Vol.30, No.1, 2004, pp.70–86.

65 South Island Native Land Claims, 1893, Folder 15, No.15, Box 2, W. A. Taylor Papers, Canterbury Museum.

66 South Island Native Land Claims, 1893.

67 South Island Native Land Claims, 1893.

68 Waitangi Tribunal, *Ngai Tahu Report 1991*, Waitangi Tribunal, Wellington, 1991, p.856.

69 Waitangi Tribunal, *Ngai Tahu Report*.

70 Waitangi Tribunal, *Ngai Tahu Report*.

71 Atholl Anderson, 'Historical and Archaeological Aspects of Muttonbirding in New Zealand', *New Zealand Journal of Archaeology*, Vol.17, 1995, pp.38–9; Michael Stevens, 'Kāi Tahu me te Hopu Tītī ki Rakiura: An Exception to the "Colonial Rule"?', *The Journal of Pacific History*, Vol.41, No.3, 2003, pp.273–91.

72 Thelma Smith, *Tai-ari Ferry and Henley 'Our Native Place': A Souvenir of the Schools Jubilee, 24th–27th January, 1941*, Otago Daily Times and Witness Newspapers, Dunedin, 1941, p.25.

73 Smith, *Tai-ari Ferry and Henley*, p.13.

74 Interview with Kath Hislop, 6 April 1994, Bill Dacker Oral History Collection, Dunedin Public Library.

75 L. B. Campbell to Under-Secretary, Native Department, 14 August 1941, cited in David Armstrong, *Supporting Papers*, Vol.2, S10, Crown Papers (Wai-27).

76 Hislop interview.

77 Brown, 'The Life of Thomas Brown'.

78 Catherine Wilson, 'Tatawai, Kai Tahu and the Claim', BA (Hons) research essay, University of Otago, 2002, p.4.

79 'Peninsula and Taieri', Newspaper Cuttings, Folder 95, No.5, Box 12, Taylor Papers, Canterbury Museum.

80 Wilson, 'Tatawai, Kai Tahu and the Claim', p.6.

81 Wilson, 'Tatawai, Kai Tahu and the Claim', p.7.

82 Wilson, 'Tatawai, Kai Tahu and the Claim', p.1.

83 Gail Tipa, *Environmental Performance Indicators: Taieri River Case Study*, Ministry for the Environment, Wellington, 1999, p.6.

84 G. F. Davis, 'Old Identities and New Iniquities: The Taieri Plain in Otago Province, 1770–1870', MA thesis, University of Otago, 1974, p.58.

85 Tiaki Kona to Tame Parata, 28 August 1891, translated 29 August 1891, Tatawai Fishing Reserve, LS 1/41749, Box 398, Archives New Zealand, Wellington.

86 'Native Affairs Committee', *AJHR*, I-2, 1885, p.24.

87 Royal Commission on Middle Island Native Land Claims, Minutes of Evidence, 26 February 1891, MA 72/1, Archives New Zealand, Wellington.

88 Tiaki Kona to Alexander Mackay, 13 September 1901, Inwards Letters to Judge Mackay, MLC 8/1, Archives New Zealand, Wellington.

89 Katie Pickles, 'The Re-Creation of Bottle Lake: From Site of Discard to Environmental Playground?', *Environment and History*, Vol. 9, 2003, pp.419–34.

90 Geoff Park, '"Swamps Which Might Doubtless Easily be Drained": Swamp Drainage and its Impact on the Indigenous', in Eric Pawson and Tom Brooking (eds), *Environmental Histories of New Zealand*, Oxford University Press, Oxford, 2002, pp.151–68.

91 Park, '"Swamps Which Might Doubtless Easily be Drained"', p.156.

92 Interview with Maraea, 24 January 2003.

93 *Wise's Directory 1894–95*, p.366.

94 *Results of a Census of the Colony of New Zealand taken for the night of the 12th April 1896*, Government Printer, Wellington, 1897, p.74.

95 Brown, 'The Life of Thomas Brown'.

96 Henley Maori Kaika Minutes, 20 June 1900, Ted Palmer, Private Collection.

97 Brown, 'The Life of Thomas Brown'.

98 *Otago Daily Times*, 10 April 1901.

99 Trustee Record Book Native Hall, 19 June 1912, Ted Palmer, Private Collection.

100 Trustee Record Book Native Hall, 19 June 1912.

101 Smith, *Tai-ari Ferry and Henley*, pp. 5, 13.

102 Hislop interview.

103 Hislop interview.

104 Robert J. C. Young, *Colonial Desire: Hybridity in Theory, Culture and Race*, Routledge, London, 1995; Ann Laura Stoler, *Carnal Knowledge and Imperial Power: Race and the Intimate in Colonial Rule*, University of California Press, Berkeley, 2002; Hannah Robert, 'Disciplining the Female Aboriginal Body: Inter-racial Sex and the Pretence of Separation', *Australian Feminist Studies*, Vol.16, No.34, 2001, pp.69–81.

Chapter 7. Migration Stories

1 Interview with Kath Hislop, 6 April 1994, Bill Dacker Oral History Collection, Dunedin Public Library.

2 General Maori Information Book 3, Herries Beattie Papers, PC-174, Hocken Library, Dunedin.

3 Probate of Ani Wellman, DAAC D239 178 4689, Archives New Zealand, Dunedin.

4 Report of the Board Representative in the Matter of Taieri, A13, 5 December 1929, Taieri, MLC AccW2218 Box 26 n.125, Archives New Zealand, Wellington.

5 Tom Brooking, *Lands for the People? The Highland Clearances and the Colonisation of New Zealand: A Biography of John McKenzie*, Otago University Press, Dunedin, 1996, pp.278–9.

6 Henley School Committee Minute Book, 14 June 1902, Henley School Records, AG-110-10, Hocken Library, Dunedin.

7 Knox Church Marriage Register, Vol.2: 1880–1891, Hocken Library, Dunedin.

8 Balclutha Old Cemetery Headstone Burial Records, Hocken Library, Dunedin.

9 General Maori Information Book 3, Herries Beattie Papers, PC-174, Hocken Library, Dunedin.

10 Succession to John Wellman, 22 May 1936, South Island Maori Land Court Minute Book 28, p.114, Macmillan Brown Library, University of Canterbury.

11 Interview with David, 23 March 2003.

12 *Dunedin Star*, 16 September 1989, p.9.

13 *Dunedin Star*, 16 September 1989, p.9.

14 Dawn to Allan, undated letter, Lavell family, Private Collection.

15 Obituary, January 1938, in Miscellaneous Death Notices, David Brown, Private Collection.

16 Succession to Sarah Robertson, 5 November 1913, South Island Maori Land Court Minute Book 18, p.198, Macmillan Brown Library, University of Canterbury.

17 Interview with Ted, 9 September 2003.

18 Interview with Allan, 20 July 2003.

19 Interview with Allan.

20 *The Press*, 17 November 1932, p.1.

21 Succession to Teone Wiwi Paraone, South Island Maori Land Court Minute Book 32, p.108, Macmillan Brown Library, University of Canterbury; *The Press*, 7 July 1934, p.1; *The Press*, 4 March 1944, p.1.

22 L. D. B. Heenan, 'The Changing South Island Maori Population', *New Zealand Geographer*, Vol.22, No.2, 1966, p.126.

23 Atholl Anderson, *Race Against Time: The Early Maori-Pakeha Families and the Development of the Mixed-race Population in Southern New Zealand*, Hocken Library, Dunedin, 1991, p.20.

24 *Results of a Census of the Dominion of New Zealand taken for the night of 17th April 1921*, Government Printer, Wellington, 1922, Appendix A: Maori Census, p.6.

25 *Dominion of New Zealand Population Census 1926, Volume XIV*, Government Printer, Wellington, 1927, p.19.

26 Thomas Brown, 'The Life of Thomas Brown (and Memory of Others) 1885–1974', Cecily Parker, Private Collection.

27 General Maori Information Book 3, Herries Beattie Papers.

28 T. M. Smith to M. J. Savage, Minister of Maori Affairs, 18 October 1939, in *Supporting Papers of David Armstrong*, Vol.2, S10, Crown Papers (Wai-27).

29 Sarah Stevenson to Maori Land Court, 20 November 1919, Taieri, MLC AccW2218 Box 26 n.125, Archives New Zealand, Wellington.

30 John Fraser to Native Land Court, 27 August 1897, Cancelled Court Applications (South Island), MLC AccW2218 Box 17, Archives New Zealand, Wellington.

31 12 December 1922, South Island Maori Land Court Minute Book 22, p.186, Macmillan Brown Library, University of Canterbury.

32 Bill Dacker, *Te Mamae me te Aroha – The Pain and the Love: A History of Kai Tahu Whānui in Otago*, 1844–1994, Otago University Press, Dunedin, 1994, p.135.

33 Tom Bennion, *The Maori Land Court and Land Boards, 1909–1952*, Waitangi Tribunal, Wellington, 1997, p.22.

34 Tom Bennion and Judy Boyd, *Succession to Maori Land, 1900–52*, Waitangi Tribunal, Wellington, 1997, p.24.

35 Application for Confirmation of Alienation, 1 February 1910, Taieri, CH270 15/2/4011, Archives New Zealand, Christchurch; Deeds Register Book, 12 April 1910, Vol.151, p.321, Land Information New Zealand, Dunedin.

36 Wilkinson to Native Land Court, 11 March 1907, Cancelled Court Applications (South Island), MLC AccW2218 Box 17, Archives New Zealand, Wellington.

37 Hakita Hutika Huria to the Registrar, Native Land Court, 27 May 1940, Taieri Native Reserve, Section 8, CH270 15/11/1119, Archives New Zealand, Christchurch.

38 Sheppard to Registrar, Native Land Court, 31 January 1939, and Alice Hariata Uru to Registrar, Native Land Court, 26 January 1939, Taieri Native Reserve, Section 8, CH270 15/11/1119, Archives New Zealand, Christchurch.

39 Papprill, Son and Corcoran to Native Land Court, 9 February 1938, Taieri Native Reserve, Block A, Section 11, CH270 15/2/1088, Archives New Zealand, Christchurch. See also John Steven Brown to Native Trustee, 30 August 1937, and John Steven Brown to Native Land Court, 13 April 1937, Taieri Native Reserve, Block A, Section 11, CH270 15/2/1088, Archives New Zealand, Christchurch.

40 W. R. Wellman to Minister of Native Affairs, 17 July 1939, Section 6, Block XIV, Waitutu, ABWN/6095 AccW5021/22/1099/15, Part 1, Box 571, Archives New Zealand, Wellington.

41 Interview with Marna Dunn, 25 November 1993, Bill Dacker Oral History Collection, Dunedin Public Library.

42 Interview with Marna Dunn.

43 Megan Woods, 'Dissolving the Frontiers: Single Maori Women's Migrations, 1942–1969', in Lyndon Fraser and Katie Pickles (eds), *Shifting Centres: Women and Migration in New Zealand History*, Otago University Press, Dunedin, 2002, pp.117–34; Joan Metge, *A New Maori Migration*, Athlone Press, London, 1964; Erik Schwimmer (ed.), *The Maori People in the Nineteen-Sixties*, Longman Paul, Auckland, 1968.

44 Erik Olssen, 'Towards a New Society', in G. W. Rice (ed.), *The Oxford History of New Zealand*, Oxford University Press, Oxford, 1995, p.258.

45 Susan Sleeper-Smith, *Indian Women and French Men: Rethinking Cultural Encounter in the Western Great Lakes*, University of Massachusetts Press, Amherst, 2001, p.9.

46 Interview with Stephen, 12 April 2003.

47 Annabel Cooper, Erik Olssen, Kirsten Thomlinson and Robin Law, 'The Landscape of Gender Politics: Place, People and Two Mobilisations', in Barbara Brookes, Annabel Cooper and Robin Law (eds), *Sites of Gender: Women, Men and Modernity in Southern Dunedin, 1890–1939*, Auckland University Press, Auckland, 2003, pp.36–7.

48 Interview with Ian, 20 June 2003.

49 Interview with Shirley, 15 June 2003.

50 'Census of the Maori Population', *AJHR*, H-14a, 1911, p.19.

51 Interview with Rona, 25 June 2003; Elizabeth to author, undated letter; interview with Dale, 11 June 2003.

52 Interview with Shirley.

53 Interview with Marna Dunn; interview with Rona.

54 Interview with Rona.

55 Interview with Allan.

56 Interview with Rona.

57 Elizabeth, undated letter to author.

58 Interview with Hazel, 19 June 2003.

59 Interview with Ian.

60 Interview with Elizabeth, 18 December 2003.

61 Interview with Hazel.

62 Interview with Hazel.

63 Interview with Martin, 8 April 2003.

64 Interview with Allan; interview with Brian, 14 December 2003; interview with Irene, 14 December 2003.

65 F. G. Hall-Jones, *Kelly of Inverkelly*, Southland Historical Committee, Invercargill, 1944, p.42.

66 Johannes Wohlers, Travel Report, 30 June–17 July 1846, Wohlers Papers, 0428-04A, Alexander Turnbull Library, Wellington.

67 Damon Salesa, 'Race Mixing: A Victorian Problem in Britain and New Zealand, 1830s–1870s', DPhil thesis, University of Oxford, 2000.

68 Edward Said in Joanna Sassoon, 'Becoming Anthropological: A Cultural Biography of E. L. Mitchell's Photographs of Aboriginal People', *Aboriginal History*, Vol.28, 2004, p.36.

69 Leonard Bell, '"Pictures as History, Settlement as Theatre": John Davis's Photo-portrait of Robert Louis Stevenson and Family at Vailima, Samoa, 1892', *Journal of New Zealand Literature*, Vol.21, 2002, p.96.

70 James R. Ryan, *Picturing Empire: Photography and the Visualization of the British Empire*, Reaktion Books, London, 1997; Joan M. Schwartz and James R. Ryan (eds), *Picturing Place: Photography and the Geographical Imagination*, I. B. Tauris, London, 2003; Eleanor M. Hight and Gary D. Sampson (eds), *Colonialist Photography: Imag(in)ing Race and Place*, Routledge, London, 2002; Elizabeth Edwards (ed.), *Anthropology and Photography, 1860–1920*, Yale University Press, New Haven, 2002; P. S. Landau, 'Empires of the Visual: Photography and Colonial Administration in Africa', in Paul S. Landau and Deborah D. Kaspin (eds), *Images and Empires: Visuality in Colonial and Postcolonial Africa*, University of California Press, Berkeley, 2002, pp.141–71; Carol J. Williams, *Framing the West: Race, Gender, and the Photographic Frontier in the Pacific Northwest*, Oxford University Press, Oxford, 2003; Jane Lydon, *Eye Contact: Photographing Indigenous Australians*, Duke University Press, Durham, 2005; Elizabeth Edwards and Janice Hart (eds), *Photographs, Objects, Histories: On the Materiality of Images*, Routledge, London, 2004.

71 Nancy Stepan, *Picturing Tropical Nature*, Cornell University Press, Ithaca, 2001, p.86.

72 Martha A. Sandweiss, *Print the Legend: Photography and the American West*, Yale University Press, New Haven, 2002, p.215.

73 J. Sutton Beets, 'Images of Maori Women in New Zealand Postcards after 1900', in Alison Jones, Phyllis S. Herda and Tamasailau Suaalii (eds), *Bitter Sweet: Indigenous Women in the Pacific*, Otago University Press, Dunedin, 2000, pp.17–33. See also William Main, *Facing an Era: Postcard Portraits from a Century Ago*, Exposures, Wellington, 2006.

74 William Main, *Maori in Focus: A Selection of Photographs of the Maori from 1850–1914*, Millwood, Wellington, 1976.

75 J. Dennis, 'McDonald, James Ingram, 1865–1935', in Claudia Orange (ed.), *The Dictionary of New Zealand Biography: Volume Three (1901–1930)*, Ministry for Culture and Heritage, Wellington, 1996.

76 Jo Spence and Patricia Holland (eds), *Family Snaps: The Meaning of Domestic Photography*, Virago, London, 1991, p.1. On the relationship between photographs, family albums, and orality, see Martha Langford, *Suspended Conversations: The Afterlife of Memory in Photographic Albums*, McGill-Queen's University Press, Montreal and Kingston, 2001.

77 Spence and Holland, *Family Snaps*, p.9. See also Julia Hirsch, *Family Photographs: Content, Meaning and Effect*, Oxford University Press, Oxford, 1981.

78 Alison Brown and Laura Peers, *'Pictures Bring Us Messages' / Sinaakssiiksi Aohtsimaahpihkookiyaawa: Photographs and Histories from the Kainai Nation*, University of Toronto Press, Toronto, 2006, p.155.

79 Sassoon, 'Becoming Anthropological', p.60.

80 Sandweiss, *Print the Legend*, p.272; H. J. Tsinhnahjnnie, 'When is a Photograph Worth a Thousand Words?', in Christopher Pinney and Nicolas Peterson (eds), *Photography's Other Histories*, Duke University Press, Durham, 2003, p.41.

81 J. R. Miller, 'Reading Photographs, Reading Voices: Documenting the History of Native Residential Schools', in Jennifer S. H. Brown and Elizabeth Vibert (eds), *Reading Beyond Words: Contexts for Native History*, Broadview Press, Peterborough, 2001, p.466.

82 Shawn Michelle Smith, *Photography on the Color Line: W. E. B. DuBois, Race, and Visual Culture*, Duke University Press, Durham, 2004, p.7.

83 Michael King, *Maori: A Photographic and Social History*, Reed, Wellington, 1996, p.2.

84 Sylvia Van Kirk, 'Tracing the Fortunes of Five Founding Families of Victoria, British Columbia', *BC Studies*, No.115/116, 1997/1998, p.151.

85 Anne Maxwell, *Colonial Photography and Exhibitions: Representations of the 'Native' People and the Making of European Identities*, Leicester University Press, London, 1999, p.13.

86 Maxwell, *Colonial Photography and Exhibitions*, p.163.

87 Barbara Brookes, 'Marriage: The Gendered Contract', in Barbara Brookes, Annabel Cooper and Robin Law (eds), *Sites of Gender: Women, Men and Modernity in Southern Dunedin, 1890–1939*, Auckland University Press, Auckland, 2003, p.354.

88 Anne Else, 'History Lessons: The Public History You Get When You're Not Getting Any Public History', in Bronwyn Dalley and Jock Phillips (eds), *Going Public: The Changing Face of New Zealand History*, Auckland University Press, Auckland, 2001, p.128. See also Deborah Chambers, 'Family as Place: Family Photograph Albums and the Domestication of Public and Private Space', in Joan M. Schwartz and James R. Ryan (eds), *Picturing Place: Photography and the Geographical Imagination*, I. B. Tauris, London, 2003, pp.96–114.

Bibliography

Archival Sources

Alexander Turnbull Library, Wellington

Coral Beattie Papers, Ms-Papers-4280-008
Mantell Family Papers, Ms-Group-0305
W. B. D. Mantell Journal, Ms-1543
W. B. D. Mantell Letterbook, qMs-1308
Edward Shortland Papers, qMs-1800
Andrew Sinclair Papers, Ms-1947
Weller Brothers Papers, Ms-Papers, 0872
J. F. H. Wohlers Papers, Ms-Papers-0428

Archives New Zealand, Christchurch

Land Alienation Files, CH 270
Probate Files: Christchurch (CH 171), Timaru (CH 729) and Greymouth (GM 3387)

Archives New Zealand, Dunedin

Commissioner of Crown Lands Outwards Letterbook, 1877–81, DAAK D124/1a
Probate Files: Otago and Southland, DAAC/D239, DAFG/9066, DAFG/9067, DAFG/9068, DAFG/9069

Archives New Zealand, Wellington

Board of Inquiry into Native Affairs in New Zealand, 1856
    G51/1: Verbatim Evidence from 33 Witnesses
    G51/2: Additional Evidence relating to Maori
Legislative Council Records Group:
    LE 1/38 1863/116 Box 31: Correspondence regarding promises of land
Lands and Surveys Department Records Group:
    LS 1/41749 Box 398: Tatawai Fishing Reserve
Maori Affairs Records Group:
    MA 1 1892/2250: Letters to Native Minister
    MA 1/78 5/5/89: Clarendon XI
    MA 13/19: Land Claims of South Island Half-Castes
    MA 13/20: Land Claims of South Island Half-Castes
    MA 13/21: Land Claims of South Island Half-Castes
    MA 23: Papers relating to the Maori Census
    MA 67: Evidence of Witnesses, Smith-Nairn Commission, 1879–80
    MA 72: Minutes of Evidence, Royal Commission on Middle Island Native Land Claims
Maori Affairs and Maori Trustee Records Group
    MA-MT 6/15: Volume of Papers relating to Native Reserves
    MA-MT 6/19: Schedule of Native Reserves in the South Island
Maori Land Court Records Group
    MLC AccW2218 Box 17: Cancelled Court Applications (South Island)
    MLC AccW2218 Box 26 n.125: Taieri
    MLC 8/1: Inwards Letters to Judge Mackay

Old Land Claims Records Group
    OLC 1: Old Land Claims Case Files
    OLC 4/20: Half-Caste Land Claims
    OLC 6/1: Registered Files, 1856–1860
Registers of Inwards Correspondence
    CS 2/1: Register of Inwards Correspondence to the Civil Secretary
    CS 2/2: Register of Inwards Correspondence to the Civil Secretary
    G 22/1: Register of Correspondence to the Governor, 1840–1870
    MA 2/1: Register of Correspondence to the Maori Affairs Department, 1840–47
Waitutu Survey District: ABWN 6095 AccW5021 22/1099/15 Part 1 Box 571

Canterbury Museum Documentary Research Centre, Christchurch

Jenny Murray, *Archival Material in the Registers of the Native Affairs Department and the Canterbury Provincial Council*, ARC1989/59
H. K. Taiaroa Papers
W. A. Taylor Papers

Hocken Library, Dunedin

Anglican Diocese of Dunedin Records
Anglican Parish Register, St Pauls Church, Dunedin, 1852–1865
Anglican Parish Registers, St Peters Church, Caversham, 1864–1912
Balclutha Old Cemetery Headstones and Burial Records
James Herries Beattie Papers, Ms-582, PC-174
Brinns Point, Karitane and Puketeraki Cemeteries and Headstones, 1840–1984
East Taieri Cemetery Headstone Transcript 1855–1999
First Church Marriage Register, 1848–1920
Henley Maori Cemetery Transcript of Headstones
Henley School Records
Charles Kettle, Letterbook, William Cargill Papers, Ms-0083
Knox Church Marriage Register Vols 1 and 2
W. B. D. Mantell Collection, Misc-Ms-0424
William Martin, Diary, Ms-0204
William Martin, Reminiscences, Ms-0206
Otokia Cemetery, Headstones and Burial Register, 1858–1980
Register of Baptisms, Ruapuke, 1850–1885
Register of Marriages, Ruapuke, 1850–1882
Ruapuke Registers (Vol.4) Miscellaneous Births, Baptisms, Deaths, Marriages 1844–1885
Taieri Beach Cemetery, Transcript of Plan, Headstones and Incomplete Burial Records, 1879–1879
G. C. Thomson Papers, Ms-0438, Ms-0439, Ms-0440, PC-025
Tokomairiro Anglican Parish Registers, St John's Church, Milton, 1864–1923
Tokomairiro Presbyterian Marriage Register Transcripts 1860–1922

Land Information New Zealand, Dunedin

Deeds Register Books

New Zealand Room, Christchurch Central Library

Holy Trinity Anglican Church, Lyttelton, Baptismal Register 1851–1858
Holy Trinity Anglican Church, Lyttelton, Marriage Registers 1880–1920
The Register of Bishop Harper's Country Baptism Book

Macmillan Brown Library, University of Canterbury, Christchurch

Te Runanga o Ngai Tahu Collection
South Island Maori Land Court Minute Books Vols 1–40
Wellington Maori Land Court Minute Books Vols 44–45
Wellington and Ikaroa Appellate Minute Book 6
Wellington and South Island Appellate Minute Book 4

McNab Room, Dunedin Public Library

Bill Dacker Oral History Collection
W. H. S. Roberts Newspaper Cuttings, Vols 2, 3 and 5

Otago Settlers Museum, Dunedin

John Bowie Papers, AB 42
Margaret Shaw Papers, AG 71
The Visitation Book of Reverend Thomas Burns, 1848–1858

Te Waipounamu Maori Land Court, Christchurch

Clarendon Block Files, Box 36
South Island Landless Natives Act Block Files
South Island Native Land Court Minute Books, Vols 41–55
Taieri Native Reserve Block Files, Boxes 256–263

Private Collections

Coral Beattie
Cath Brown
David Brown
Jenny Garth
Allan Lavell

Ted Palmer
Cecily Parker
Te Maire Tau
Shirley Tindall

Informants

Written Communications

Alex, 3 June 2003
Beverley, 10 June 2003
Cecily, 10 June 2003
Chris, 25 June 2003
Claire, 3 June 2003
Colin, 24 July 2003
Colin B., 14 July 2003
Dale, 3 June 2003
Dianne, 31 August 2003
Elizabeth, undated
Ian, 10 June 2003
Ian M., 2 July 2003
Janelle, 24 June 2003
Jeanette, undated

Jim, 31 May 2003
Joy, 5 June 2003
Justine, 24 July 2003
Kevin, 2 July 2003
Lillian, 10 June 2003
Marilyn, 27 January 2004
Marna, 10 March 2003
Nora, 3 June 2003
Rex, 17 June 2003
Murray, 4 June 2003
Noeline, 29 June 2003
Shirley A., 6 June 2003, 7 June 2003
Stu, 6 June 2003
Ted, 4 March 2003

Interviews

Allan, 20 July 2003
Brian, 14 December 2003
Coral, 22 June 2003
Dale, 11 June 2003
David, 23 March 2003, 25 April 2003
Elizabeth, 18 December 2003
Hazel, 19 June 2003
Ian, 20 June 2003

Irene, 14 December 2003
Malcolm, 12 June 2003
Maraea, 24 January 2003, 14 May 2003
Martin, 8 April 2003
Rona, 25 June 2003
Shirley, 15 June 2003
Stephen, 12 April 2003
Ted, 9 April 2003

Official Publications

Appendices to the Journals of the House of Representatives (AJHR)
British Parliamentary Papers. Colonies: New Zealand
New Zealand Census, 1871–1936
New Zealand Parliamentary Debates (NZPD)
New Zealand Gazette
New Zealand Official Yearbook
New Zealand Statistics
New Zealand Statutes
Statistics of New Zealand, 1857–1867

Periodicals

Otago Daily Times
Otago Witness
The Press, (Christchurch)
Wise's New Zealand Post Office Directory, 1878–1925
Stone's Otago and Southland Directory, 1890–1929

Published Secondary Sources

Acker Family Reunion Committee, *Acker Family, 1834–1984*, Acker Family Reunion Committee, Invercargill, 1984

Anderson, Atholl and Te Maire Tau (eds), *Ngāi Tahu: A Migration History. The Carrington Text*, Bridget Williams Books, Wellington, 2008

Anderson, Atholl, 'Historical and Archaeological Aspects of Muttonbirding in New Zealand', *New Zealand Journal of Archaeology*, Vol.17, 1995, pp.35–55

Anderson, Atholl, 'Maori Settlement in the Interior of Southern New Zealand from the Early 18th to Late 19th Centuries A.D.', *Journal of the Polynesian Society*, Vol.91, 1982, pp.53–80

Anderson, Atholl, *Race against Time: The Early Maori-Pakeha Families and the Development of the Mixed-race Population in Southern New Zealand*, Hocken Library, Dunedin, 1991

Anderson, Atholl, *The Welcome of Strangers: An Ethnohistory of Southern Maori A.D. 1650–1850*, Otago University Press, Dunedin, 1998

Anderson, Atholl, 'Towards an Explanation of Protohistoric Social Organisation and Settlement Patterns Amongst the Southern Ngai Tahu', *New Zealand Journal of Archaeology*, Vol.2, 1980, pp.2–23

Anderson, Atholl, *When All the Moa Ovens Grew Cold: Nine Centuries of Changing Fortune for the Southern Maori*, Otago Heritage Books, Dunedin, 1983

Anderson, Benedict, *Imagined Communities: Reflections on the Origin and Spread of Nationalism*, Verso, London, 1991

Armstrong, M. Jocelyn, 'Maori Identity in the South Island of New Zealand: Ethnic Identity Development in a Migration Context', *Oceania*, Vol.57, No.3, 1987, pp.195–216

Axtell, James, 'The White Indians of Colonial America', in Peter C. Mancall and James H. Merrell (eds), *American Encounters: Natives and Newcomers from European Contact to Indian Removal*, Routledge, London, 2000, pp.324–50

Backhouse, Constance, *Colour-Coded: A Legal History of Racism in Canada, 1900–1950*, University of Toronto Press, Toronto, 1999

Ballantyne, Tony and Antoinette Burton (eds), *Bodies in Contact: Rethinking Colonial Encounters in World History*, Duke University Press, Durham, 2005

Ballantyne, Tony and Antoinette Burton (eds), *Moving Subjects: Gender, Mobility and Intimacy in an Age of Empire*, University of Illinois Press, Urbana, 2008

Ballara, Angela, *Iwi: The Dynamics of Maori Tribal Organization from c. 1769 to c. 1945*, Victoria University Press, Wellington, 1998

Ballara, Angela, *Proud to be White? A Survey of Pakeha Prejudice in New Zealand*, Heinemann, Auckland, 1986

Ballhatchet, Kenneth, *Race, Sex and Class Under the Raj: Imperial Attitudes and Policies and their Critics, 1793–1905*, Weidenfeld & Nicolson, London, 1980

Barman, Jean, *Stanley Park's Secret: The Forgotten Families of Whoi Whoi, Kanaka Ranch and Brockton Point*, Harbour Publishing, Vancouver, 2005

Barman, Jean, 'Taming Aboriginal Sexuality: Gender, Power, and Race in British Columbia, 1850–1900', *BC Studies*, No.115/116, 1997/98, pp.237–66

Beaglehole, Ernst and Pearl Beaglehole, *Some Modern Maoris*, New Zealand Council for Educational Research, Wellington, 1946

Beattie, Coral, 'Palmer, William McLeur (1815–1903)', in J. Thomson (ed.), *Southern People: A Dictionary of Otago Southland Biography*, Dunedin City Council/Longacre Press, Dunedin, 1998, pp.375–6

Beattie, James Herries, *The First White Boy Born in Otago: The Story of T.B. Kennard*, Reed, Dunedin, 1939

Beattie, James Herries, *Traditional Lifeways of the Southern Maori*, Atholl Anderson (ed.), Otago University Press, Dunedin, 1994

Beattie, Herries, *Maori Place-names of Otago*, Otago Daily Times & Witness Newspapers, Dunedin, 1944

Beattie, Herries, *Our Southernmost Maoris*, Otago Daily Times & Witness Newspapers, Dunedin, 1954

Belich, James, *Making Peoples: A History of the New Zealanders from Polynesian Settlement to the End of the Nineteenth Century*, Penguin, Auckland, 1996

Bell, Leonard, '"Pictures as History, Settlement as Theatre": John Davis's Photo-Portrait of Robert Louis Stevenson and Family at Vailima, Samoa, 1892', *Journal of New Zealand Literature*, Vol.21, 2002, pp.93–111

Bennion, Tom and Judy Boyd, *Succession to Maori Land, 1900–52*, Waitangi Tribunal, Wellington, 1997

Bennion, Tom, *The Maori Land Court and Land Boards, 1909–1952*, Waitangi Tribunal, Wellington, 1997

Bentley, Trevor, *Pakeha Maori: The Extraordinary Story of the Europeans who Lived as Maori in Early New Zealand*, Penguin, Auckland, 1999

Bhabha, Homi K., *The Location of Culture*, Routledge, London, 1994

Biggs, Bruce, *Maori Marriage: An Essay in Reconstruction*, Reed, Wellington, 1960

Binney, Judith, 'Contested Ground: Australian and Aborigines under the British Crown. Edited by Ann McGrath', *New Zealand Journal of History*, Vol.30, No.1, 1996, p.87

Binney, Judith, '"In-Between" Lives: Studies from within a Colonial Society', in Tony Ballantyne and Brian Moloughney (eds), *Disputed Histories: Imagining New Zealand's Pasts*, Otago University Press, Dunedin, 2006, pp.93–118

Bishop, Russell, *Collaborative Research Stories: Whakawhanaungatanga*, Dunmore Press, Palmerston North, 1996

Brooking, Tom, *Lands for the People? The Highland Clearances and the Colonisation of New Zealand: A Biography of John McKenzie*, Otago University Press, Dunedin, 1996

Brookes, Barbara and Margaret Tennant, 'Maori and Pakeha Women: Many Histories, Divergent Pasts?', in Barbara Brookes, Charlotte Macdonald and Margaret Tennant (eds), *Women in History 2*, Bridget Williams Books, Wellington, 1992, pp.25–48

Brookes, Barbara, 'Marriage: The Gendered Contract', in Barbara Brookes, Annabel Cooper and Robin Law (eds), *Sites of Gender: Women, Men and Modernity in Southern Dunedin, 1890–1939*, Auckland University Press, Auckland, 2003, pp.348–55

Brookes, Barbara, 'Taking Private Life Seriously: Marriage and Nationhood', *History Compass*, Vol.1, No.1, November 2003, pp.1–4

Brown, Alison and Laura Peers, *'Pictures Bring Us Messages'/Sinaakssiiksi Aohtsimaahpihkookiyaawa: Photographs and Histories from the Kainai Nation*, University of Toronto Press, Toronto, 2006

Brown, Jennifer S. H., *Strangers in Blood: Fur Trade Company Families in Indian Country*, University of British Columbia Press, Vancouver, 1980

Brownlie, Robin Jarvis, 'Intimate Surveillance: Indian Affairs, Colonization, and the Regulation of Aboriginal Women's Sexuality', in Katie Pickles and Myra Rutherdale (eds), *Contact Zones: Aboriginal and Settler Women in Canada's Colonial Past*, University of British Columbia Press, Vancouver, 2006, pp.160–78

Burton, Antoinette, 'Rules of Thumb: British History and "Imperial Culture" in Nineteenth- and Twentieth-century Britain', *Women's History Review*, Vol.3, No.4, 1994, pp.483–501

Burton, Antoinette, 'Some Trajectories of "Feminism" and "Imperialism"', *Gender and History*, Vol.10, No.3, 1998, pp.558–68

Burton, Antoinette, 'Thinking Beyond the Boundaries: Empire, Feminism and the Domains of History', *Social History*, Vol.26, No.1, 2001, pp.60–71

Byrnes, Giselle, *Boundary Markers: Land Surveying and the Colonisation of New Zealand*, Bridget Williams Books, Wellington, 2001

Byrnes, Giselle, '"The Imperfect Authority of the Eye": Shortland's Southern Journey and the Calligraphy of Colonisation', *History and Anthropology*, Vol.8, Nos 1–4, 1994, pp.207–35

Caldwell, Russell, *Whakapapa Ngai Tahu: A Guide to Enrolment and Research*, Te Runanga o Ngai Tahu, Christchurch, 1996

Campbell, I. C., *'Gone Native' in Polynesia: Captivity Narratives and Experiences from the South Pacific*, Greenwood Press, Connecticut, 1998

Campbell, Matthew, 'A Site Survey of Whaling Stations on the Southern Coast of the South Island', *Archaeology in New Zealand*, Vol.36, No.3, 1993, pp.135–46

Carrick, R. O., *Historical Records of New Zealand South prior to 1840*, Otago Daily Times & Witness Newspapers, Dunedin, 1903

Carter, Sarah A., 'Creating "Semi-Widows" and "Supernumerary Wives": Prohibiting Polygamy in Prairie Canada's Aboriginal Communities to 1900', in Katie Pickles and Myra Rutherdale (eds), *Contact Zones: Aboriginal and Settler Women in Canada's Colonial Past*, University of British Columbia Press, Vancouver, 2006, pp.131–59

Carter, Sarah, *The Importance of Being Monogamous: Marriage and Nation Building in Western Canada to 1915*, University of Alberta Press, Edmonton, 2008

Chambers, Deborah, 'Family as Place: Family Photograph Albums and the Domestication of Public and Private Space', in Joan M. Schwartz and James R. Ryan (eds), *Picturing Place: Photography and the Geographical Imagination*, I. B. Tauris, London, 2003, pp.96–114

Christie, John, *History of Waikouaiti*, Christchurch Press Company, Christchurch, 1929

Clarke, George, *Notes on Early Life in New Zealand*, Walch & Sons, Hobart, 1903

Colley, Linda, 'Going Native, Telling Tales: Captivity, Collaborations and Empire', *Past and Present*, No.168, 2000, pp.170–93

Coney, Sandra, *I Do: 125 Years of Weddings in New Zealand*, Hodder Moa Beckett, Auckland, 1995

Coney, Sandra (ed.), *Standing in the Sunshine: A History of New Zealand Women since They Won the Vote*, Viking, Auckland, 1993

Cooper, Annabel, Erik Olssen, Kirsten Thomlinson and Robin Law, 'The Landscape of Gender Politics: Place, People and Two Mobilisations', in Barbara Brookes, Annabel Cooper and Robin Law (eds), *Sites of Gender: Women, Men and Modernity in Southern Dunedin, 1890–1939*, Auckland University Press, Auckland, 2003, pp.15–49

Cott, Nancy F., *Public Vows: A History of Marriage and the Nation*, Harvard University Press, Cambridge, MA, 2000

Coutts, P. J., 'Merger or Takeover: A Survey of the Effects of Contact Between European and Maori in the Foveaux Strait Region', *Journal of the Polynesian Society*, Vol.78, No.4, 1969, pp.495–516

Coutts, Peter J. F., 'An Approach to the Investigation of Colonial Settlement Patterns: Whaling in Southern New Zealand', *World Archaeology*, Vol.7, No.3, 1976, pp.291–305

Dacker, Bill, 'H. K. Taiaroa and Te Kerema: Crisis and Leadership in the Nineteenth Century', in Michael Reilly and Jane Thomson (eds), *When the Waves Rolled in Upon Us: Essays in Nineteenth-century Maori History*, Otago University Press, Dunedin, 1999, pp.75–91

Dacker, Bill, *Te Mamae me te Aroha: The Pain and the Love: A History of Kai Tahu Whānui in Otago, 1844–1994*, Otago University Press, Dunedin, 1994

Dalziel, Raewyn, '"Making Us One": Courtship and Marriage in Colonial New Zealand', *Turnbull Library Record*, Vol.19, No.1, 1986, pp.7–26

Dalziel, Raewyn, 'Men, Women and Wakefield', in Friends of the Turnbull Library, *Edward Gibbon Wakefield and the Colonial Dream: A Reconsideration*, GP Books, Wellington, 1997, pp.77–86

Dawson, Lew, *Taproots Revisited: The Whakapapa of Wharetutu and George Newton, 1828 to the Present*, Taproots Research, Invercargill, 1986

Dennis, J., 'McDonald, James Ingram, 1865–1935', in Claudia Orange (ed.), *The Dictionary of New Zealand Biography: Volume Three (1901–1930)*, Ministry for Culture and Heritage, Wellington, 1996

Dieffenbach, Ernst, *Travels in New Zealand*, first published in 1845, reissued by Capper Press, Christchurch, 1974

Durwood, Elizabeth W., 'The Maori Population of Otago', *Journal of the Polynesian Society*, Vol.42, 1933, pp.49–82

Eber, Dorothy Harley, *When the Whalers Were Up North: Inuit Memories from the Eastern Artic*, McGill-Queen's University Press, Kingston, 1989

Eccles, Alfred and A. H. Reed, *John Jones of Otago: Whaler, Coloniser, Shipowner and Merchant*, Reed, Wellington, 1949

Edwards, Elizabeth and Janice Hart (eds), *Photographs, Objects, Histories: On the Materiality of Images*, Routledge, London, 2004

Edwards, Elizabeth (ed.), *Anthropology and Photography, 1860–1920*, Yale University Press, New Haven, 2002

Ellinghaus, Katherine, 'Margins of Acceptability: Class, Education, and Interracial Marriage in Australia and North America', *Frontiers*, Vol.23, No.3, 2002, pp.55–75

Ellinghaus, Katherine, 'Reading the Personal as Political: The Assimilationist Views of a White Woman Married to a Native American Man, 1880s–1940s', *Australasian Journal of American Studies*, Vol.18, No.2, 1999, pp.23–42

Ellinghaus, Katherine, *Taking Assimilation to Heart: Marriages of White Women and Indigenous Men in the United States and Australia, 1887–1937*, University of Nebraska Press, Lincoln, 2006

Ellis, Georgina, *Time and Tide: Ramblings, Recollections and Reminiscences of the Spencer Family*, Georgina Ellis, Invercargill, 2000

Else, Anne, 'History Lessons: The Public History You Get When You're Not Getting Any Public History', in Bronwyn Dalley and Jock Phillips (eds), *Going Public: The Changing Face of New Zealand History*, Auckland University Press, Auckland, 2001, pp.123–40

Entwisle, Peter, *Behold the Moon: The European Occupation of the Dunedin District, 1770–1848*, Port Daniel Press, Dunedin, 1998

Evans, Rex, Adriene Evans and Janet Old, *A Haberfield Genealogy*, Evagean Publishers, Auckland, 1996

Evison, Harry C., *The Long Dispute: Maori Land Rights and European Colonisation in Southern New Zealand*, Canterbury University Press, Christchurch, 1993

Evison, Harry C., *Te Wai Pounamu: The Greenstone Island. A History of the Southern Maori during the European Colonization of New Zealand*, Aoraki Press, Christchurch, 1993

Faragher, John Mack, 'The Custom of the Country: Cross-Cultural Marriage in the Far Western Fur Trade', in Lillian Schlissel, Vicki L. Ruiz and Janice Monk (eds), *Western Women: Their Land, Their Lives*, University of New Mexico Press, Albuquerque, 1988, pp.199–216

Fargher, Ray, *The Best Man Who Ever Served the Crown? A Life of Donald McLean*, Victoria University Press, Wellington, 2007

Fenton, F. D., *Observations on the State of the Aboriginal Inhabitants of New Zealand*, Government Printer, Auckland, 1859

Gibbons, Peter, 'The Far Side of the Search for Identity: Reconsidering New Zealand History', *New Zealand Journal of History*, Vol.37, No.1, 2003, pp.38–49

Goodall, Maaire and George Griffiths, *Maori Dunedin*, Otago Heritage Books, Dunedin, 1980

Grady, Don, *Sealers and Whalers in New Zealand Waters*, Reed Methuen, Auckland, 1986

Grimshaw, Patricia, 'Interracial Marriage and Colonial Regimes in Victoria and Aotearoa/New Zealand', *Frontiers*, Vol.23, No.3, 2002, pp.12–28

Haines, David, 'In Search of the "Whaheen": Ngai Tahu Women, Shore Whalers, and the Meaning of Sex in Early New Zealand', in Tony Ballantyne and Antoinette Burton (eds), *Moving Subjects: Gender, Mobility, and Intimacy in an Age of Global Empire*, University of Illinois Press, Urbana, 2009

Hall, Catherine (ed.), *Cultures of Empire: Colonizers in Britain and the Empire in the Nineteenth and Twentieth Centuries: A Reader*, Manchester University Press, Manchester, 2000

Hall-Jones, F. G., *Kelly of Inverkelly*, Southland Historical Committee, Invercargill, 1944

Hall-Jones, John, *Bluff Harbour*, Southland Harbour Board, Bluff, 1976

Hall-Jones, John, *Stewart Island Explored*, Craig Printing, Invercargill, 1994

Hall-Jones, John, *The South Explored*, Reed, Wellington, 1979

Hamel, Jill, *The Archaeology of Otago*, Department of Conservation, Wellington, 2001

Hanning, Tony, *'The Whaler and the Princess': Irihapeti Patahi and Edwin Palmer*, Tony Hanning, Dunedin, 2000

Harrē, John, *Maori and Pakeha: A Study of Mixed Marriages in New Zealand*, Reed, Wellington, 1966

Harrē, John, 'Maori-Pakeha Intermarriage', in E. Schwimmer (ed.), *The Maori People of the Nineteen-Sixties*, Longman Paul, Auckland, 1968, pp.118–31

Harrē, John, 'The Relevance of Ancestry as a Factor in Social and Cultural Choice', *Journal of the Polynesian Society*, Vol.74, No.1, 1965, pp.3–20

Harris, Cole, *Making Native Space: Colonialism, Resistance, and Reserves in British Columbia*, University of British Columbia Press, Vancouver, 2002

Hawes, Christopher, *Poor Relations: The Making of a Eurasian Community in British India, 1773–1833*, Curzon Press, Richmond, 1996

Heenan, L. B. D., 'The Changing South Island Maori Population', *New Zealand Geographer*, Vol.22, No.2, 1966, pp.125–65

Heuer, Berys E., 'Maori Women in Traditional Family and Tribal Life', *Journal of the Polynesian Society*, Vol.78, No.4, 1969, pp.448–94

Hight, Eleanor M. and Gary D. Sampson (eds), *Colonialist Photography: Imag(in)ing Race and Place*, Routledge, London, 2002

Hirsch, Julia, *Family Photographs: Content, Meaning and Effect*, Oxford University Press, Oxford, 1981

Hirsch, Marianne (ed.), *Family Frames: Photography, Narrative and Postmemory*, Harvard University Press, Cambridge, MA, 1997

Hocken, Thomas M. *Contributions to the Early History of New Zealand (Settlement of Otago)*, Sampson, Low, Marston and Company, London, 1898

Hodes, Martha, 'Fractions and Fictions in the United States Census of 1890', in Ann Laura Stoler (ed.), *Haunted By Empire: Geographies of Intimacy in North American History*, Duke University Press, Durham, 2006, pp.240–70

Holm, Janet, *Caught Mapping: The Life and Times of New Zealand's Early Surveyors*, Hazard Press, Christchurch, 2005

Hohepa, Pat and David V. Williams, *The Taking into Account of Te Ao Maori in Relation to the Reform of the Law of Succession*, Law Commission, Wellington, 1996

Horowitz, Helen Lefkowitz and Kathy Peiss (eds), *Love Across the Color Line: The Letters of Alice Hanley to Channing Lewis*, University of Massachusetts Press, Amherst, 1996

Howard, Basil, *Rakiura: A History of Stewart Island, New Zealand*, Reed, Dunedin, 1940

Jacobs, Margaret D., 'The Eastmans and the Luhans: Interracial Marriage between White Women and Native American Men, 1875–1935', *Frontiers*, Vol.23, No.3, 2002, pp.29–54

Johnson, Ralph, *The Trust Administration of Maori Reserves, 1840–1913*, Waitangi Tribunal, Wellington, 1997

Kelly, Robert, *John Kelly, Sealer, Whaler, Trader, Boatman: Piecing Together the Jig-saw of an Early Southland Pioneer*, Weranui Publications, Waiwera, 2001

Kelm, Mary-Ellen, *Colonizing Bodies: Aboriginal Health and Healing in British Columbia, 1900–50*, University of British Columbia Press, Vancouver, 2001

King, Michael, 'Between Two Worlds', in G.W. Rice (ed.), *The Oxford History of New Zealand*, 2nd edn, Oxford University Press, Auckland, 1995, pp.285–307

King, Michael, *Maori: A Photographic and Social History*, Reed, Wellington, 1996

King, Michael, *The Penguin History of New Zealand*, Penguin, Auckland, 2003

Knight, Hardwicke, *Photography in New Zealand: A Social and Technical History*, John McIndoe, Dunedin, 1971

Landau, P. S., 'Empires of the Visual: Photography and Colonial Administration in Africa', in Paul S. Landau and Deborah D. Kaspin (eds), *Images and Empires: Visuality in Colonial and Postcolonial Africa*, University of California Press, Berkeley, 2002, pp.141–71

Langford, Martha, *Suspended Conversations: The Afterlife of Memory in Photographic Albums*, McGill-Queen's University Press, Montreal and Kingston, 2001

Lydon, Jane, *Eye Contact: Photographing Indigenous Australians*, Duke University Press, Durham, 2005

MacIntosh, Joan, *A History of Fortrose*, Times Printing, Invercargill, 1975

Mackay, Alexander, *A Compendium of Official Documents Relative to Native Affairs in the South Island: Volume I*, Government Printer, Wellington, 1872

Mackay, Alexander, *A Compendium of Official Documents Relative to Native Affairs in the South Island: Volume II*, Government Printer, Wellington, 1872

Main, William, *Facing an Era: Postcard Portraits from a Century ago*, Exposures, Wellington, 2006

Main, William, *Maori in Focus: A Selection of Photographs of the Maori from 1850–1914*, Millwood, Wellington, 1976

Malloch, Donald W., *Early Waikouaiti*, Otago Daily Times, Dunedin, 1940

Margolis, Eric and Jeremy Rowe, 'Images of Assimilation: Photographs of Indian Schools in Arizona', *History of Education*, Vol.33, No.2, 2004, pp.199–204

Margolis, Eric, 'Looking at Discipline, Looking at Labour: Photographic Representations of Indian Boarding Schools', *Visual Studies*, Vol.19, No.1, 2004, pp.72–96

Mawani, Renisa, 'In Between and Out of Place: Mixed-Race Identity, Liquor, and the Law in British Columbia, 1850–1913', in Sherene H. Razack (ed.), *Race, Space and the Law: Unmapping a White Society*, Between the Lines, Toronto, 2002, pp.47–70

Maxwell, Ann, *Colonial Photography and Exhibitions: Representations of the 'Native' and the Making of European Identities*, Leicester University Press, London, 1999

McAloon, Jim, 'Resource Frontiers, Environment and Settler Capitalism: 1769–1860', in Eric Pawson and Tom Brooking (eds), *Environmental Histories of New Zealand*, Oxford University Press, Oxford, 2002, pp.52–68

McClintock, Anne, *Imperial Leather: Race, Gender and Sexuality in the Colonial Conquest*, Routledge, London, 1995

McGrath, Ann, 'Consent, Marriage and Colonialism: Indigenous Australian Women and Colonizer Marriages', *Journal of Colonialism and Colonial History*, Vol.6, No.3, 2005

McLean, Gavin, *Moeraki: 150 Years of Net and Plough Share*, Otago Heritage Books, Dunedin, 1986

McLintock, A. H., *The History of Otago: The Origins and Growth of a Wakefield Class Settlement*, Otago Historical Centennial Publications, Dunedin, 1949

McManus, Sheila, *The Line Which Separates: Race, Gender, and the Making of the Alberta-Montana Borderlands*, University of Nebraska Press, Lincoln, 2005

McNab, Robert, *Murihiku and the Southern Islands*, William Smith, Invercargill, 1907

McNab, Robert, *The Old Whaling Days: A History of Southern New Zealand from 1830 to 1840*, Whitcombe & Tombs, Christchurch, 1913

McRae, Jane, '"E Manu, Tena Koe! O Bird, Greetings to You": The Oral Tradition in Newspaper Writing', in Jenifer Curnow, Ngapare Hopa and Jane McRae (eds), *Rere Atu, Taku Manu! Discovering History, Language and Politics in the Maori-language Newspapers*, Auckland University Press, Auckland, 2002, pp.42–59

Metge, Joan, *New Growth From Old: The Whanau in the Modern World*, Victoria University Press, Wellington, 1995

Metge, Joan, *The Maoris of New Zealand*, Keegan & Paul, London, 1967

Middleton, Angela, *Two Hundred Years on Codfish Island (Whenua Hou): From Cultural Encounter to Nature Conservation*, Department of Conservation, Wellington, 2007

Midgley, Clare (ed.), *Gender and Imperialism*, Manchester University Press, Manchester, 1998

Miller, J. R., 'Reading Photographs, Reading Voices: Documenting the History of Native Residential Schools', in Jennifer S.H. Brown and Elizabeth Vibert (eds), *Reading Beyond Words: Contexts for Native History*, 2nd edn, Broadview Press, Peterborough, 2001, pp.460–82

Mohammed, Patricia, '"But most of all mi love me browning": The Emergence in Eighteenth- and Nineteenth-century Jamaica of the Mulatto Woman as the Desired', *Feminist Review*, No.65, 2000, pp.22–48

Monin, Paul, *This Is My Place: Hauraki Contested, 1769–1875*, Bridget Williams Books, Wellington, 2001

Morton, Harry, *The Whale's Wake*, Otago University Press, Dunedin, 1982

Murphy, Lucy Eldersveld, 'Public Mothers: Native American and Metis Women as Creole Mediators in the Nineteenth Century Midwest', *Journal of Women's History*, Vol.14, No.2, 2003, pp.142–66

Murray, J. E., *Crown Policy on Maori Reserved Lands, 1840 to 1865, and Lands Restricted From Alienation, 1865 to 1900*, Waitangi Tribunal, Wellington, 1997

Natusch, Sheila, *Brother Wohlers: A Biography of J. F. H. Wohlers of Ruapuke*, 2nd edn, Caxton Press, Christchurch, 1992

Natusch, Sheila, 'Wohlers, Johann Friedrich Heinrich, 1811–1885', in W. H. Oliver (ed.), *The Dictionary of New Zealand Biography: Volume 1, 1769–1869*, Allen & Unwin/Department of Internal Affairs, Wellington, 1990, pp.606–7

Nobles, Melissa, 'Racial Categorization and Censuses', in David I. Kertzer and Dominique Arel (eds), *Census and Identity: The Politics of Race, Ethnicity and Language in National Censuses*, Cambridge University Press, Cambridge, 2002, pp.43–70

Olssen, Erik and Andree Levesque, 'Towards a History of the European Family in New Zealand', in Peggy G. Koopman-Boyden (ed.), *Families in New Zealand Society*, Methuen, Wellington, 1978, pp.1–25

Olssen, Erik, *A History of Otago*, John McIndoe, Dunedin, 1984

Olssen, Erik, *Building the New World: Work, Politics and Society in Caversham 1880s–1920s*, Auckland University Press, Auckland, 1995

Olssen, Erik, 'Families and the Gendering of European New Zealand in the Colonial Period, 1840–1880', in Caroline Daley and Deborah Montgomerie (eds), *The Gendered Kiwi*, Auckland University Press, Auckland, 1999, pp.37–62

Olssen, Erik, 'Towards a New Society', in G.W. Rice (ed.), *The Oxford History of New Zealand*, 2nd edn, Oxford University Press, Oxford, 1995, pp.254–84

Olssen, Erik, 'Women, Work and Family: 1880–1920', in Phillida Bunkle and Beryl Hughes (eds), *Women in New Zealand Society*, George Allen & Unwin, Auckland, 1980, pp.159–83

Olssen, Erik, 'Where to from Here? Reflections on the Twentieth-century Historiography of Nineteenth-century New Zealand', *New Zealand Journal of History*, Vol.26, No.1, 1992, pp.54–77

O'Regan, Hana, *Ko Tahu, Ko Au*, Horomaka Press, Christchurch, 2001

O'Regan, Tipene, 'Old Myths and New Politics: Some Contemporary Uses of Traditional History', *New Zealand Journal of History*, Vol.26, No.1, pp.5–27

Orbell, Margaret, 'The Traditional Maori Family', in Peggy G. Koopman-Boyden (ed.), *Families in New Zealand Society*, Methuen, Wellington, 1978, pp.104–19

Page, Dorothy, Howard Lee and Tom Brooking, 'Schooling for a Gendered Future: Gender, Education and Opportunity', in Barbara Brookes, Annabel Cooper and Robin Law (eds), *Sites of Gender: Women, Men and Modernity in Southern Dunedin, 1890–1939*, Auckland University Press, Auckland, 2003, pp.91–122

Park, Geoff, *Effective Exclusion? An Exploratory Overview of Crown Actions and Māori Responses Concerning the Indigenous Flora and Fauna, 1912–1983*, Waitangi Tribunal, Wellington, 2001

Park, Geoff, '"Swamps which might doubtless easily be drained": Swamp Drainage and its Impact on the Indigenous', in Eric Pawson and Tom Brooking (eds), *Environmental Histories of New Zealand*, Oxford University Press, Oxford, 2002, pp.151–68

Parkes, Win and Kath Hislop, *Taieri Mouth and its Surrounding Districts*, Otago Heritage Books, Dunedin, 1980

Parsonson, Ann, 'Ngāi Tahu – The Whale that Awoke: From Claim to Settlement (1960–1998)', in John Cookson and Graeme Dunstall (eds), *Southern Capital: Christchurch. Towards a City Biography, 1850–2000*, Canterbury University Press, Christchurch, 2000, pp.248–76

Parsonson, Ann, 'Stories for Land: Oral Narratives in the Maori Land Court', in Bain Attwood and Fiona Magowan (eds), *Telling Stories: Indigenous History and Memory in Australia and New Zealand*, Bridget Williams Books, Wellington, 2001, pp.21–40

Pascoe, Peggy, 'Miscegenation Law, Court Cases, and Ideologies of "Race" in Twentieth-century America', in Martha Hodes (ed.), *Sex, Love, Race: Crossing Boundaries in North American History*, New York University Press, New York, 1999, pp.464–90

Paterson, Lachy, *Colonial Discourses: Niupepa Māori, 1855–1863*, Otago University Press, Dunedin, 2006

Paterson, Lachy, 'Kiri Mā, Kiri Mangu: The Terminology of Race and Civilisation in the Mid-nineteenth-century Maori-language Newspapers', in Jenifer Curnow, Ngapare Hopa and Jane McRae (eds), *Rere Atu, Taku Manu! Discovering History, Language and Politics in the Maori-language Newspapers*, Auckland University Press, Auckland, 2002, pp.78–97

Perry, Adele, *On the Edge of Empire: Gender, Race, and the Making of British Columbia, 1849–1871*, University of Toronto Press, Toronto, 2001

Petrie, Hazel, *Chiefs of Industry: Māori Tribal Enterprise in Early Colonial New Zealand*, Auckland University Press, Auckland, 2006

Peterson, Jacqueline and Jennifer S. H. Brown (eds), *The New Peoples: Being and Becoming Métis in North America*, University of Manitoba Press, Winnipeg, 1985

Pickens, K. A., 'Marriage Patterns in a Nineteenth-century British Colonial Population', *Journal of Family History*, Vol.5, 1980, pp.180–96

Pickles, Katie and Myra Rutherdale (eds), *Contact Zones: Aboriginal and Settler Women in the Canadian Colonial Past*, University of British Columbia Press, Vancouver, 2005

Pickles, Katie, 'Locating Widows in Mid-nineteenth Century Pictou County, Nova Scotia', *Journal of Historical Geography*, Vol.30, No.1, 2004, pp.70–86

Pickles, Katie, 'The Re-Creation of Bottle Lake: From Site of Discard to Environmental Playground?', *Environment and History*, Vol.9, 2003, pp.419–34

Pool, Ian, *Te Iwi Maori: A New Zealand Population Past, Present and Projected*, Auckland University Press, Auckland, 1991

Porter, Frances and Charlotte Macdonald, with Tui MacDonald (eds), *My Hand Will Write What My Heart Dictates: The Unsettled Lives of Women in Nineteenth-century New Zealand as revealed to Sisters, Family and Friends*, Auckland University Press, Auckland, 1996

Posel, Deborah, 'A Mania for Measurement: Statistics and Statecraft in the Transition to Apartheid', in Saul Dubow (ed.), *Science and Society in South Africa*, Manchester University Press, Manchester, 2000, pp.116–42

Potiki, Tahu, 'Karetai Family of Otakou', in Jane Thomson (ed.), *Southern People: A Dictionary of Otago Southland Biography*, Dunedin City Council/Longacre Press, Dunedin, 1998, pp.263–5

Pratt, Mary Louise, *Imperial Eyes: Travel Writing and Transculturation*, Routledge, London/New York, 1992

Pybus, T. A., *Maori and Missionary: Early Christian Missions in the South Island of New Zealand*, Reed, Wellington, 1954

Pybus, T. A., *The Maoris of the South Island*, Reed, Wellington, 1954

Reid, Ken W., *The Reids of West Taieri*, Ken W. Reid, Mosgiel, 1990

Rice, Geoffrey W., *Heaton Rhodes of Otahuna: The Illustrated Biography*, Canterbury University Press, Christchurch, 2001

Riddell, Kate, '"Improving" the Maori: Counting the Ideology of Intermarriage', *New Zealand Journal of History*, Vol.34, No.1, 2000, pp.80–97

Robert, Hannah, 'Disciplining the Female Aboriginal Body: Inter-racial Sex and the Pretence of Separation', *Australian Feminist Studies*, Vol.16, No.34, 2001, pp.69–81

Roberts, W. H. S., *Maori Nomenclature: Early History of Otago*, Otago Daily Times & Witness Newspapers, Dunedin, 1910

Roberts, W. H. Sherwood, *Place Names and Early History of Otago and Southland with Other Interesting Information*, Southland Times, Invercargill, 1913

Russell, Lynette (ed.), *Colonial Frontiers: Indigenous-European Encounters in Settler Societies*, Manchester University Press, Manchester, 2001

Ryan, James R., *Picturing Empire: Photography and the Visualization of the British Empire*, University of Chicago Press, Chicago, 1997

Said, Edward W., *Culture and Imperialism*, Vintage, London, 1994

Salesa, Toeolesulusulu D., 'Half-Castes Between the Wars: Colonial Categories in New Zealand and Samoa', *New Zealand Journal of History*, Vol.34, No.1, 2000, pp.98–116

Sandweiss, Martha A., *Print the Legend: Photography and the American West*, Yale University Press, New Haven, 2002

Sassoon, Joanna, 'Becoming Anthropological: A Cultural Biography of E. L. Mitchell's Photographs of Aboriginal People', *Aboriginal History*, Vol.28, 2004, pp.59–86

Schwartz, Joan M. and James R. Ryan (eds), *Picturing Place: Photography and the Geographical Imagination*, I. B. Tauris, London, 2003

Scott, Linda J., Finlay Bayne and Michael J. F. O'Connor, *Nathaniel Bates of Riverton: His Families and Descendants*, Bates Reunion Committee, Christchurch, 1994

Shaw, Margaret S., *The Taieri Plain: Tales of the Years that are Gone*, Otago Centennial Publications, Dunedin, 1949

Shortland, Edward, *The Southern Districts of New Zealand: A Journal with Passing Notices of the Customs of the Aborigines*, Longman, Brown, Green and Longmans, London, 1851

Sleeper-Smith, Susan, *Indian Women and French Men: Rethinking Cultural Encounter in the Western Great Lakes*, University of Massachusetts Press, Amherst, 2001

Sleeper-Smith, Susan, 'Women, Kin and Catholicism: New Perspectives on the Fur Trade', *Ethnohistory*, Vol.47, No.2, 2000, pp.423–52

Smith, Linda Tuhiwai, *Decolonizing Methodologies: Research and Indigenous Peoples*, Otago University Press, Dunedin, 2001

Smith, Shawn Michelle, *Photography on the Color Line: W. E. B. DuBois, Race, and Visual Culture*, Duke University Press, Durham, 2004

Smith, Thelma, *Tai-ari Ferry and Henley 'Our Native Place': A Souvenir of the Schools Jubilee, 24th–27th January, 1941*, Otago Daily Times & Witness Newspapers, Dunedin, 1941

Sorrenson, M. P. K., 'How to Civilize Savages: Some "Answers" from Nineteenth-century New Zealand', *New Zealand Journal of History*, Vol.9, No.2, 1975, pp.97–110

Sorrenson, M. P. K., *Integration or Identity? Cultural Interaction: New Zealand Since 1911*, Heinemann, Auckland, 1977

Sorrenson, M. P. K., 'Land Purchase Methods and their Effect on Maori Population, 1865–1901', *Journal of the Polynesian Society*, Vol.65, No.2, 1956, pp.183–99

Sorrenson, M. P. K., *Maori and European since 1870: A Study in Adaptation and Adjustment*, Heinemann, Auckland, 1967

Spence, Jo and Patricia Holland (eds), *Family Snaps: The Meaning of Domestic Photography*, Virago, London, 1991

Spiller, Peter, Jeremy Finn and Richard Boast, *A New Zealand Legal History*, Brookers, Wellington, 1996

Stack, J. W., *South Island Maoris: A Sketch of their History and Legendary Lore*, Whitcombe & Tombs, Christchurch, 1898

Stenhouse, John, '"A Disappearing Race Before We Came Here": Doctor Alfred Kingcombe Newman, the Dying Maori, and Victorian Scientific Racism', *New Zealand Journal of History*, Vol.30, No.2, 1996, pp.124–40

Stepan, Nancy Leys, *Picturing Tropical Nature*, Reaktion Books, London, 2001

Stepan, Nancy Leys, *'The Hour of Eugenics': Race, Gender and Nation in Latin America*, Cornell University Press, Ithaca, 1991

Stevens, Michael, 'Kāi Tahu me te Hopu Tītī ki Rakiura: An Exception to the "Colonial Rule"?', *The Journal of Pacific History*, Vol.41, No.3, 2003, pp.273–91

Stoler, Ann Laura and Frederick Cooper, 'Between Metropole and Colony: Rethinking a Research Agenda', in Frederick Cooper and Ann Laura Stoler (eds), *Tensions of Empire: Colonial Cultures in a Bourgeois World*, University of California Press, Berkeley, 1997, pp.1–56

Stoler, Ann Laura, *Carnal Knowledge and Imperial Power: Race and the Intimate in Colonial Rule*, University of California Press, Berkeley, 2002

Stoler, Ann Laura, *Haunted By Empire: Geographies of Intimacy in North American History*, Duke University Press, Durham, 2006

Stoler, Ann Laura, 'Making Empire Respectable: The Politics of Race and Sexual Morality in 20th-century Colonial Cultures', *American Ethnologist*, Vol.16, 1989, pp.634–60

Stoler, Ann Laura, 'Sexual Affronts and Racial Frontiers: European Identities and the Cultural Politics of Exclusion in Colonial Southeast Asia', in Frederick Cooper and Ann Laura Stoler (eds), *Tensions of Empire: Colonial Cultures in a Bourgeois World*, University of California Press, Berkeley, 1997, pp.198–237

Stoler, Ann Laura, 'Tense and Tender Ties: The Politics of Comparison in North American History and (Post) Colonial Studies', *Journal of American History*, Vol.88, No.3, 2001, pp.829–65

Strobel, Margaret, *Gender, Sex and Empire*, American Historical Association, Washington, DC, 1993

Stuart, Ronald J., *Henley, Taieri Ferry and Otokia: A Schools and District History*, Reunion Committee, Outram, 1981

Sutherland, Gwen, *Coast, Road and River: The Story of Taieri Mouth, Taieri Beach, Glenledi and Akatore*, Clutha Leader Print, Invercargill, 1962

Sutton Beets, Jacqui, 'Images of Maori Women in New Zealand Postcards after 1900', in Alison Jones, Phyllis S. Herda and Tamasailau Suaalii (eds), *Bitter Sweet: Indigenous Women in the Pacific*, Otago University Press, Dunedin, 2000, pp.17–33

Swainson, William, *New Zealand and its Colonization*, Smith, Elder & Co., London, 1859

Tau, Rawiri Te Maire, *Ngā Pikitūroa o Ngāi Tahu: The Oral Traditions of Ngāi Tahu*, Otago University Press, Dunedin, 2003

Tau, Te Maire, 'Ngāi Tahu and the Canterbury Landscape – A Broad Context', in John Cookson and Graeme Dunstall (eds), *Southern Capital: Christchurch. Towards a City Biography, 1850–2000*, Canterbury University Press, Christchurch, 2000, pp.41–59

Taylor, W. A., *Lore and History of the South Island Maoris*, Bascands, Christchurch, 1950

Thomas, Nicholas, *Colonialism's Culture: Anthropology, Travel and Government*, Princeton University Press, New Jersey, 1994

Thomas, Nicholas, *Possessions: Indigenous Art/Colonial Culture*, Thames & Hudson, London, 1999

Thomson, Arthur S., *The Story of New Zealand Past and Present – Savage and Civilized Vol. II*, John Murray, London, 1859

Thorne, Tanis C., 'For the Good of Her People: Continuity and Change for Native Women of the Midwest, 1650–1850', in Lucy Eldersveld Murphy and Wendy Hamand Venet (eds), *Midwestern Women: Work, Community, and Leadership at the Crossroads*, Indiana University Press, Bloomington, 1997, pp.95–120

Thorp, Daniel, 'Going Native in New Zealand and America: Comparing Pakeha Maori and White Indians', *Journal of Imperial and Commonwealth History*, Vol.31, No.3, 2003, pp.1–23

Tipa, Gail, *Environmental Performance Indicators: Taieri River Case Study*, Ministry for the Environment, Wellington, 1999

Tsinhnahjnnie, H. J., 'When is a Photograph Worth a Thousand Words?', in Christopher Pinney and Nicolas Peterson (eds), *Photography's Other Histories*, Duke University Press, Durham, 2003, pp.40–52

Van Kirk, Sylvia, 'A Transborder Family in the Pacific North West: Reflecting on Race and Gender in Women's History', in Elizabeth Jameson and Sheila McManus (eds), *One Step Over the Line: Toward a History of Women in the North American Wests*, University of Alberta Press, Edmonton, 2008, pp.81–93

Van Kirk, Sylvia, 'From "Marrying-in" to "Marrying-out": Changing Patterns of Aboriginal/Non-aboriginal Marriage in Colonial Canada', *Frontiers*, Vol.23, No.3, 2002, pp.1–11

Van Kirk, Sylvia, '"What if Mama is an Indian?" The Cultural Ambivalence of the Alexander Ross Family', in Jacqueline Peterson and Jennifer S. H. Brown (eds), *The New Peoples: Being and Becoming Mētis in North America*, University of Manitoba Press, Winnipeg, 1985, pp.207–20

Van Kirk, Sylvia, *Many Tender Ties: Women in Fur-Trade Society, 1670–1870*, University of Oklahoma Press, Norman, 1980

Van Kirk, Sylvia, 'Tracing the Fortunes of Five Founding Families of Victoria', *BC Studies*, No.115/116, Autumn/Winter 1997/98, pp.148–79

Van Toorn, Penny, *Writing Never Arrives Naked: Early Aboriginal Cultures of Writing*, Aboriginal Studies Press, Canberra, 2006

Waitangi Tribunal, *The Ngai Tahu Ancillary Claims Report 1995*, Waitangi Tribunal, Wellington, 1995

Waitangi Tribunal, *The Ngai Tahu Report 1991*, Waitangi Tribunal, Wellington, 1991

Wakefield, E. J., *Adventure in New Zealand from 1839 to 1844*, Whitcombe & Tombs, Christchurch, 1908

Walker, Ranginui, *Ka Whawhai Tonu Matou: Struggle Without End*, Penguin, Auckland, 1990

Wanhalla, Angela, 'Marrying "In": The Geography of Intermarriage at Taieri, 1830s–1920s', in Tony Ballantyne and Judith A. Bennett (eds), *Landscape/Community: Perspectives from New Zealand History*, Otago University Press, Dunedin, 2005, pp.73–94

Wanhalla, Angela, 'The "natives uncivilize me": Missionaries and Interracial Intimacy in Early New Zealand', in Patricia Grimshaw and Andrew May (eds), *Missions, Indigenous Peoples and Cultural Exchange*, Sussex Academic Press, Eastbourne, 2010

Wanhalla, Angela, 'The Politics of "Periodical Counting": Race, Place and Identity in Southern New Zealand', in Penelope Edmonds and Tracey Banivanua Mar (eds), *Making Space: Settler-colonial Perspectives on Land, Place and Identity*, Palgrave Macmillan, London, 2010

Ward, Alan, *A Show of Justice: Racial 'Amalgamation' in Nineteenth Century New Zealand*, Auckland University Press, Auckland, 1995

White, Pat, 'Sizemore, Richard (c.1800–1861)', in J. Thomson (ed.), *Southern People: A Dictionary of Otago Southland Biography*, Dunedin City Council/Longacre Press, Dunedin, 1998, p.458

White, Richard, *The Middle Ground: Indians, Empires, and Republics in the Great Lakes Region, 1650–1815*, Cambridge University Press, Cambridge, 1991

Williams, Carol J., *Framing the West: Race, Gender, and the Photographic Frontier in the Pacific Northwest*, Oxford University Press, Oxford, 2003

Williams, David V., *'Te Kooti Tango Whenua': The Native Land Court 1864–1909*, Huia, Wellington, 1999

Wilson, Eva, *Hakoro Ki te Iwi: The Story of Captain John Howell and his Family*, Eva Wilson, Invercargill, 1976

Wohlers, Johann and John Houghton, *Memories of the Life of J. F. H. Wohlers, Missionary at Ruapuke, New Zealand: An Autobiography*, Otago Daily Times & Witness Newspapers, Dunedin, 1895

Young, Robert J. C., *Colonial Desire: Hybridity in Theory, Culture and Race*, Routledge, London, 1995

Unpublished Secondary Sources

Waitangi Tribunal Evidence and Reports

Alexander, J. A., Supporting Papers to Evidence of David James Alexander regarding Otakou, Murihiku and Rakiura, Ngai Tahu Claim Crown Papers, Vol.26, (WAI-27)

Anderson, Atholl, Kin and Border: Traditional Land Boundaries in East Polynesia and New Zealand with Particular Reference to the Northern Boundary of Ngai Tahu, (WAI-785)

Anderson, Atholl, Mahinga Kai: Evidence for the Ngai Tahu Claim to the Waitangi Tribunal, April 1988, (WAI-27)

Anderson, Atholl, Otakou: Evidence for the Ngai Tahu Claim Before the Waitangi Tribunal, November 1987, (WAI-27)

Anderson, D. A., Ngai Tahu Fishing in the Twentieth Century: An Overview, Ngai Tahu Claim Crown Papers, Vol.41, (WAI-27)

Armstrong, D. A., Evidence of David A. Armstrong re Crown's Reserve Policy 1890–1944, Ngai Tahu Claim Crown Papers, Vol.9 (WAI-27)

Armstrong, D. A., Supporting Papers to Evidence of David Anderson Armstrong, Ngai Tahu Claim Crown Papers, Vol.41 (WAI-27)

Armstrong, D. A., Supporting Papers to Evidence of David Anderson Armstrong, Ngai Tahu Claim Crown Papers, Vol.42, (WAI-27)

Dacker, Bill, Evidence for the Ngai Tahu Claim Before the Waitangi Tribunal, Otakou Marae, February 1988, (WAI-27)

Parsonson, Ann, Otakou Tenths: Evidence for the Ngai Tahu Claim to the Waitangi Tribunal, November 1987, (WAI-27)

Walzl, Anthony, Supporting Papers to Evidence of Tony Walzl, Ngai Tahu Claim Crown Papers, (WAI-27)

Academic theses and papers

Campbell, Matthew L., 'A Preliminary Investigation of the Archaeology of Whaling Stations on the Southern Coast', MA thesis, University of Otago, 1992

Chapman, R. W., 'The South Island Maoris and their Reserved Lands, 1860–1910', MA thesis, University of Canterbury, 1966

Dacker, Bill, 'Chapters in Nineteenth Century South Island Maori History', BA (Hons) long essay, University of Otago, 1980

Davis, G. F., 'Old Identities and New Iniquities: The Taieri Plain in Otago Province 1770–1870', MA thesis, University of Otago, 1974

Kelly, Stephanie, 'Weaving Whakapapa and Narrative in the Management of Contemporary Ngai Tahu Identities', PhD thesis, University of Canterbury, 2002

Owen, Emily V., 'Intermarriage: Its Role and Importance within Early New Zealand Shore Whaling Stations', MA thesis, Massey University, 2007

Riddell, Kate A., 'Marriage of the Races'? Aspects of Intermarriage, Ideology and Reproduction on the New Zealand Frontier', MA thesis, Victoria University of Wellington, 1996

Rutherford, D. W., 'The South Island Maori Population', MA thesis, University of Otago, 1941

Salesa, Damon, 'Race Mixing: A Victorian Problem in Britain and New Zealand, 1830s–1870s', DPhil thesis, University of Oxford, 2000

Wilson, Catherine Tatawai, 'Kai Tahu and the Claim', BA (Hons) research essay, University of Otago, 2002

Index